THE
1910s

Other books in this series:

THE
1910s

John F. Wukovits, *Book Editor*

David L. Bender, *Publisher*
Bruno Leone, *Executive Editor*
Bonnie Szumski, *Series Editor*
David M. Haugen, *Managing Editor*

Greenhaven Press, Inc., San Diego, California

AMERICA'S DECADES

Every effort has been made to trace the owners of copyrighted material. The articles in this volume may have been edited for content, length, and/or reading level. The titles have been changed to enhance the editorial purpose.

Library of Congress Cataloging-in-Publication Data

The 1910s / John F. Wukovits, book editor.
    p.   cm. — (America's decades)
    Includes bibliographical references and index.
    ISBN 0-7377-0296-6 (lib. : acid-free paper) —
    ISBN 0-7377-0295-8 (pbk. : acid-free paper)
    1. United States—Civilization—1865–1918. 2. United States—
Civilization—1918–1945. 2. Nineteen tens. I. Wukovits, John F.,
1944–   . II. Series

E169.1 .A1125 2000
973.91'3—dc21
                                                                99-055859
                                                                    CIP

Cover photo: 1. Stock Montage, Inc. 2. Corbis/Bettman
Library of Congress, 47, 56, 76, 118
National Archives, 239

©2000 by Greenhaven Press, Inc.
P.O. Box 289009, San Diego, CA 92198-9009

Printed in the U.S.A.

Contents

Chapter 2: Entertainment and Technology

Chapter 3: America Enters the World Arena

among nations. His idea intrigued European leaders, but he could not garner sufficient support in his own country.

Chapter 5: A Nation Isolated

Foreword

In his book *The American Century*, historian Harold Evans maintains that the history of the twentieth century has been dominated by the rise of the United States as a global power: "The British dominated the nineteenth century, and the Chinese may cast a long shadow on the twenty-first, but the twentieth century belongs to the United States." In a 1998 interview he summarized his sweeping hypothesis this way: "At the beginning of the century the number of free democratic nations in the world was very limited. Now, at the end of the century, democracy is ascendant around the globe, and America has played the major part in making that happen."

As the new century dawns, historians are eager to appraise the past one hundred years. Evans's book is just one of many attempts to assess the historical impact that the United States has had in the past century. Although not all historians agree with Evans's characterization of the twentieth century as "America's century," no one disputes his basic observation that "in only the second century of its existence the United States became the world's leading economic, military and cultural power." For most of the twentieth century the United States has played an increasingly larger role in shaping world events. The Greenhaven Press America's Decades series is designed to help readers develop a better understanding of America and Americans during this important time.

Each volume in the ten-volume series provides an indepth examination of the time period. In compiling each volume, editors have striven to cover not only the defining events of the decade—in both the domestic and international arenas—but also the cultural, intellectual, and technological trends that affected people's everyday lives.

Essays in the America's Decades series have been chosen for their concise, accessible, and engaging presentation of the facts. Each selection is preceded by a summary of the article's content. A comprehensive index and an annotated table of contents also aid readers in quickly locating material of interest. Each volume begins with an introductory essay that presents the broader themes of each decade. Several research aids are also present, including an extensive bibliography and a timeline that provides an at-a-glance overview of each decade.

Each volume in the Greenhaven Press America's Decades series serves as an informative introduction to a specific period in U.S. history. Together, the volumes comprise a detailed overview of twentieth century American history and serve as a valuable resource for students conducting research on this fascinating time period.

Introduction: Change at Home and Abroad

The decade from 1910 to 1920 produced vast changes in the United States. Politicians and social activists successfully promoted legislation that improved lives of youths, laborers, and women. The nation burst onto the international scene as a world power, helping to defeat Germany and its allies in World War I and contributing the inspiration for the League of Nations before reverting to a self-imposed isolation in the twenties.

Although the decade opened with hope and vitality created by reformers who saw the opportunity to make the nation a better place in which to live, it closed with fear and disillusionment brought about by a catastrophic war and a resulting desire to rid the nation of foreign influence. In between, though, the 1910s produced enormous changes that altered the path of the nation.

The Progressive Reformers

In the years following the Civil War, the United States exploded in a flurry of activity. Much of the South had to be rebuilt, and western lands beckoned with their dreams of adventure and financial opportunities. At the same time numerous problems plagued society, but they became overshadowed by the desire to take advantage of the economic climate. New factories produced tons of steel for the booming railroad industry, but poorly paid workers lived in slums and children labored ten to twelve hours a day in horrendous conditions.

To rectify these and other ills, reformers battled in the Political and social arenas to effect needed changes. Called Progressives because of their desire to eradicate evil from American society and make true progress toward equality, the reformers succeeded in focusing attention on abuses such as the denial of basic rights to women and African

11

Americans and, most prominently, the unfair and often unscrupulous treatment of the nation's working class. One historian of this period wrote, "The Progressive movement, then, may be looked upon as an attempt to develop the moral will, the intellectual insight, and the political and administrative agencies to remedy the accumulated evils and negligences of a period of industrial growth."[1]

Reformers fought a formidable foe in big business. For half a century industry magnates wielded enormous power. Since they accumulated such fantastic wealth, men such as banker J.P. Morgan and oilman John D. Rockefeller influenced many politicians, who then passed laws helping big business. When confronted with the challenge that their economic empires created vast seas of slums and urban blight, industrialists responded that only laziness kept people from achieving a happy life.

Progressives, who countered that people were good by nature but outmuscled by big business, argued that only the federal government, combined with the efforts of reform-minded individuals, was powerful enough to force change on the industrialists. Progressives believed that if these two groups joined forces, no problem was too large to be solved.

In the first ten years of the new century, a series of journalists wrote magazine articles and books exposing some of the problems infecting the nation. Novelist Upton Sinclair criticized the meatpacking industry, political writer Ida Tarbell targeted Standard Oil, social critic Jacob Riis powerfully painted an image of the dismal life in slums and tenements, and reformer John Spargo wrote of the horrors of child labor.

Reform-minded politicians listened. In an August 31, 1910, speech, Theodore Roosevelt, again in the hunt for the presidency after a two-year absence, introduced what he called "the New Nationalism." The former president, who had broken several business monopolies while in office, stated, "I mean not merely that I stand for fair play under the present rules of the game, but . . . for having those rules changed so as to work for a more substantial equality of opportunity and of reward for [everyone]."[2] Roosevelt proposed an eight-hour workday, laws preventing child labor in factories, and stricter rules regulating big business. Though he did not win reelection, his ideas influenced other reformers who carried on the battle.

The 1912 Commission on Industrial Relations, established by President William H. Taft, conducted hearings for 154 days into the state of business and concluded that workers had been unfairly treated. In its report, the commission asked, "Have the workers received a fair share of the enormous increase in wealth which has taken place in this country as a result largely of their labors? The answer is emphatically No!" The report claimed that one-third of the workers lived in "abject poverty," and it compared owner-labor strife to a "civil war."[3]

When Woodrow Wilson took office in 1913, he targeted big business's power. Lower tariffs, or taxes, on foreign products entering the country ensured that American businesses faced competition; the Federal Reserve Bank Act created a central federal bank and twelve regional banks to diminish the control wielded by New York bankers; the newly created Federal Trade Commission more closely regulated commerce; the Clayton Antitrust Act handed the government increased power to supervise business and gave labor unions the right to strike; and a 1916 law prohibited the transportation across state lines of goods made from child labor.

Because of these reform efforts, conditions improved by 1920. Two million children worked in factories in 1910, but the number was reduced in half by 1920. Wages, which had hovered around the one-dollar-per-day level, steadily rose, led by automaker Henry Ford's revolutionary five-dollars-a-day offer. A U.S. Supreme Court ruling in 1917 upheld the constitutionality of a ten-hour workday and helped abolish twelve- and fourteen-hour days.

Changes for Women

The desire for change did not rest only in the industrial field. Throughout the entire decade the National American

Woman Suffrage Association staged protests and marches to bring the issue of suffrage—the right for women to vote—before the public and politicians. In 1912 more than fifteen thousand women marched down New York's Fifth Avenue, and three years later over forty thousand women protested in the same city. Women had been permitted to vote in only four states in 1910, but by the end of the decade they had made rapid strides toward equality.

Though protest marches and letters to politicians proved effective, nothing that women did carried more impact than their labor on the home front during World War I. By heading war committees, selling war bonds, and even knitting socks for soldiers, women proved that they were vital, contributing members of society. At war's end they argued that if they had been expected to do their share for democracy, the least the nation could do was permit them to exercise democracy's most precious gift—the right to vote. In 1919, one year after the war ended, Congress passed the Nineteenth Amendment to the Constitution, granting women the right to vote. When the amendment was ratified the following year, for the first time in the country's history women enjoyed the same political rights as men.

The Limits of the Progressive Era

One group lost in the reform shuffle in this decade was African Americans. Still suffering deep hatreds and prejudices rooted primarily in the South, between 1900 and 1915, more than one thousand blacks were lynched, burned, or shot to death. Though the National Association for the Advancement of Colored People was established in 1909, it only had about six thousand members by 1914 and did not yet hold sufficient power to effect much change. Even President Wilson, who was a strong advocate for social reform, retreated from a campaign promise to improve conditions for America's blacks, claiming that segregation was desirable because it reduced animosity between whites and blacks.

America's entrance into World War I in 1917 ended the

Progressive Era of reform. The nation turned its attention from domestic issues and focused overseas. However, the reform movement that had dominated American life in the century's first seventeen years left a proud legacy. Investigative journalism and social criticism gained acceptance and became important features of the nation's media. More importantly, the notion took hold that the federal government had an obligation to assist its citizens in achieving a better life.

Technology for the Masses

While reform from within and war from without rocked the nation, advances in technology brought sweeping changes to the United States by 1920. One man—automaker Henry Ford—so profoundly altered American society with two measures that by 1920 the nation was vastly different than it had been in 1910.

First of all, Ford made the automobile, which had once been an expensive toy enjoyed solely by the rich, available to almost everyone by introducing the assembly line in his Highland Park, Michigan, plant in 1913. "When I'm through everybody will be able to afford [a car], and about everyone will have one,"[4] Ford promised, and his innovative method of production resulted in 250,000 cars each year, almost as many as all his competitors combined. As a result, he reduced the vehicle's cost to a level that was within reach for the average consumer. Whereas only a handful of people owned automobiles in 1910, almost 10 million consumers had purchased a vehicle by 1920.

Ford's impact on society went beyond the automobile, however. Labor reformers had battled for years to guarantee a living wage for workers, and in one step in 1914 Ford granted his employees what they sought. To battle the tediousness of the assembly line job, which asked the worker to repeat the same motion over and over again, Ford revolutionized the industry by offering workers the fantastic wage of five dollars per day. Thousands of applicants rushed to Ford headquarters in Dearborn, Michigan. For the first time workers enjoyed a decent salary, and Ford's wage became the standard by which other businesses were measured.

The laborer earned his lofty salary, though, because he had to maintain the grueling pace set by the assembly line. The wife of one laborer wrote Henry Ford in 1914, "That $5 a day is a blessing—a bigger one than you know but oh they earn it."[5]

No two people better symbolized the dramatic change brought by the automobile than Presidents Taft and Wilson. In 1909 Taft rode to the Capitol for his inauguration in a horse-drawn carriage, a device that had been used by ancient Egyptians, Greeks, and Romans. Only four years later, Wilson sat in a car and, in the words of a contemporary historian, "rode to the Capitol in a complicated product of physics and chemistry, compounded of gears, levers, pedals, rubber, cloth, glass, wire; and powered by an engine which generated motion as a result of electrically induced explosions of gasoline in expansion cylinders." The historian added that "the distance between the Wilson automobile and the Taft carriage was, in time, four years; in material change, it was fully twenty centuries."[6]

Technology Overcomes Distance

The airplane kept pace with the automobile with rapid changes of its own. In the first five years after the Wright brothers first succeeded in flying in 1903, the nation paid little attention to the new device. Many people thought the airplane was a new toy that would soon disappear, and they considered anyone crazy who wished to step into a cockpit. The airplane was dangerous, expensive, and not worth much attention. Few newspapers even reported aviation's first few steps between 1903 and 1910.

Due to a succession of developments, that view disappeared by 1920. Instead of dismissing the invention, people saw the airplane as an important addition to society. In 1911 Calbraith R. Rodgers became the first man to fly coast to coast (although it took seven weeks); Glenn H.

Curtiss lifted his airplane from the waters near San Diego, California, circled overhead for a time, then safely landed on the water; and a man leaped from an airplane with a parachute and safely landed on the ground. Within six years the airplane would add its terrifying potential to war over Europe's battlefields in World War I.

Technology also spurred developments in radio and telephone. Growing from the infant experiments of innumerable local inventors, by 1915 the U.S. Navy transmitted voices from Washington, D.C., to the Panama Canal Zone. Five years later the nation's first radio station, WWJ, opened for business in Detroit, Michigan.

The telephone industry made equally rapid advances. On January 25, 1915, Alexander Graham Bell repeated the words he made famous in 1876, "Mr. Watson, come here, I want you." Rather than uttering that sentence to his assistant in the next room, Bell stood in a room in New York and spoke that phrase to Watson, who listened from his room in San Francisco, California. The first transcontinental conversation, traversing 3,400 miles of copper wire stretched across 130,000 poles, had occurred, and for the first time in the nation's history coast-to-coast telephone service became available to the public.

The Entertainment Industry

Another industry that spread from one side of the nation to the other was moviemaking. This decade saw the film industry in Hollywood, California, grow from a struggling concern to a nationwide phenomenon complete with matinee idols such as Tom Mix, Douglas Fairbanks, Mary Pickford, and the immortal Charlie Chaplin. "Going to see Charlie Chaplin has become a habit all over the country," proclaimed *Photoplay Magazine* in 1915. "With his doleful countenance, his heavy feet, his characteristic French kick, his diminutive moustache, and his ridiculous actions, he has earned a place all his own in the realm of motion pictures."[7]

In 1915 legendary film director D.W. Griffith produced his three-hour epic movie *The Birth of a Nation*. By using close-ups, flashback, fade-outs, and scenes containing fantastic action, Griffith changed the way movies would be made. Though the movie created enormous controversy by glorifying the Ku Klux Klan and portraying African Americans as a threat to white people, millions paid to view the spectacle.

The low admission price of a nickel enticed people who could not afford live entertainment, and since pictures could be simultaneously seen around the nation, the stars gained large groups of enthusiastic admirers. By the middle of the decade almost 25 million people attended a picture each day, and Hollywood changed from a quiet little California community to the site of fifty-two movie companies.

World War I

For most of its history the United States remained out of European conflicts. Safely sheltered by the Atlantic Ocean, the country felt confident that whatever occurred in distant Europe would have minimal impact on the nation. However, one event altered that manner of thinking. World War I, which flared into a continent-wide struggle in Europe in 1914, slowly and steadily drew a hesitant President Wilson and the nation into the strife.

One of President Wilson's first public statements urged his countrymen to be "impartial in thought, as well as in action"[8] and stated to the world that the United States would take no side in the conflict. Many Americans supported this view. The League to Limit Armaments was formed by pacifists to keep the nation out of the war and to fight against any increase in military spending, and other peace groups organized in many large cities. Prominent reformers such as Carrie Chapman Catt and Jane Addams lent their support to these enterprises.

The nation was by no means united in this opposition to war, however. A vocal minority claimed that the nation would inevitably be drawn into the conflict and that the time to prepare was at hand. Former president Theodore Roosevelt crisscrossed the land in an effort to awaken his countrymen from what he considered a catastrophic apathy, and the National Defense League attempted to counter the peace groups. Most citizens who wanted the country involved in the war favored joining on the side of Great Britain, but even Germany had its supporters, especially in large cities like Milwaukee, Wisconsin, the home of a large German American contingent.

Events dragged a reluctant America into world war. The first episode startled the nation and did much to increase anti-German sentiment. On May 7, 1915, a German submarine sank the British liner *Lusitania* off of Ireland's coast. Of the 1,198 killed, 128 were Americans. A New York minister declared from his pulpit that "this sinking . . . is not war; it is . . . organized murder and no language is too strong for it."[9] Wilson fired off a strong letter of protest to Germany, and followed with another blunt warning in May after a second sinking in which two Americans died. As a result, Germany agreed to cease its unrestricted submarine warfare.

In late 1915 President Wilson, still hoping to avoid war, took steps to ensure that his country would be prepared for hostilities. He ordered an increase in the regular army to more than 140,000 men and the creation of a reserve army of 400,000. Wilson still longed for peace, but events had begun to pull him along the path to war.

Germany aggravated the situation the next March when it broke the agreement by sinking the unarmed French steamer *Sussex*, in which eighty Americans were among the dead and wounded. On January 31, 1917, Germany severed the final hopes for peace by announcing that its submarines would attack without warning any ship entering British waters. When Wilson learned that Germany had offered to help Mexico recover the land it had lost to the United States in the Mexican-American War (Texas, New Mexico, and Arizona) in return for Mexican assistance against the United States, and when Germany sank four unarmed American merchant ships, Wilson knew all hopes for peace had been shattered.

On April 2, 1917, Wilson stood before Congress and, in a somber voice, asked the legislators to vote for war. The man of peace realized that he was sending young men to their deaths, but he believed that he could no longer avoid bloodshed. "Property can be paid for; the lives of peaceful and innocent people cannot be," he mentioned to a still chamber. "The present German submarine warfare against commerce is a warfare against mankind." He declared that the United States had a duty to fight "for the rights of nations great and small and the privilege of men everywhere to choose their way of life." Then, in words now famous, he mentioned that "the world must be made safe for democracy."[10] As the president departed the podium amidst raucous applause, he muttered to an adviser, "Isn't it strange that men should cheer for war?"[11] Back in his office, the weary president placed his head on his desk and wept.

The nation quickly geared for war. The military contained few officers with combat experience. Outdated weapons plagued training efforts, and the infant air corps boasted a mere 55 planes and 130 pilots. Congress took steps to alleviate the problem by passing the Selective Service Act in May, and within eighteen months more than 24 million men had registered. Of this, 3 million were drafted into the military by lottery.

General John J. Pershing led the American expeditionary force into European battle at a crucial moment in the conflict. Internal political revolution had knocked Russia out of the war, which enabled Germany to shift its armies from the Russian front to Western Europe. In a spring offensive, confident German forces punched through British and French lines and advanced to within fifty-five miles of Paris. However, newly arrived American forces helped stop the Germans, first at Cantigny, then at Château-Thierry and Belleau Wood. In September 1918 Pershing opened the American offensive with successful thrusts against German lines at Saint-Mihiel and the Meuse-Argonne region.

Germany could no longer successfully battle the combined strength of its European foes and the United States. Rather than continue a hopeless fight, on November 11, 1918, Germany surrendered to the Allies and World War I ended.

A Lasting Peace

Realizing that his nation had emerged as a world power and that he carried newfound influence among leaders, Woodrow Wilson traveled to Europe intent on producing a lasting peace. In what is known as his Fourteen Points speech, Wilson called for an emphasis on the rights of all nations and the reduction of weapons. He also asked world leaders to form an international peacekeeping organization that would prevent disputes from flaring into war. Called the League of Nations, the idea gained widespread acceptance among the people of Europe.

However, Wilson's ideas were not as popular with French and British political leaders. They had emerged victorious from a vicious and costly war, and they were determined to make Germany pay for what it had done. In their views, Wilson's ideas may have been appropriate for a nation protected on two sides by immense oceans, but for nations living in proximity to each other, as they had with Germany, other measures had to be taken. They intended to so weaken Germany that it could never again start a war.

Eventually Wilson had to drop most of his Fourteen Points in the face of this opposition. However, he convinced Europe's leaders to form the League of Nations. Wilson warned that "within another generation, there will be another world war if the nations of the world do not concert the method by which to prevent it."[12]

Wilson's problems intensified when he returned to the United States. Weary of the bloody war and suspicious of foreign crises, the public wanted to withdraw from the world scene and focus on national issues. Wilson futilely tried to convince Congress to accept the League of Nations, but a sense of isolationism was too imbedded. Though he tirelessly traveled and spoke on behalf of the League, his opponents in the Senate voted it down.

An exhausted President Wilson, on the verge of a collapse that would almost kill him, commiserated, "We had a chance to gain the leadership of the world. We have lost it, and soon we shall be witnessing the tragedy of it all."[13]

The Nation Turns Inward

Reformer Jane Addams, who gained fame with her tireless efforts on behalf of the country's downtrodden, asserted that U.S. involvement in World War I would smother the desire for reform at home. "The spirit of fighting burns away all those impulses . . . which foster the will to justice."[14]

Woodrow Wilson took the notion a step further and cautioned that rather than simply turn away from positive change, the nation would enact restrictive rules:

> Once lead this people into war and they'll forget there ever was such a thing as tolerance. To fight you must be brutal and ruthless, and the spirit of the ruthless brutality will enter into the very fiber of our national life, infecting Congress, the courts, the policeman on the beat, the man in the street. Conformity would be the only virtue, and every man who refused to conform would have to pay the penalty.[15]

The change was apparent long before the war ended. Anti-immigrant feelings, especially toward those with German ties, led to actions that bordered on the absurd. Americans bearing German-sounding names fretted about keeping their jobs. Orchestras refused to play musical pieces by German composers like Bach, Mozart, and Beethoven. Citizens started calling German measles liberty measles.

Even former president Theodore Roosevelt joined the fray by attacking what he called "hyphenated Americans"—German-Americans, Italian-Americans, Polish-Americans—as being harmful to the nation. "Once it was true," he claimed, "that this country could not endure half free and half slave. Today it is true that it cannot endure half American and half foreign. The hyphen is incompatible with patriotism."[16] The nation waged a ghastly European war against "foreigners," and many citizens demanded that America shut its doors to immigrants.

More frightening were the steps taken by Congress in clear violation of the First Amendment to the Constitution. The Espionage Act of 1917 and the Sedition Act of 1918 made it illegal to mention anything disloyal or critical of the war. When the Reverend Clarence Waldron told a Bible class that Christians should not participate in war, he received a fifteen-year prison term. A noted Columbia University professor lost his job because he spoke out against the war.

Fear of foreign influence reached a frenzy when the Communists swept to power in Russia following the Russian Revolution and threatened to spread their ideology throughout the world. In what historians have labeled "the Red Scare," citizens and authorities suspected anyone who looked or sounded different as being a Communist sympathizer. People with accents or foreign-style clothing, or those who attended radical lectures and rallies, were in danger of being arrested. Reformers who had been respected were now shunned, in part because many reformers had opposed the war. A. Mitchell Palmer, the attorney general, headed a new drive to locate "disloyal" individuals and throw them behind bars.

The Red Scare gradually died down, and Americans quickly turned from serious world issues to fun, games, relaxation, and entertainment. The twenty-year battle to reform the nation by wrestling with evils at home, followed by the fight for democracy on Europe's battlefields, was about to be nudged aside by the Roaring Twenties and its flappers, bathtub gin, and the Charleston. A decade-long spree, induced in part because of events from 1910 to 1920, was about to begin with the arrival of the 1920s.

1. Quoted in Richard Hofstadter, ed., *The Progressive Movement, 1900–1915.* Englewood Cliffs, NJ: Prentice-Hall, 1963, pp. 2–3.

2. Quoted in Michael V. Uschan, *A Cultural History of the United States Through the Decades: The 1910s.* San Diego: Lucent Books, 1999, p. 16

3. Quoted in Uschan, *A Cultural History of the United States Through the Decades,* p. 30.

4. Quoted in Gerald A. Danzer et al., *The Americans: Reconstruction Through*

the Twentieth Century. Evanston, IL: McDougal Littell, 1999, p. 333.

5. Quoted in Danzer et al., *The Americans*, p. 333.

6. Quoted in Mark Sullivan, *Our Times*, vol. 4, *The War Begins, 1909–1914*. New York: Charles Scribner's Sons, 1932, pp. 268–69.

7. Quoted in Mark Sullivan, *Our Times*, vol. 5, *Over Here, 1914–1918*. New York: Charles Scribner's Sons, 1933, p. 600.

8. Quoted in Page Smith, *America Enters the World: A People's History of the Progressive Era and World War I*. New York: McGraw-Hill, 1985, p. 440.

9. Quoted in Danzer et al., *The Americans*, pp. 399–400.

10. Quoted in Danzer et al., *The Americans*, p. 401.

11. Quoted in Joy Hakim, *An Age of Extremes*. New York: Oxford University Press, 1994, p. 182.

12. Quoted in Uschan, *A Cultural History of the United States Through the Decades*, p. 94.

13. Quoted in Uschan, *A Cultural History of the United States Through the Decades*, p. 109.

14. Quoted in Danzer et al., *The Americans*, p. 359.

15. Quoted in Danzer et al., *The Americans*, p. 412.

16. Quoted in Uschan, *A Cultural History of the United States Through the Decades*, p. 73.

CHAPTER 1

Reform and Reaction

AMERICA'S DECADES

The Progressive Movement Changes America

Richard Hofstadter

After fifty years of incredible economic growth and territorial expansion following the Civil War, the nation turned its gaze to unsolved problems which accompanied the rapid development. While some Americans accumulated enormous profit, others labored and lived in squalor. Government had become too closely allied with the interests of big business, and individual rights suffered. To rectify these and other problems, the Progressive Movement appeared. Acclaimed historian of reform movements, Richard Hofstadter, explains the origins of the Progressive Movement in this introduction to a book about the era.

For a long time historians have written of the period roughly between 1900 and 1914 as the Progressive era, and of its variety of reform agitations, as the Progressive movement. In these designations the historians have followed the example of many of the period's leading figures, who liked the ring of the word "Progressive" as applied to themselves. The men of that age were proudly aware, even as they were fighting their battles, that there was something distinctive about the political and social life of their time which sharply marked it off from the preceding era of materialism and corruption.

Excerpted from *The Progressive Movement, 1900–1915*, by Richard Hofstadter. Copyright ©1963 by Prentice-Hall, Inc. Reprinted with permission from Simon & Schuster, Inc.

The Need for Change

From the end of the Civil War to the close of the nineteenth century, the physical energies of the American people had been mobilized for a remarkable burst of material development, but their moral energies had lain relatively dormant. Certain moral facets of the American character had become all but invisible. It was as though the controversy over slavery, the Civil War itself, and the difficulties and failures of Reconstruction had exhausted the moral and political capacities of the people and left them relieved to abandon crusades and reforms and to plunge instead into the rewarding tasks of material achievement.

During this period American settlers and entrepreneurs had filled up a vast area of land between the Mississippi River and California and had spanned the country with a railroad network of more than a quarter of a million miles. The number of farms, as well as the number of acres under cultivation, had doubled between 1870 and 1900, and the production of wheat, cotton, and corn had increased from two to two-and-a-half times.

Still more impressive was the growth of the urban and industrial segment of the economy. Whole systems of industry and whole regions of industrial production were created. Between 1870 and 1900 the production of bituminous coal increased five times, of crude petroleum twelve times, of steel ingots and castings more than 140 times. The urban population jumped from 9.9 million to 30.1 million, and thoughtful observers could see that the day was not very far off when the rural population would be outnumbered and the characteristic problems of the nation would be city problems. The larger cities grew at an almost alarming speed, and the pace of their growth seemed to outstrip their means of administration. Chicago, for example, more than doubled its population in the single decade 1880 to 1890, and a growth rate for that decade alone of from 60 to 80 per cent was not uncommon for the newer cities of the Middle West.

Toward the turn of the century it became increasingly

evident that all this material growth had been achieved at a terrible cost in human values and in the waste of natural resources. The land and the people had both been plundered. The farmers, whose products had not only fed the expanding national working force but had also paid abroad for much of the foreign capital that financed American industrialization, had received pathetic returns for their toil. They had had little or no protection against exploitation by the railroads, against the high cost of credit, or against an unjust burden of taxation. At the same time the cities that grew with American industry were themselves industrial wastelands—centers of vice and poverty, ugly, full of crowded slums, badly administered. Industry, after a period of hectic competition, was rapidly becoming concentrated, a process which was hastened by the power of finance capital. Big business choked free competition and concentrated political power in a few hands. Stirred by such works as Ida Tarbell's account of the methods of the Standard Oil Company, men began to realize how ruthless were the methods by which some great enterprises and great fortunes had been built, how business competitors and industrial workers alike had been exploited by the captains of industry. Moreover, business, great and small, had debased politics: working with powerful bosses in city, state, and nation, it had won favors and privileges in return for its subsidies to corrupt machines. Domination of affairs by political bosses and business organizations was now seen to be a threat to democracy itself.

What had happened, as a great many men of good will saw it at the beginning of the Progressive era, was that in the extraordinary outburst of productive energy of the last few decades, the nation had not developed in any corresponding degree the means of meeting human needs or controlling or reforming the manifold evils that come with any such rapid physical change. The Progressive movement, then, may be looked upon as an attempt to develop the moral will, the intellectual insight, and the political and administrative agencies to remedy the accumulated evils and negligences of a period of industrial growth. Since the Progressives were not revolutionists, it was also an attempt to work out a strategy for orderly social change.

A Broad Umbrella

Of course, not everyone looked at the evils that burdened society from quite the same point of view, and it would be a mistake to exaggerate the measure of agreement among those who were called, or chose to call themselves, Progressives. The larger their numbers, the more likely serious differences among them would be. And in a short time their numbers became large indeed. Perhaps the most remarkable thing about the Progressive movement was that it became so pervasive, that so many people could, at some time and on some issue, be called "Progressive." In the three-cornered presidential election of 1912, the two most popular candidates, Woodrow Wilson and Theodore Roosevelt, both ran on Progressive platforms and made Progressive-sounding speeches, and between them they had almost 70 per cent of the popular votes. Even the third candidate, President Taft, who had offended the Progressives in his own party and was inevitably cast in the conservative role, had been identified with some Progressive issues. Significantly, his party's leaders thought it wise to declare in their platform that they were "prepared to go forward with the solution of those new questions, which social, economic, and political development have brought to the forefront of the nation's interest," and to promise "to satisfy the just demand of the people for the study and solution of the complex and constantly changing problems of social welfare." Thus even the conservatism of 1912 thought it would be to its advantage to present itself as being, in some degree, "Progressive."

When a term becomes as widely adopted as this, we may justifiably be suspicious of the precision of its meaning. To speak of any two men of this era as being "Progressives" in their general political direction, does not mean that they will be in agreement on all social or political issues. One

cannot forget the great heterogeneity of the country, or ignore the possibility that Progressivism could mean something different in the countryside from what it meant in the
city, that it might have different principles in the Northeast
as opposed to the South and West, that businessmen who
favored some Progressive measures might have different
hopes from those of professional and middle-class Progressives, and that Progressives in the farm country would have
some special interests of their own.

It is necessary also to bear in mind the variety of issues
about which one might or might not have taken a "Progressive" point of view: trusts and finance capital; bosses
and popular control of politics; taxation and tariffs; conservation; railroad rates and rebates; vice and corruption;
the conditions of labor and the role of labor unions;
woman suffrage; the rights of Negroes; referendum and recall; city reform; even Prohibition. The diversity of these issues, and the diversity of social classes and social interests
that were at play in the political system, multiply the possibilities for disagreement within the Progressive movement. A businessman and a labor leader might have common notions about a campaign against corruption but have
diametrically opposed ideas about the position of trade
unions. A small-town banker and a farmer might see eye-
to-eye on certain matters of financial reform, but have
wholly different views on the referendum and recall. Two
harassed shippers might agree heartily on the necessity of
doing something about railroad rates but fall out over tariff policy. No doubt there were at work in the Progressive
movement some persons who deserve the generic label of
"reformers" for having given enthusiastic support to most
of the proposals for change that were being agitated in
their day. But there were also one-interest and one-issue
people, who worked arduously to advance this or that reform and remained quite indifferent to the others.

Historians have rightly refused to allow such complica-
tions to prevent them from speaking of the Progressive
movement and the Progressive era. It is the historian's busi-

ness not only to take careful account of particulars but also to assess the general direction of social movements in the past. For all its internal differences and counter-currents, there were in Progressivism certain general tendencies, certain widespread commitments of belief, which outweigh the particulars. It is these commitments and beliefs which make it possible to use the term "Progressive" in the hope that the unity it conveys will not be misconstrued.

Progressivism's Unique Qualities

What were these distinguishing qualities that mark Progressivism? The name itself may be slightly misleading here: of course, the Progressives believed in progress; but so did a great many conservatives, who argued that they had a sounder understanding of how progress works and of the pace at which it goes on. The distinguishing thing about the Progressives was something else, which for lack of a better term might be called "activism": they argued that social evils will not remedy themselves, and that it is wrong to sit by passively and wait for time to take care of them. As Herbert Croly put it, they did not believe that the future would take care of itself. They believed that the people of the country should be stimulated to work energetically to bring about social progress, that the positive powers of government must be used to achieve this end. Conservatives generally believed in time and nature to bring progress; Progressives believed in energy and governmental action.

The basic mood of Progressivism was intensely optimistic. One can, to be sure, find in the writings of some Progressives a note of anxiety as to what might happen to the country if various proposed reforms should fail to relieve the most threatening evils. Some of them feared that a continued concentration of power in the hands of investment banking firms—which they called "the money trust"—might in the long run undermine American democracy and the spirit of enterprise. But the dominant note is one of confidence, of faith that no problem is too difficult to be overcome by the proper mobilization of energy and intelligence in the citizenry. And when one thinks of the outstanding political leaders of the Progressive era—men like Theodore Roosevelt, Woodrow Wilson, William Jennings Bryan, and Robert M. La Follette—one thinks mainly of men with a certain faith, serene, militant, or buoyant, in the possibilities of the future. The movement was animated with the sense that something new and hopeful was being created—with a faith that found itself embodied in party slogans or the titles of important books: *The Old Order Changeth, The New Democracy, The New Freedom, The New Nationalism, The Promise of American Life.*

This promise of social progress was not to be realized by sitting and praying, but by using the active powers—by the exposure of evils through the spreading of information and the exhortation of the citizenry; by using the possibilities inherent in the ballot to find new and vigorous popular leaders; in short, by a revivification of democracy. . . .

Politicians and Thinkers Join Hands

Progressivism was largely the creation of a new and younger generation of politicians, who had come of age after the problems of Reconstruction had been largely settled, who had grown up along with post–Civil War industrialization, and who had never acquiesced in the crass and ruthless materialism of its captains of industry. These politicians were very often of well-established families, the sons of well-to-do professionals or business men, who were inspired by the high civic ideals kept alive since the Civil War by the Mugwump reformers. They saw that their own political careers were not to be made by catering to money makers, but by some more disinterested contribution either in the reform of industrial and political evils or in the promotion of America's interests in the arena of world politics—or, as in the case of Theodore Roosevelt, by both. Hence the Progressive movement was led by young men. In 1900 Robert M. La Follette was 45, Woodrow Wilson and Louis D. Brandeis were 44, Roosevelt 42, Bryan 40, [Albert] Beveridge and Hughes 38, Borah 35, Hiram Johnson 34,

Joseph W. Folk 31. The writers who did so much to shape the tone of the period were even younger; for Ida M. Tarbell was 43 in 1900, Herbert Croly 35, Lincoln Steffens 34, David Graham Phillips 33, Ray Stannard Baker 30, Walter Weyl 27, and Upton Sinclair only 22.

What politicians were doing in the field of public leadership, and what writers were doing in the field of reporting and exposure, a new generation of thinkers and scholars was doing in the academic world. Men like Charles A. Beard and J. Allen Smith in history and political science, Richard T. Ely, John R. Commons, and the acidulous Thorstein Veblen in economics, John Dewey in philosophy and education, Lester F. Ward, Edward A. Ross and Charles H. Cooley in sociology, and the admirers of Oliver Wendell Holmes, Jr., in jurisprudence, were together developing a kind of social criticism that transcended the formalistic doctrines and methods of their predecessors and tried to cope with the sordid and often unacknowledged realities of the world. Men such as these were concerned not so much with formal political philosophies and the texts of constitutions as with the interests behind them, not so much with old-fashioned economic doctrine as with the actual development of economic institutions, not so much with the elaboration of philosophical or educational systems as with the progressive use of thought in action, not so much with the preaching of high social principles as with the development of detailed knowledge of the operation of social forces, not so much with the elaboration of legal traditions as with the way in which legal decisions were actually arrived at. New political writers emerged, like Herbert Croly, the founder of the *New Republic* and his colleagues Walter Lippmann and Walter Weyl, who used the newer thought to analyze for a broad public the problems of the day, writing of the Progressives sometimes sympathetically and sometimes in a spirit of keen criticism.

Hardly less important than the work of academic and journalistic critics was the influence of social Christianity. For some time, large segments of the Protestant clergy had been alarmed at the violence of labor conflict, appalled at city living conditions, and troubled by the failure of the churches to win an adequate following among urban workers. During the 1890's the clerical conviction that Christianity, to make a contribution to solving the new moral problems of industrialism, must become a social force as well as a religious creed, had precipitated a strong movement to make the churches socially effective. The writings of such leaders of the social gospel as Washington Gladden and Walter Rauschenbush helped to give the Progressive movement the character of an evangelical revival in politics and economics. In the Progressive protest, the voice of the Christian conscience was heard more clearly than at any time since the days of the abolitionist movement.

Another notable feature of the era was the increasing role of women in American politics. Women had, of course, long been interested in reform movements, and had played a prominent part in abolitionism. But the numbers of women active in political affairs had been very limited. Now the educated, middle-class woman was beginning to grow tired of the passivity that was expected of her and sought to express herself in civic affairs. Her own interests as a mother were brought into play by her concern over the education and welfare of her children, the urban environment in which they lived, and such municipal facilities as playgrounds, schools, and parks. Her interests as a consumer were alerted by political struggles over tariffs, taxes, monopolies, and graft. But more important than her interests were her sympathies, for she was shocked by the revelations that were being made almost every day about the conditions of labor of women and children in the mills and mines of the country, of the conditions under which the urban poor lived in the tenement-house districts. Women were beginning to develop their own heroes of philanthropic action, like Jane Addams, the founder of the famous social settlement at Hull House in Chicago, and also to feel more strongly about their political rights. Believing that they were far better equipped than men to introduce into politics the note of morality and humane concern that the state of American society seemed to need so badly, women in increasing numbers began to demand the vote for themselves. By 1914 they had the vote in eleven states, and their efforts were crowned with final success in the Nineteenth Amendment, which was ratified in 1920.

Government by the People

If one examines the historical course of Progressive politics, one finds that the Progressive movement began in the cities, spread rapidly to the states, and reached the federal level most effectively in its later phases. Indeed, if one looks at the history of American cities, one is impressed with the fact that there Progressivism was really well under way in the 1890's, when the city governments of New York, Chicago, Detroit, Milwaukee, and others were reformed. By 1895 over seventy citizens' organizations had been formed to work for the improvement of city conditions.

But in law the cities were simply the creations of the states, and efforts to better municipal life forced reformers time and again to confront the power of the allies of local bosses who sat in the state legislatures. Moreover, many of the business abuses, from extortionate railroad rates to the exploitation of woman and child labor, were by their nature susceptible to reform only on the state level through statewide laws. Around the turn of the century, several of the reform leaders were elected state governors. Among the first of these was Robert M. La Follette, who was elected governor of Wisconsin in 1900, and who waged a courageous and moderately successful battle to regulate the railroads and public utilities of his state and tighten its tax system. Similar battles were fought in California by Hiram Johnson, in New York by Charles Evans Hughes, who had previously done notable work in exposing the corrupt practices of insurance companies, in Missouri by Joseph Folk, in Oregon by William S. U'Ren, and still later in New Jersey by Woodrow Wilson and in Ohio by James M. Cox.

In their struggles against railroads, utilities, insurance

companies, and other business organizations, reformers were driven to do constant battle with the political machines fed by contributions from businessmen. They became convinced that in order to achieve lasting success, control of the political parties and the state and local governments must be taken out of the hands of venal bosses and put into the hands of the people. To this end, they proposed and succeeded in getting passed in many states democratic reforms of varying degrees of effectiveness. Corrupt practices acts were intended to attack the illicit relation between money and politics. The direct primary was intended to put the choice of political candidates in the hands of the people, rather than the party machines, and thus raise the level of political leadership. The initiative made it possible for citizens' organizations to propose legislation, while the referendum made it possible for voters to pass on state laws. The short ballot was adopted to make it easier for the voter to perform his function intelligently. The recall of public officials was widely adopted as a means of removing corrupt or incompetent officials before the expiration of their terms of office. Finally, since many reform measures were being turned down by courts throughout the country, more advanced reformers began to advocate even the public recall of judges, and seven western states actually made provision for such recall. This proposal, which seemed to threaten the independence of the judiciary, was particularly shocking to conservatives, though the controversy it aroused was meaningless, since to judge of any superior or supreme court of any of the states having such laws was ever recalled. When Theodore Roosevelt, attempting to arrive at a compromise on the issue, suggested the recall of judicial *decisions* in 1912, he lost many of his Republican friends.

The demand for returning government to the people was carried from state government into national affairs. In the House of Representatives insurgents under the leadership of Champ Clark of Missouri and George W. Norris of Nebraska struck a blow at bossism when they took away from "Uncle Joe" Cannon, the Speaker, the power to control the workings of its vital Rules Committee. The Senate itself, which had long been stigmatized as a "millionaire's club" and a haunt of reactionary allies of big business, was at last touched by the reform movement when the Seventeenth Amendment took the power to appoint Senators out of the hands of the legislatures and required direct election by the people. . . .

On a National Scale

Certain national problems, especially those involving big business, railroads, tariff, finance capital, and the like, were too large to be dealt with effectively in the states. At the turn of the century it was already clear that the demand for reform would reach national political leaders. When the conservative McKinley was assassinated in 1901, his replacement by a representative of the new generation, Theodore Roosevelt, only released forces that were already in existence. Roosevelt himself was a combination of moderate conservative and moderate Progressive, who did not believe that trust-busting on a large scale was practicable or desirable and who looked with some anxiety upon the discontent stirred up by the muckrakers and other reformers. But he was also opposed to plutocratic arrogance, corruption, civic indifference, and materialism, and he understood the need of right-thinking Americans to be reassured about the ability of their government to cope with bosses, bankers, and trusts. Although he did not act on a large scale against trusts, his prosecution of the Northern Securities Company, one of the biggest and best-known, established the point, as he said "that the most powerful men in this country were held to accountability under the law." Again, his settlement of the ominous anthracite strike of 1902, in the face of arrogance and intransigent conduct by the mine owners, confirmed the impression that the country at last had a President big enough to stand up to the great capitalist interests.

During Roosevelt's administration, Congress also set the basis for effective railroad regulation by passing the Hepburn Act, which, though it failed to satisfy the demands of ardent reformers like La Follette, gave the Interstate Commerce Commission enough power to begin the substantial reduction of many rates. Congress responded to public pressures aroused by such muckrakers as Upton Sinclair and Samuel Hopkins Adams by enacting a Pure Food and Drug Act in 1906. A reform about which Roosevelt did have unbounded enthusiasm was the conservation of natural resources, which had been squandered for generations. Roosevelt set aside millions of acres of timber and other lands as governmental reserves, put the zealous conservationist Gifford Pinchot in charge of the national forests, and in 1907 called a national conference of governors and others interested in conservation, which elevated the concern for conservation to a national movement.

Under William Howard Taft, Roosevelt's chosen successor, Progressivism seemed to be marking time, so far as the federal government was concerned. It was true that Taft pushed anti-trust activities far more vigorously than Roosevelt, and extended some conservation policies. But he failed ignominiously to win real tariff reform—an issue Roosevelt had entirely ducked—and his acceptance of the leadership of Senate conservatives offended Progressives. Increasingly, the insurgents within his own party struck off on their own. On a few issues, they were successful. Not only did they break the power of "Uncle Joe" Cannon in the House, but they strengthened the power of the ICC with the Mann-Elkins Act and passed a Physical Evaluation Act, long sought by La Follette, which set up a more realistic framework for railroad regulation, based on the true value of railroad properties rather than on watered stock. They also pushed through (with some support from Taft) the Sixteenth Amendment, authorizing an income tax, which was ratified in 1913; and the Seventeenth Amendment, providing for popular election of Senators, was ratified the same year.

Taft's inability to command the loyalty of Progressives in his own party led to a Republican split, manifest in the in-surgency of 1910, and finally in the formation of a new, though short-lived party, the Progressive party, whose 1912 platform may be taken almost as a consummatory statement of the social aims of the Progressive movement. The split in the Republican party between the followers of Theodore Roosevelt and those of Taft was a welcome opportunity to the Democrats, who had not elected a president since Cleveland in 1892. The forces of Western and Southern agrarianism were still strong in the Democratic party, and Democratic Progressivism was somewhat more colored than that of the Republicans by old rural animosities. Like the Progressive party, the Democratic party endorsed a wide variety of reform proposals; but many Democrats considered Roosevelt's acceptance of bigness in business as a betrayal of what they felt to be the central goal in the Progressive movement—the restoration of a truly competitive business world. Woodrow Wilson's campaign speeches were a masterly restatement of this view; he argued that no government would be strong enough to regulate the interests satisfactorily if they were not broken up through antitrust action and the restoration of competition. In this way, the main argument between the two progressive-minded candidates in 1912 became an argument between regulated monopoly and regulated competition.

Wilson's Presidency

Backed by widespread Progressive sentiment in both parties, the Wilson administration set out vigorously to redeem its promises of business and tariff reform. In 1913, responding to an appeal by Wilson for real tariff reform, Congress passed the Underwood Tariff, the first satisfactory downward revision since the Civil War. Its passage was probably made possible by an unprecedented act on Wilson's part: a bold appeal to the American public against the activities of business lobbyists, activities of the sort which had crippled all previous attempts at tariff revision. Banking and credit reforms followed: with the creation of the Federal Reserve System in 1913 the United States devised, for the first time in its long history of unsatisfactory banking, a sound central banking system with adequate governmental direction. To make sure that farm credit facilities were adequate, Congress also passed the Federal Farm Loan Act in 1916 which enabled farmers to secure loans against farm lands and buildings, and the Warehouse Act, which made loans available against stored farm products.

To meet the demand for anti-trust legislation, the administration secured the passage of two laws in 1914. The first, the Federal Trade Commission Act, was intended to prevent unfair trade practices by creating a commission empowered to investigate corporations and to issue "cease and desist" orders when it found that such practices prevailed. Wilson's own appointees to this body, however, proved relatively lax, and in later years the Commission was frequently used as a way of encouraging business consolidation. The second law, the Clayton Act, was intended to expand the legal foundation for anti-trust action laid in the Sherman Act of 1890. A notable provision, demanded by A.F.L. head Samuel Gompers, seemed to exempt labor unions from prosecution as conspiracies in restraint of trade, but later decisions by the Court nullified its force. Since the Clayton Act was passed just on the eve of World War I, however, it came into being just at a time when, in the interests of wartime production, anti-trust activities were largely suspended.

Progressivism's Legacy

The Progressive movement was dependent upon the civic alertness and the combative mood of a great part of the public. Such a mood cannot last forever; perhaps what was most remarkable about the Progressives was their ability to sustain reformist enthusiasm as long as they did. Even the first World War, which in the end helped to destroy the Progressive movement, was conducted with true Progressive fervor and under the cover of Progressive thinking: for the war too became a crusade against autocracy, an attempt to make the world safe for democracy. When the reaction finally did come, it was sharp and decisive. The war left the people fatigued with Wilsonian idealism and ready for a return to "normalcy."

During the 1920's, as the public relaxed into a mood of acquiescence in business domination, the transient character of much of Progressivism became apparent. The Progressive movement had never succeeded in remedying the maldistribution of wealth, which was increasing even as its reforms were being passed. Now its very efforts to establish an apparatus for the effective regulation of business were constantly frustrated. The Federal Trade Commission, for example, far from preventing unfair practices, as was intended, became an agency of business consolidation. The heroic efforts of the Progressives to uproot the bosses and put government in the hands of the people also seemed to have failed, though the Progressive legislation remained on the books as a possible check to corrupt machines. The most durable aspect of Progressivism seems to have been its social legislation; for even during the conservative 1920's much of this legislation was extended, and in some states its enforcement was improved.

Despite the transiency of many of its achievements, the heritage of the Progressive movement cannot be considered small or unimportant. The Progressives developed for the first time on a large scale a type of realistic journalism and social criticism that has become a permanent quality of American thinking. They gave renewed strength to a climate of opinion hostile to monopoly and suspicious of arbitrary aggregates of business power, which forced big business to operate circumspectly and even to exercise some self-restraint. The traditions of responsible government and forceful leadership exemplified by men like Theodore Roosevelt and Woodrow Wilson established unforgettable high points in American statesmanship. Finally, the reforms of the Progressive era established a basis and a precedent for further reforms to be passed when the need for them was felt. Franklin D. Roosevelt's New Deal owed a heavy debt to its Progressive forerunners both for moral inspiration and for some of its administrative devices.

The men and women of the Progressive movement must be considered, in this regard, to be pioneers of the welfare state. This was not because they sought to foster big government for its own sake. But they were determined to remedy the most pressing and dangerous social ills of industrial society, and in the attempt they quickly learned that they could not achieve their ends without using the power of the administrative state. Moreover, they asserted—and they were the first in our history to do so with real practical success—the idea that government cannot be viewed merely as a cold and negative policing agency, but that it has a wide and pervasive responsibility for the welfare of its citizens, and for the poor and powerless among them. For this, Progressivism must be understood as a major episode in the history of the American conscience.

Child Labor: A National Disgrace

Walter Lord

One of the worst features of American society in the first two decades of the twentieth century was the employment of the nation's young boys and girls in factories and mines. Rather than shielding its youth in their formative years, the nation for too long turned its gaze from the blatant abuses of a system that fueled industry with the labor of children. Investigative journalists and politicians placed this issue at the top of their agendas. Some wrote articles exposing child labor, while others sought legislation to correct the situation. Noted historian Walter Lord, who authored a succession of best-selling books on American history, examines the steps taken to eliminate child labor.

1913 . . . Children at Work

> "The golf links lie so near the mill
> That almost every day
> The laboring children can look out
> And see the men at play."
> —Sarah N. Cleghorn

Woodrow Wilson stood for freedom; so it was not surprising early in 1913 when a group of social workers asked him to help free the children from the nation's factories. The new President politely declined. No one was more

Excerpted from *The Good Years*, by Walter Lord (New York: Bantam, 1960). Copyright ©1960 by Walter Lord. Reprinted with permission from Sterling Lord Literistic, Inc.

idealistic, but an important part of his idealism was a deep, almost sacred belief in states' rights. "It is plain," he told the reformers, "that you would have to go much further than most interpretations of the Constitution would allow, if you were to give the government general control over child labor throughout the country."

So the children worked on, unhampered by federal interference. Twelve-year-old Owen Jones tore and bruised his hands in the breakers of a West Virginia coal mine. Tiny Anetta Fachini twisted the stems for artificial flowers under the lonely lamp bulb of a New York tenement sweatshop. Eleven-year-old Sam Bowles did his best in the weaving room of Georgia's White City Manufacturing Company—for forty cents a day.

At an Atlanta cotton mill one nimble-fingered boy stretched three thousand flour bags a shift; but he had plenty of practice, for he worked a sixty-hour week. In Pittsburgh an unknown little girl rolled one thousand stogies a day—which meant, looking at it another way, that one thousand times a day she had to bite off the end of a cigar.

Somehow in these years of thrilling reform, there were still areas of extreme poverty. Worst of all, children were lost in the shuffle. Perhaps the economists were bored—it was so much more stimulating to rewrite the tariff or draw up the Federal Reserve. Perhaps labor was to blame; Samuel Gompers was a rugged individualist who had little use for social welfare laws. Perhaps the children were too quiet.

In any case, by 1913 some 20 per cent of all the children in America were earning their own living. And the number was growing all the time. In 1900 the Census listed 1,750,178 "gainfully occupied children aged ten to fifteen"; in 1910 the figure jumped to 1,990,225. To many this was sad but inevitable. The average family needed $800 a year to get along, yet most unskilled jobs paid less than $500 a year. Unless general wage levels went up, the children had to fill the gap. As the Clarke County Mississippi *Tribune* realistically asked, "What are the children going to do to keep from starving and going naked?"

Reform Efforts

A small band of dedicated people refused to go along with all this. They felt that child labor was one reason why wages were so low; get the children out of the factories and the general level would rise. These reformers had set up the National Child Labor Committee in 1904, and in the years since then had waged a tireless crusade. They roamed through the factories. They talked to the children. They heard out the foremen. They prepared model bills. They badgered state legislatures. And occasionally they even pushed through a law.

But so many of the "victories" were hollow. Massachusetts had only eighteen inspectors for fifty-six thousand plants. The New York law against tenement work listed some ninety exceptions. In Alabama a twelve-year-old girl might still put in a sixty-hour week.

The cotton mills posed the biggest problem. Hot competition and little call for skill—the perfect climate for cheap child labor. And the children came: five thousand little girls between ten and twelve worked at the spindles in Southern plants. In the North, nearly seventeen thousand mill hands were under sixteen.

More meaningful, perhaps, were the figures on injuries. One Southern surgeon estimated that he had amputated the fingers of more than one hundred children. "We don't have many accidents," a mill foreman countered, "once in a while a finger is mashed or a foot, but it does not amount to anything."

No wonder the reform groups were elated in 1913 when two leading cotton textile states—Massachusetts and Georgia—began to consider stronger child labor curbs. Best of all, public interest was growing, and this time it looked as if something might really be done.

The Massachusetts bill came up first. It restricted street trades, raised school requirements, and most important of all, set an eight-hour day for anyone under sixteen—the highest standard yet reached by a cotton mill state. As expected, the law passed in June, and the New England conscience basked in a glow of self-congratulation.

All eyes now turned to Georgia. The bill here was not quite as strong—it gradually raised the working age to fourteen—but it was a big step forward and its prospects were bright. Early in August the Atlanta *Journal* predicted that the measure would definitely pass, and child labor groups everywhere prepared to celebrate the biggest victory yet. Then, on the afternoon of August 5, word was flashed that the Georgia State Senate had unexpectedly killed the bill.

Reaction to Reform

What had happened? Many Southerners were sure that the Senate had discovered in the nick of time that child labor reform was really sponsored by hypocritical Yankees, hoping to increase Southern labor costs and cut the South's competitive advantage. Northerners were equally convinced that Georgia's failure to act was one more example of Southern backwardness.

Actually, both theories were wrong. No Northern mill ever gave a dollar to the National Child Labor Committee. And some of the most active reformers—not only in the South but throughout the nation—were dedicated Southerners . . . men like Senator Hoke Smith of Georgia, Dr. A.J. McKelway from Atlanta, and Dr. Edgar Gardner Murphy, the Alabama clergyman who organized the whole movement.

Moreover, the men who led the fight against reform in Georgia were not necessarily "backward" Southerners by any means. Often they were upstanding New Englanders who pointed with pride to "enlightened Massachusetts". . . but applied different standards to the mills they ran down South.

There was, perhaps, no nicer man in Columbus, Georgia, than Frederick B. Gordon, a transplanted Bostonian who ran the Columbus Manufacturing Company's cotton mill. Active in civic affairs, Mr. Gordon helped found the Primary Industrial School. His big new plant, a local historian proudly recorded, "responds liberally to all civic calls—even some that do not directly benefit its own business." And it prospered mightily . . . quickly repaying its Northern investors dollar for dollar, plus a 100 per cent stock dividend. Relaxing in his colonnaded mansion appropriately called "Gordonido," Mr. Gordon undoubtedly fitted the description supplied by his authorized biographer: "He possesses a genial, sympathetic nature and has found life well worth living, making the most of it every day."

a child miner, bent from years of toil

Down at the factory, life was a little different. "I have never seen so many children in any one mill as there were here," wrote the Reverend Harvey P. Vaughn, a gentle Tennessee minister, after a visit in April, 1913. The children worked, it turned out, a twelve-hour day—from 5:30 A.M. to 5:30 P.M. There was no time off even for lunch; if anything went wrong while they were snatching a bite, they had to stop eating to fix it.

When Dr. Vaughn indelicately asked how many of the mill hands were under fourteen, Mr. Gordon politely declined to answer. As he once explained, "The millowners do not feel that there is any reason for spasms on the part of the paid agitators, the newspaper preachers, or our gentle and zealous friends, the clubwomen."

Mr. Gordon had always felt that way. It was 1902 when he first tried to set the record straight. Writing to the magazine *Social Service*, he denied that the children were exploited. On the contrary, they were often hired "purely as a matter of charity" and they were much better off in the mill than running loose, "learning the first lessons of a vagrant's life."

As for the people stirring up all this trouble, Mr. Gordon

felt that at best they were "a noble and disinterested class made up of the clergy and the clubwomen, with whom it is quite a drawing room fad." At worst, they were "paid and prejudiced agitators." And with perhaps a slight bow toward the Confederate flag, he added that these agitators were "backed to some extent by New England competitors of Southern mill interests." This was always a good argument in Georgia, and Mr. Gordon wisely did not add that he was a Northerner backed by Northern capital.

As for any abuses, he pointed out that the millowners had a "gentlemen's agreement" that was far more effective than any law. It limited the employment of ten-year-olds to sixty-six hours a week . . . and the owners could be trusted to observe it. "Legislation based on oversentimentality and disregard of actual conditions," Mr. Gordon concluded sternly, "would prove a severe menace to Southern industrial progress.". . .

Opposition Mounts

Visiting the Lindale Mills a few year later, investigator Lewis W. Hine saw "youngsters by the dozen, tiny little chaps, sweeping, doffing, spinning—there were twenty-five of them that I judged to be under twelve in the three spinning rooms alone, and I found some more in the weave rooms, helping."

At that, the Lindale management was more advanced than some, for at least it allowed Hine to poke around. Other mills didn't let outsiders in, and since they usually owned not only the factories but the houses, stores and streets as well, their orders were final. When the Reverend Alfred E. Seddon visited the Porterdale Mills in 1908, he was refused a room at the local hotel and advised to take the next train out of town.

Whole communities seemed mesmerized. In Winona, Mississippi (not Georgia, but typical), a local doctor declared that the longer the children were in a factory, the healthier they grew. "Why, one bright little girl told me she gained ten pounds in four months after going to work in the mill."

In 1911 Georgia again considered the child labor question, and the reform groups again found themselves up against ingenious opposition. This time petitions poured in to the legislature ostensibly from mill workers all over the state. They begged the lawmakers not to shorten hours, not to stop night work, not to set any age limitations. Some were all signed by the same hand, but others seemed genuine—painfully scrawled signatures by the few who could write, rows of X's for the many who couldn't.

Somewhere along the line the owners also picked up a poet laureate. He was Thomas Dawley, who specialized in obtaining rapturous testimonials from enthusiastic child workers. One little victim of reform in Tennessee was quoted as pleading, "Oh, kind sir, can't you do something to have the law changed so that I can go back to the cotton mill?"

Against this sort of talent not much could be done. By the end of the 1911 session the reform elements did manage to win a sixty-hour work week. But the eleven-hour day remained, and it was still legal for a ten-year-old child to work in a Georgia cotton mill.

But the reform groups kept chipping away, and in 1912 it seemed as if something might be done. The progressive movement was at flood tide and, best of all, the millowners appeared to see the light. Not just liberal manufacturers like Harry L. Williams of Swift Company—he had always understood—but even Frederick B. Gordon, the transplanted Bostonian. As president of the Georgia Cotton Manufacturers Association, Mr. Gordon indicated that his organization would not oppose a reasonable bill.

Just to make sure, the reformers met with the association's officials and went over the provisions together. When the manufacturers objected to parts of the proposed bill, a compromise was worked out. In its final form the measure gradually raised the age limit to fourteen. Everybody seemed agreeable.

The bill sailed through the House with one minor amendment—store help was exempted to allow for delivery boys, bootblacks, stock clerks, and the like. Although disappointed, the progressives felt half a loaf was better than none and let the change stand.

But not Frederick B. Gordon. He vigorously complained that the bill was no longer in its original shape. Then he appeared at the Senate hearings on behalf of the children who worked in the stores, as the reform leaders watched in wide-eyed amazement. They soon learned what was up. Since these lads in the stores weren't covered, Mr. Gordon felt reluctantly compelled to withdraw his support. The Cotton Manufacturers Association fell in line and the bill was defeated. Once again Georgia had no effective child labor law.

When the Reverend Harvey Vaughn resumed his tireless investigations of mill conditions the following April, Mr. Gordon cheerfully described his role in beating the 1912 bill. But he announced that he was now definitely going to work for a law. Hence the reformers' optimism when the new bill came up in August, 1913—and their surprise when it lost like so many others. They might have known better, for certainly the pattern was familiar: Again a compromise approved by everybody . . . again a minor amendment . . . again defeat.

Senator Spinks, one of the measure's opponents, tried to placate the progressives. He said that the bill was "beautiful in theory but it would not stand the test." And he added that Georgia was not ready.

Support for Reform Grows

Maybe not, but almost. Each successive defeat had awakened more interest, and now public support was strong. Georgia labor leaders and newspapers threw their weight behind the battling clergymen and progressive politicians.

By December sentiment was hot enough for an interesting meeting to take place at the National Child Labor Committee headquarters. Mr. Edward Lovering of the Massachusetts Mills of Lowell and Harry Meikleham of the firm's Lindale Mills (he who had earlier warned so darkly of Northern mills) together called on the committee leaders and strongly complained about the drive. They especially resented any comparison of the company's Massachusetts and Georgia mills. They couldn't see why the same age limits should apply to both. The committee couldn't see why not.

The movement continued to build up steam, and in the summer of 1914 the Atlanta *Georgian* went all-out in support of reform. All through July the paper ran immensely effective articles, editorials, and cartoons. By August the battle was won. A new bill was proposed and this time passed by the Legislature. There were loopholes—and the educational requirement was a little weak—but at least children under fourteen (with a few exceptions) were kept out of the mills and factories. Georgia at last had its law.

A great day, but poor children were still a long way from rich children. . . .

But if America was still a land of extremes, there was at least a great moral awakening. Ordinary people in every walk of life felt a growing sense of social responsibility. It was not so much a political movement as a purely humanitarian revolt against poverty . . . a warmhearted crusade for a finer, cleaner life.

Child labor reform was only one sign. Another was the spate of laws governing factory safety, minimum hours for women, and workmen's compensation. . . .

Reviewing the fervid feeling of the times, the January 24, 1914, issue of *Collier's* proudly declared, "Fifty years from now the future historian will say that the ten years ending about January 1, 1914, was the period of the greatest ethical advances made by this nation in any decade."

But all too soon no one even noticed. For in the hot, languid summer of 1914—in fact on the very day the Georgia Senate Committee finally approved the child labor bill—Germany unexpectedly invaded Belgium, and within a few brief years the tramp of marching feet stamped out such pleasant thoughts.

Females Demand Their Rights: The Women's Suffrage Movement

Elizabeth Frost and Kathryn Cullen-DuPont

For many years, females in the United States had endured a second-class citizenship. Rights which males took for granted were denied to females. Gradually, following the lead of champions like Susan B. Anthony and Elizabeth Cady Stanton, women began demanding equal treatment. By the first decades of the twentieth century, women had organized into a powerful suffrage movement. Elizabeth Frost and Kathryn Cullen-DuPont studied the origins and effects of the suffrage movement, and published their findings in a 1992 book. This selection is an excerpt from that book.

When Lucy Stone, Elizabeth Cady Stanton and Susan B. Anthony died, their natural rights argument for suffrage was replaced by one stressing its usefulness. Where the earliest leaders had looked for authority to the Declaration of Independence, their successors looked to any number of investigatory reports about the wages and hours of working women. Women's lives had changed, these new leaders argued, and women needed the ballot in order to deal with the consequences. In 1892 Elizabeth Cady Stanton said that "[t]he strongest reason why we ask for woman a voice in the government under which she lives; in the religion she is asked to believe; equality in social life . . .

---

a place in the trades and professions . . . is because of her birthright to self-sovereignty . . .￾" By the early part of the 20th century, Melinda Scott, a hat trimmer in a New York factory, had found, in her "place in the trades," reasons of her own. "If women had the ballot," she explained, ". . . [they] would have dared to pass the 54-hour bill . . . I do not want to be governor of the State . . . but I do want the ballot to be able to register my protest against the [working] conditions that are killing and maiming. . . ."

Working conditions were, indeed, dreadful for many women. Garment workers, for example, frequently worked 11- and 12-hour days, six or seven days a week, in buildings that were poorly maintained, dimly lit and often in violation of safety codes. They not only were paid meager wages but were also expected to use those funds to purchase their own sewing supplies.

Initial Steps to Equality

Thousands of women went on strike. As the winter of 1909 began, the employees of the Triangle Shirtwaist Company of New York "left the factories from every side, all of them walking down toward Union Square . . . the spirit of a conqueror led them on." The shirtwaist workers of Philadelphia struck that same winter; the following year, 14 women walked out on Hart, Schaffner and Marx in Chicago, and 8,000 co-workers followed; and in 1912, women were among the 20,000 textile workers to strike in Lawrence, Massachusetts.

There had been strikes before, but none, of men or women, to equal these strikes in size or duration. Women stayed out on strike despite arrests, beatings and the need for wages with which to feed their children. This last need was real: During the winter of the Chicago strike, 1,250 strikers or wives of strikers gave birth. One newly-delivered woman explained her continued support of the strike: "It is not only bread we give our children. . . . We live by freedom, and I will fight till I die to give it to my children."

The members of the Women's Trade Union League

(WTUL) worked to ensure that women *didn't* die in this particular fight. The WTUL was an organization that joined women factory workers with women from the middle and upper classes, including such well-known society women as Anne Morgan, Alva Belmont, Mrs. Henry Morgenthau and Helen Taft (the president's daughter). Those from the monied half of the partnership were called "allies."

Although some of the factory workers found some of their "allies" patronizing, there is no dispute about the amount of aid rendered. In New York, 75 of what some called the "mink brigade" joined the picket lines, and many were arrested along with the strikers. Others raised bail money for the arrested factory workers and secured legal representation for them. They did what they could to end the police brutality taking place daily. Individually, they acted as witnesses, brought charges against abusive foremen and police and monitored the courts day and night to ensure fair treatment of the arrested strikers. When police brutality continued, the WTUL and 10,000 sympathizers

A Woman's Pledge

To gain equality, women adopted many measures. One way was to sign a pledge promising certain actions. The following, used in 1910, provides an example of such pledges.

I hereby promise that:

1. I WILL give what I can and do my share of the work to gain Votes for Women.

2. I WILL NOT give either money or service to any other cause until the women of New York State have been enfranchised.

> *Pledge prepared by the Women's Political Union, made available for signature December 10, 1910, in Blatch and Lutz's* Challenging Years, *137.*

Elizabeth Frost and Kathryn Cullen-DuPont. *Women's Suffrage in America: An Eyewitness History.* New York: Facts On File, Inc., 1992.

marched in protest to City Hall. (Not all the women active in the labor movement appreciated efforts to link labor rights and women's suffrage. Mother Jones, for example, heartily resented it.)

Militant methods found their way into the women's suffrage campaign as well. In 1887 Elizabeth Cady Stanton had written, "If all the heroic deeds of women recorded in history and our daily journals . . . have not yet convinced our opponents that women are possessed of superior fighting qualities, the sex may feel called upon in the near future to give some further illustrations of their prowess. Of one thing they may be assured, that the next generation will not argue the question of woman's rights with the infinite patience we have had for half a century. . . ." One younger person notably lacking in patience was Cady Stanton's own daughter, Harriot.

Because American graduate schools were largely closed to women, Harriot Stanton Blatch had attended graduate school in England. There, in 1882, she married a British citizen (losing her own United States citizenship in the process, since a woman's citizenship followed her husband's) and became involved in the English women's movement. In 1902, the last year of her mother's life, Blatch returned to the United States with her husband and daughter Nora; when Elizabeth Cady Stanton died, Harriot was at her side.

Eight weeks after Cady Stanton's funeral, Susan B. Anthony complained about Blatch's failure to attend a convention in New Orleans. "I thought," Anthony wrote, "she should be there & *represent her mother.*" Gradually, Blatch began to do that and more.

The National American Woman Suffrage Association (NAWSA) Blatch found upon her return to the United States had become, she believed, the staid organization her mother had predicted. Blatch thereupon founded the Equality League of Self-Supporting Women, which was joined by a large number of factory women who wanted suffrage. (When it became clear that many other would-be members were not yet self-supporting, the name was changed to the Women's Political Union.) In 1910 the Women's Political Union held the first suffrage parade in New York City. A year later there was another one, with "3,000 marchers and perhaps 70,000 onlookers."

Women Strike Back

There was also a funeral parade in New York City in 1911. It was in memory of 146 victims, mostly female, of the Triangle Shirtwaist Company fire.

The employees of this company had gone on strike two years before, but their working conditions had not changed. The building had inadequate fire escapes and no sprinkler system. Worse, the doors were locked from the outside to prevent the women from leaving during working hours. When the fire broke out on March 25, 1911, the women were trapped. They clung to the breaking fire escapes on the ninth floor. Fire fighters tried to reach them, but their ladders stopped at the sixth floor. Women jumped from the windows and died on the sidewalk. Other

The New York City suffrage parade of 1912 drew 20,000 marchers and one half million spectators.

women, remaining inside, died of burns or suffocation. That night, the 26th Street pier was filled with 146 corpses and 2,000 people in search of their loved ones' bodies.

It took a week to identify the dead, and seven women could not be identified at all. The outraged members of the New York Women's Trade Union League and the International Ladies Garment Workers Union planned a funeral for the unnamed women. When Mayor Gaynor had the bodies buried in a city plot, the women's funeral procession was conducted with an empty hearse. New York's grieving population turned out in full on the rainy, cold day, April 5, 1911. Through the steady downpour, they marched. The Washington Square Arch was the agreed point of merger for marchers from all across the city to become members of one parade. There were so many people at that spot by 3:20 P.M. that the last person had to wait until 6:00 P.M. to pass below the arch. Almost half a million people lined the sidewalks in silence to witness the procession.

Afterward, Max Blanck and Isaac Harris, the owners of the company, were acquitted of manslaughter charges. (Max Blanck was charged two years later for once again locking his female employees in their work room. He was fined $20.00.) Even before the acquittal, female labor leaders such as Leonora O'Reilly demanded woman suffrage with an increased sense of urgency.

March Toward Parity

When the next New York City suffrage parade was held in 1912, there were 20,000 marchers and another half million people lining the sidewalks. The 1913 New York City suffrage parade was even larger. Then, in Washington, D.C., on March 13, 1913, the day before President Wilson's inauguration, there was another parade. Women would be so badly harassed during this parade that a special session of the United States Congress would conduct hearings to investigate the behavior of the District of Columbia police department, and the chief of police would be dismissed. One woman, however, was particularly ill-treated—and by the women's rights activists themselves. That woman was Ida B. Wells-Barnett.

Wells-Barnett, prominent newspaper owner, journalist

 Clarence Darrow on Suffrage

Clarence Darrow was an outspoken proponent of fair play, yet he spouted ambiguous views when it came to women's suffrage. The following selection from a biography of the legal giant illustrates the point.

George Briggs, the single taxer, met Darrow one Sunday morning at an atheist-science service and accompanied him and three of Darrow's women friends to the Auditorium Hotel for luncheon. Briggs had a five-dollar ticket in his pocket to hear Mary Garden sing but let it lapse because he preferred arguing with Darrow. At the end of an afternoon of intense discussion Darrow turned to Briggs and, indicating his three women admirers who had filled so admirably the role of audience, commented:

"These women have laughed in the right places; they have nodded their heads in the right places; they've asked the right questions—but none of them knows a damn thing of what we've been talking about."

"If you give votes to women," he said, "they will bring prohibition down upon us." Another friend relates, "I remember making some remarks about the desirability of women having the same rights, privileges and duties as men. Darrow replied:

"'I'm not so sure about that. We notice that nature makes the least differentiation between the sexes in her lowest orders. As we rise in the scale the differences become greater until, when we reach the human animal, it is greatest of all. I think possibly it is better that way.'"

He confided to Gertrude Barnum that "votes for women would put progress back fifty years"—but voted for suffrage anyway.

Irving Stone, *Clarence Darrow for the Defense.* Garden City, NY: Garden City Publishing Co., Inc., 1941.

and president of the first African-American women's suffrage organization, the Alpha Suffrage Club of Chicago, stood with the Illinois section as preparations for the parade began. When women from the Southern states refused to participate in an integrated event, NAWSA officials asked Wells-Barnett to join a special "Negro women's contingent." Fellow suffragists of European descent argued among themselves about the need to keep as many Southern women as possible in the suffrage movement; few of these women spoke up to say that Wells-Barnett should be welcomed regardless of potential Southern defection. Wells-Barnett finally said that she would join Illinois' contingent or none at all. Then she left.

When the parade started, Ida B. Wells-Barnett was among the many bystanders. As her state's contingent passed before her, she left the crowd and took her place in the parade. Two European-American women then left their assigned places to march at her side.

The parade Wells-Barnett joined had not been going smoothly. Passage through the streets had been arranged in advance with the police department. Police officers on duty were instructed to "give every attention to protecting those comprising the parade against embarrassments and afford them every security." Those orders were not obeyed.

Instead, as participants in the parade began to walk down Pennsylvania Avenue, hordes of people filled the center of the street. Men, many of them drunk, poked and jeered at the suffragists. Only an occasional police officer tried to control the crowd. As one woman recalled for U.S. Senators, "there was no space whatever. There was not 10 inches . . . between us and the crowd . . . I had with me a number of young girls in our division—my daughter and one or two others—and the crowd did hoot and jeer and make the most insulting remarks to these girls. They tried to grab their flowers away from them, and one man stuck his foot out. . . . She was tripped but did not fall . . . because the crowd was too dense . . . there were two policemen standing together that were egging the crowd on to jeer, and they themselves were making remarks to us and jeering."

Asked why she didn't complain to the police, the witness said, "None of us complained. I simply told the young girls to keep out of their way. I was just as much alarmed at those policemen as I was at the crowd."

Even after this experience, people who were becoming militant suffragists continued to use whatever methods they could to call attention to their cause. Emmeline Pankhurst, the self-described "Hooligan woman" from England, was invited to speak in Carnegie Hall. Mrs. Richard Hornsby and several of her suffragist friends flew an airplane above President Wilson's yacht and dropped petitions on board.

These were strategies of which Carrie Chapman Catt, the reelected president of NAWSA and, by now, a superb tactition, did not approve. Working through a network of state organizations between 1907 and 1916, NAWSA and its affiliates had helped secure suffrage in Washington, California, Arizona, Kansas, Oregon, Montana, Nevada, Illinois and Alaska Territory. Moreover, by 1916, she had quietly established a rapport with President Wilson.

Instead, she very privately addressed the NAWSA's Executive Council after the organization's 1916 convention. The convention would "not adjourn, should it sit until Christmas," Catt told her national officers and state chapter presidents, unless it adopted "a logical and sensible policy toward the Federal Amendment. . . ." Catt herself had devised such a plan. Using military metaphor, she described a new campaign to secure women's suffrage in at least 36 states, the number needed to ratify a Federal Amendment. Once this was accomplished, voting women would apply organized pressure to get a Federal Amendment passed by their representatives and senators and ratified by the members of their state legislatures. In secret, more than 36 state chapter presidents signed a document pledging themselves to the campaign. It would be Carrie Chapman Catt's "Winning Plan."

Denied at Work, Denied at Home: The Reasons People Strike

Philip S. Foner

Although the nation's economic expansion of the late 1800s improved the lifestyle of many people, factory workers did not share in the benefits. Laboring under conditions that bordered on the criminal, men, women, and children battled to subsist from week to week. In the following selection, labor historian Philip S. Foner graphically details the reasons why workers organized a 1912 strike in Lawrence, Massachusetts.

Situated in the Merrimack River Valley, about 30 miles north of Boston, Lawrence had the reputation in 1912 of being "the worsted center of the world." The American Woolen Co., Morgan-controlled, the most powerful textile corporation in America, had three of its largest woolen mills in Lawrence: The Washington, employing about 6,500 hands; the Wood, with 5,200 operatives, and the Ayer, with 2,000 hands. The only independent woolen mill was the George E. Kunhardt, employing about 950. There were four large cotton mills in Lawrence: The Arlington, employing about 6,500 workers; the Pacific, the largest producer of cotton-print goods in the world, with 5,200 employees; the Everett, employing 2,000 operatives, and the Atlantic, giving employment to 1,300 hands. There were also two small cotton mills employing together 1,100

Excerpted from *History of the Labor Movement in the United States,* vol. 4, *The Industrial Workers of the World, 1905–1917,* by Philip S. Foner. Copyright ©1965 by International Publishers Co., Inc. Reprinted with permission.

people, and a large textile dyeing establishment, owned by the U.S. Worsted Co., employing 600 workers. All told, the 12 mills in Lawrence, when operating at maximum capacity, furnished employment to approximately 32,000 men, women and children.

The mill owners reaped huge profits. Dudley Holman, secretary to Governor Foss of Massachusetts, proved this statistically by disclosing that in 1902 when its capital stock was valued at $49,501,000, the American Woolen Co. paid out $1,400,000 in dividends, while in 1911, when the capital stock was valued at $60,000,000, it paid dividends of $2,800,000. Thus in the course of ten years, dividends increased 100 per cent while the capital invested rose less than 20 per cent. In 1911, the American Woolen Co.'s dividend was seven per cent; that of Pacific Mills, 12 per cent, and that of the Arlington Mill, eight per cent.

Portrait of the Factory Worker

The character of the working population in Lawrence's textile mills had undergone a sharp change in the nearly seven decades between the founding of the city in 1845 and the great strike of 1912. Until the 1880's, the native Americans, English, Irish, Scotch, and French-Canadians were the dominant elements in the textile factories, and many of them were skilled workers. With the technological advances of the 1880's, the skilled personnel were rapidly displaced, and, after 1890, the Italians, Greeks, Portuguese, Russians, Poles, Lithuanians, Syrians and Armenians took their places. By 1912, the Italians, Poles, Russians, Syrians, and Lithuanians had definitely replaced the native Americans and Western Europeans as the predominant groups in the textile mills of Lawrence. Within a one-mile radius of the mill district, there lived 25 different nationalities, speaking a half hundred different languages. The largest ethnic group in the city was Italian.

To induce the new immigrants to work in Lawrence, the American Woolen Co. had posted placards in the towns throughout Southern Europe which pictured the textile workers holding bags of gold, displaying bankbooks with substantial bank accounts and standing outside handsome homes which they were said to own. What was the real state of affairs these foreign-born workers found awaiting them in Lawrence? They can be summed up succinctly: Inadequate wages, difficult working conditions, sub-human housing facilities, and a community unsympathetic, when not hostile, to their needs.

The U.S. Bureau of Labor Statistics made a study of the payroll reports from four woolen and three cotton mills in Lawrence for the week ending nearest to November 25, 1911, about seven weeks before the strike. It covered a total of 21,922 workers (excluding overseers and clerks)— or about two-thirds of the total number in the mills on the eve of the strike. The average rate per hour of 16,578 operatives, skilled and unskilled, in the four woolen and worsted mills was 16 cents, and the average amount earned for the week under study was $8.75. The average hourly rate of 5,344 employees, skilled and unskilled, in the cotton mills was 15.8 cents, and the average weekly earnings were $8.78. These wages included premiums or bonuses! But 59.8 per cent of the operatives in the woolen mills earned less than 15 cents an hour, and 14 percent of those in the cotton mills less than 12 cents. Almost one-third— 33.2 per cent—of both woolen and cotton operatives received less than $7.00 per week. The average weekly wages revealed by this study were based on earnings during a week when the mills were running full time. But none of the mills worked full time throughout the year. Although the Bureau declared that it could not ascertain the amount of unemployment, it conceded that there was a serious curtailment of earnings due to lost time, and concluded that the $8.75 and $8.78 average wages for the week under study were far too high for an annual average.

The Lawrence textile industry was a "family industry." But this pleasant-sounding phrase had a deadly meaning for the workers. To keep the family alive, the husbands, wives, and children worked in the mills. On the eve of the strike in 1912, one-half of all children in Lawrence between 14 and 18 were employed in the mills; 44.6 per cent of the textile workers were females, and 11.5 percent were boys and girls under 18. If the earnings of the wives were pitifully small, those of the children were even less. Testimony before a Congressional Committee revealed that the youngsters, boys and girls, 14 to 16 years of age, earned seven and five dollars or less per week when the mills were running full time!

Confronted with such frightening statistics, the mill owners claimed that competition from other New England states and the South forced wages down. But they did not mention that this did not keep profits from soaring, and that they were expanding their operations in Lawrence rather than reducing them because of this competition. Actually, profits had gone up, while wages had gone down in the face of rising living costs. Congressman Victor Berger, Socialist, Wisc., revealed that in 1890, when the industry showed a profit of $164,598,665, labor received 22 per cent of the gross profit. In 1905, when profits had increased to $212,690,048, wages accounted for only 19.5 per cent of the total profits.

Workers' Grievances

According to the U.S. Bureau of Labor, the average work week in the mills of Lawrence was 56 hours. But 21.6 per cent worked more than 56 hours, and none of the workers were paid a rate higher for overtime than the regular scale. While the demand for a shorter work week was not an important issue in the strike—a fact which is hardly surprising since with hourly rates as low as they were, the workers needed a lengthened week not a shorter one to earn enough to stay alive—one of the strikers' demands was for double pay for all overtime.

Chief among the grievances of the Lawrence workers was the premium or bonus system which was introduced by William M. Wood, president of the American Woolen Co., and was used extensively in the mills. Essentially a speed-up plan, designed to obtain the highest possible production from each employee, it provided, in the case of the better-paid occupations such as the weavers, loom-fixers, warp dressers, assistant overseers, slashers, and menders, for a bonus to the worker whose output exceeded some fixed standard. In the other occupations the bonus was paid for regular attendance. Any employee who had not missed more than one day during a four-week period received a premium. . . .

Various other complaints were voiced by workers appearing as witnesses at the Congressional hearings. Water supplied by the mills was usually so warm, due to the presence of numerous steampipes in the weaving rooms, that the workers were forced, in order to quench their thirst, to buy cold drinking water at a weekly charge of ten cents. The mills held back a week's wages on all new workers, thus imposing a heavy burden on them during the first two weeks of employment. Workers, especially children, were "docked" one hour's pay for coming five or ten minutes late, and if the lateness was repeated three times, they were fired. And all witnesses expressed severe indignation at the tyrannical attitude of the foremen in their dealings with the workers. The overseers insisted that the women workers sleep with them as a condition of holding on to their jobs, swore at the men, women and children alike, constantly cursed at the foreign-born workers, calling them "ignorant Dagoes and Hunkies," and treating them as if they were "dumb cattle."

We have already seen enough of the conditions in the Lawrence mills to understand how inevitable it was that a mass uprising of the workers should occur. But even this is only part of the story. What sort of life did the earnings of the mill workers permit?

Living Conditions

Nearly all the textile workers lived in a slum area so congested that two tenements were erected on the same lot— one in front, the other on the rear of the lot. A dark alley between the front houses provided the only entrance for the rear buildings. The rooms in these wooden firetraps were gloomy and dingy. Toilet facilities were totally inadequate and plumbing defective. One or two toilets, placed in the dark tenement halls, for a four-story tenement, was not unusual. In his report for the year 1912, the Lawrence Inspector of Buildings wrote: "Conditions in the congested districts of the city are drawing close to the danger line in the manner of building construction for tenement purposes. The tendency of some property owners to use every inch of available space has in some quarters developed conditions that are not alone a menace to health, but to life itself." "Each year," he complained, "I have recommended that the City Council take up the matter of revising the Building Ordinances." But each year the proposal was buried by a Council dominated by property owners loath to increase taxes,* and convinced that these conditions were good enough for "Hunkeys, Poles and Wops."

Rents were so high that most families had to take in boarders and lodgers to meet the payment. They ranged from $2.75 per week for four-room flats to $4.50 for five, and $5.00 for six-room flats. Little wonder that the Health Department found that four or five persons lived in a room. The U.S. Bureau of Labor discovered that the Italians in Lawrence paid more per room than did their countrymen in the crowded sections of Chicago, Cleveland, Buffalo, Milwaukee, and other large cities.

The cost of food, clothing and fuel was equally excessive. Testimony before the Congressional Committee revealed that the price of meat was so high, even of stew-beef (a cheap grade which sold at ten to 14 cents a pound and for which there was a great demand by the foreign workers) that its presence on the table was more or less regarded as an occasion for a holiday. Meat usually appeared only at

---

*The mill owners, living in Boston or in New York, paid no personal taxes to the city and the mills paid only a moderate property tax. The shopkeepers and property owners of Lawrence frowned on higher expenditures for services for the foreign-born since this would increase their tax burden.

Sunday dinner; for the rest of the week the diet consisted of black bread, coffee, molasses or lard. Milk, selling at seven cents a quart, was out of reach of most workers' families who depended entirely on condensed or evaporated milk. "Often," one witness reported, "the children went hungry; there were days when only bread and water kept them alive." There being no place for the storage of coal in the crowded tenements, coal and wood had to be purchased in small quantities. This naturally increased the cost tremendously. For a 20-pound bag of coal the common price was ten to 13 cents, that is, from $10 to $13 per ton, an increase of from 40 to 80 per cent over the price of coal if purchased by the ton.

As for clothing, the comment of one student of conditions in Lawrence aptly sums up the situation: "Ironically enough, in the greatest woolen center in the country the producers of suits could not afford the price of $15.00 which was prohibitive to them, nor could the women who made the cotton dresses pay $3.00 for them. Cotton shirts sold at exorbitant prices ranging from $2.00 to $5.00. As for overcoats, they were out of the question, and to the spectator, it appeared that most of the workers of Lawrence wore sweaters beneath the coats of their suits."

Public charitable institutions failed, from lack of funds and indifference to the needs of the workers to supplement inadequate wages. Rev. Clark Carter, Director of Public Health and Charity, who defended child labor as a beneficent influence in the community, declared that the standard of living of the factory workers was all that should be expected.

Lawrence had two dubious honors. One was that it was a leading contender for being the most congested city in the nation, with 33,700 people, one-third of the population, dwelling on less than one-thirteenth of the city's area—the slum area. The other was that the infant mortality death rate in Lawrence was one of the highest of the industrial cities of the nation. Of the 1,524 deaths in Lawrence in 1910, 711 or 46.6 percent were of children less than six years. Indeed, in that year, the total deaths in Lawrence was exceeded, according to the U.S. Census office, by only six cities out of 40 selected.

Unquestionably, the foul tenements, poor diet, and lack of warm clothing were important factors in the high number of deaths. Overcrowded housing—in 1912, the Director of Public Safety found only four rooms without beds in them on a whole block of tenements—and an inadequate diet probably accounted for the high tuberculosis rate. In 1912, the Department of Health estimated that 800 people in the city had tuberculosis. The Lawrence Survey, conducted in 1911, fixed the number of deaths due to this disease at 150 yearly.

The Workers Take a Stand

Here, then, were the conditions which led to the great upheaval of the Lawrence textile workers. (These conditions, one might add, were no better in other New England textile centers.) In explaining why they finally revolted, the strikers stated:

"For years the employers have forced conditions upon us that gradually and surely broke up our homes. They have taken away our wives from the homes, our children have been driven from the playground, stolen out of schools and driven into the mills, where they were strapped to the machines, not only to force the fathers to compete, but that their young lives may be coined into dollars for a parasite class, that their very nerves, their laughter and joy denied, may be woven into cloth. . . .

"We hold that as useful members of society, and as producers we have the right to lead decent and honorable lives; that we are to have homes and not shacks; that we ought to have clean food and not adulterated food at high prices; that we ought to have clothes suited to the weather."

Mother Jones and the Fight for Workers' Rights

Dale Fetherling

Labor reformers were mostly men, but a handful of women also joined the cause of promoting workers' rights. One combative female, Mary Jones, so fiercely worked for the labor movement in America that she became known as Mother Jones. Dale Fetherling wrote a comprehensive biography of the reformer. The following selection is from his account of Mother Jones's work in West Virginia.

Paint and Cabin Creeks were the yin and yang of central West Virginia's Kanawha Valley in 1912. Eight miles apart and separated by a razorback ridge, the two streams each extended southward from the Kanawha River for some 25 miles. Through the coal-laden mountains, they carved narrow gorges, just wide enough in some spots for railroad tracks and a road. Thanks in part to Mother Jones, the Kanawha Valley—including the two creeks—had been unionized in the 1902 strike. But two years later, a brief strike by the Cabin Creek miners caused the union to lose all its organization there. Paint Creek remained a union bastion. But on Cabin Creek, the operators hired mine guards to prevent organizers from getting another foothold. Along these two streams, the mines soon would spew out many of their 7,500 miners and in so doing mark the beginning of the state's worst coal war. Before there

Excerpted from *Mother Jones: The Miners' Angel*, by Dale Fetherling. Copyright ©1974 by Southern Illinois University Press. Reprinted by permission of the publisher.

would be a truce, scores of men would die violently, a heavy economic loss would be incurred, and Mother Jones would fight—and be fought—fiercely.

Another Battle to Fight

The aged agitator, now eighty-two years old, was touring the West and the Pacific Northwest in 1912, aiding striking railway employees and addressing mass meetings. Returning to Denver by the first of June, she then went among the copper miners in Butte, Montana, prior to a scheduled speaking tour in San Francisco. But then, labor news from West Virginia broke, as it did on and off for the next decade and a half, onto the front pages of the nation's newspapers. "Now the battle had to be fought all over again," she later wrote, so I "tied up all my possessions in a black shaw—I like traveling light—and went immediately to West Virginia." Prompting her urgency was a dispute which had been smouldering particularly since 1907 when coal-mine operators in the central competitive field—western Pennsylvania, Ohio, Indiana, and Illinois—reportedly offered financial aid to the UMW [United Mine Workers] for organizing West Virginia. Forced to recognize the union as early as 1898, the central operators continued to face competition from the high-grade, cheaply dug West Virginia coal, especially after the opening of the rich Logan field in southern West Virginia in 1904. The state's coal production rose from 6,000,000 tons in 1888 to 70,000,000 by 1912, and 90 percent of that was sold in competition with the central field operators.

A UMW contract with the Kanawha field operators expired April 1, 1912. When the mine owners refused to agree to improve upon the old contract, the miners struck on April 18 throughout the Kanawha district, except, of course, for nonunion Cabin Creek. For nearly a month the strike was conducted without violence. Soon, all strike-bound operators came to terms except those on Paint Creek. They maintained that with unorganized Cabin Creek so near, they could not afford to jeopardize further their competitive position. With the battle lines narrowed to just Paint Creek, the operators there hired mine guards from the Baldwin-Felts Detective Agency in Bluefield. The first assignment of guards arrived May 7 and began bolstering the companies' defenses. Violence began in late May and escalated until, by July, miners and guards alternately were attacking one another in armylike battles. The threat of civil war gripped the state, and Mother Jones, who arrived about this time, did little to ease tensions. By the Fourth of July, she was reported "working night and day" encouraging the miners' resolve. She also may have encouraged no little violence.

Addressing strikers in Charleston, she denounced Governor William E. Glasscock for not meeting with them. "You can expect no help from such a goddamned dirty coward," she reportedly told them, "whom, for modesty's sake, we shall call 'Crystal Peter.' But I warn this little Governor that unless he rids Paint Creek and Cabin Creek of these goddamned Baldwin-Felts mine-guard thugs, there is going to be one hell of a lot of bloodletting in this hills." On another occasion on Cabin Creek, Mother Jones is said to have held up a blood-soaked coat discarded by a wounded mine guard and told the crowd: "This is the first time I ever saw a goddamned mine guard's coat decorated to suit me." Then she had the coat cut into pieces which she threw to the audience for lapel emblems.

West Virginia Explodes

For weeks the carnage grew in pitch. More than once, the miners attacked Mucklow, five miles up Paint Creek, where the guards had built a fort, complete with a machine gun, and where one of the largest collieries was headquartered. One observer noted that when Mother Jones addressed the miners, she "encouraged them to keep up the shootings and keep up the trouble. If she found some weak-kneed fellow who were [sic] hanging around the tents, she went after him and drove him off into the mountains. In one instance she was heard to say, 'Get your guns, you cowardly sons of b——s, and get into the woods.'"

Viewing the Paint Creek operators' recalcitrance as an attempt to drive a wedge into the state's slender union strength, Mother Jones again veered close to an outright call to violence during an August 1 meeting on the Charleston levee. "I am not going to say to you don't molest the operators," she stated. "It is they who hire the dogs to shoot you. (applause) I am not asking you to do it; but if he is going to oppress you, deal with him."

Socialist editor and IWW leader Ralph Chaplin was on the same program that day with Mother Jones and he later described her speech.

> She might have been any coal miner's wife ablaze with righteous fury when her brood was in danger. Her voice shrilled as she shook her fist at the coal operators, the mine guards, the union officials. . . . She prayed and cursed and pleaded, raising her clenched and trembling hands, asking heaven to bear witness. She wore long, very full skirts and a black shawl and her tiny bonnet bobbed up and down as she harangued the crowd. The miners loved it and laughed, cheered, hooted, and even cried as she spoke to them.

Sensing the rapport, Mother Jones grew yet bolder and climbed up on a box in the bed of a wagon. Then she began:

> I say to the policemen: "Get all the ammunition you can; get all the ammunition and lie quiet; for one of these days you will come over with us, and we are going to give the other fellows hell.". . . We are law-abiding citizens, we will destroy no property, we will take no life, but if a fellow comes to my home and outrages my wife, by the eternal he will pay the penalty. I will send him to his God in the repair shop. (loud applause) The man who doesn't do it hasn't got a drop of revolutionary blood in his veins. . . .

Mother Jones, at least in the early part of this long strike, was not representing the UMW but only herself. To the miners this seemingly made little difference. Still an aggressive organizer, she did not always adhere to the policy of waiting for the optimal opportunity. She told one UMW organizer to stop playing preacher and telling the miners "that silly trash" about justice eventually righting all wrongs. And at one point, when told she could not legally organize a local because she did not have a copy of the UMW ritual, she retorted, "The ritual, hell. I'll make one up!"

The union by late July turned its attention toward persuading Cabin Creek's miners to join the walkout. But by setting up guard stations at strategic spots, the operators had made Cabin Creek virtually inaccessible. In a countermove, Mother Jones scheduled an August 6 speech at Eskdale, a "free" city within the Cabin Creek territory. As one miner put it, "The only thing beautiful about Eskdale was its name. It was smoky, sooty and grimy." But it also was incorporated and thus became a refuge for miners above Eskdale who had been assaulted or driven out. Beyond it was a no-man's-land and organizers so feared the company gunmen beyond the town that union headquarters could not produce a single volunteer to venture past Eskdale on an organizing foray.

Preceding Mother Jones's expeditions, union broadsides beseeched the Cabin Creek men "in the name of the outraged women and murdered miners of Paint Creek to lay down your tools and join your striking brothers." Mother Jones's exhortations apparently were effective. Charles Cabell, general manager of the nearby Carbon Coal Company, later told Congressional investigators that the men on Cabin Creek were peaceful and content until Mother Jones began holding her meetings. After one such August meeting his men came back "very much exercised over the outlook and worried," Cabell said. Some of them left the next day. "After that time there was a great deal of unrest among our men, from that time on."

The Legend Grows

But if the first Eskdale meeting was successful in persuading the miners to unite, the next one led to the further embellishment of the legend of Mother Jones. When the second meeting broke up on August 13, someone suggested a march to the Red Warrior mining camp in the no-man's-land. Leading the marchers in a buggy, Mother Jones soon ran into a group of 50 or more mine guards with a machine gun pointed at the advancing column. As one miner recalled, Mother Jones drove her rig up to the gun emplacement, and a miner, helped her step down. "She surveyed the scene with a critical eye and walked straight up to the muzzle of one of the machine guns and patting the muzzle of the gun, said to the gunman behind it, 'Listen here, you, you fire one shot here today and there are 800 men in those hills (pointing to the almost inaccessible hills to the east)

A Woman's Place, but Not Hers

While Mother Jones spent most of her time away from her home and children, she did not believe that other females should be as active. Therefore, she opposed the suffrage movement, as this excerpt from Linda Atkinson's biography makes clear.

"In no sense of the word am I in favor of women's suffrage," she said. "Women already have a great responsibility on their shoulders. Home training of the child should be their task, and it is the most beautiful of tasks."

It was strange to hear this view from a woman who had lived a decidedly "public" life, who had urged women to join their husbands on picket lines, who had unionized working women, who had in fact done her best to change an entire culture—and who had not had a home, or even a permanent address, for over fifty years. It was the traditional view of "woman's place," and it would not have been surprising from a woman who had lived a traditional life. But from the famous—and to some people infamous—Mother Jones, such a statement was astonishing.

Linda Atkinson, *Mother Jones: The Most Dangerous Woman in America*. New York: Crown Publishers, Inc., 1978.

who will not leave one of your gang alive.'"

The hoary bluff worked. Mother Jones later admitted that if there were miners up in those hills, she did not know about them. The basis of some controversy, and perhaps hyperbole, the machine gun incident seemed to grow in Mother Jones's memory. "I realized that we were up against it," she confided, "and something had to be done to save the lives of these poor wretches, so I pulled the dramatic stuff on them thugs. Oh! how they shook in their boots, and while they were shaking in their boots I held my meeting and organized the miners who had congregated to hear me." The machine gun operator, J.H. Mayfield, however, later told a Congressional subcommittee that Mother Jones got out of the buggy and talked quietly with the guards. She "told us that when she left Eskdale that these fellows with the guns followed her up there, hot heads, and she told us she didn't want no trouble." At any rate, a tale was born and Mother Jones was allowed to continue to Red Warrior alone while the crowd had to return to Eskdale.

The joining of the Cabin Creek miners with the strike, whether done out of sympathy or coercion, was a blow to the operators. Cabell, who had about 1,000 employees, distributed questionnaires to his men when it was obvious that the UMW was going to seek to proselytize them. The results, he claimed, showed that 90 to 95 percent of the workers were satisfied with conditions. One contemporary historian said, "Through distortion of facts, the union agitators had so aroused the passions of the miners that men who were usually cool-headed threw all self-restraint to the winds and followed these leaders with the blind faith of children."

That "Horrible Old Woman" Speaks

Two days after the machine gun incident, Mother Jones delivered an hour-and-a-half address to a throng of miners gathered on the steps of the capitol in Charleston. Following several socialist speakers, she demanded the abolition of the mine guards and berated the establishment in a resolute and imaginative speech which claimed the labor movement to be a mandate from God and stated that the star of Bethlehem had been a portent of the industrial revolution. She pledged that some day the miners would take over the mines, and she poked fun at the operators' wives. "They wear $5.00 worth of makeup and have toothbrushes for their dogs, and they say, 'Oh, them horrible miners. Oh, that horrible old Mother Jones, that horrible old woman,'" she chided.

Taking an even harder than usual crack at the clergy, Mother Jones said the operators "give your missionary women a couple of hundred dollars and [they] rob you under pretense of giving it to Jesus. Jesus never sees a penny of it, and never heard of it. . . . I wish I was God Almighty, I would throw down something some night from heaven and get rid of the whole blood-sucking bunch. (Laughter and applause.)" In a stirring climax that moved her audience to both tears and rage, she told them: "And instead of the horrible homes you have got we will build on their ruins homes

Mother Jones

for you and your children to live in. . . . The day of oppression will be gone. I will be with you whether true or false. I will be with you at midnight or when the battle rages, when the last bullet ceases, but I will be in my joy, as an old saint said:

O'God, of the mighty clan,
   God grant that the woman who suffered for you,
Suffered not for a coward, but oh, for a man.
   God grant that the woman who suffered for you,
Suffered not for a coward, but oh, for a fighting man.

Then she asked the crowd to pass the hat for miners in

the throng who were broke and needed a glass of beer or who could not pay their way back home. Then a man came out of the audience and told Mother Jones: "Here is $10. I will go and borrow more. Shake hands with me, an old union miner. My children are able to take care of themselves, and I will take care of myself."

"Fight, fight, right," he said. "I have a good rifle, and I will get more money. If I don't have enough to pay my railroad fare I will walk. I don't care if this was the last cent I had, I will give it to 'Mother' and go and get some more." Such was the response Mother Jones got to her impassioned and inflammatory speeches during this long and bloody strike. As an orator, she was at her peak. Lawrence Lynch, a contemporary writer, stated:

> Head and shoulders above all the other agitators in ability and forcefulness stands "Mother" Jones, the heroine of many similar strikes. Her eighty or more years have not dimmed her eye, weakened the strength of her personality or tempered the boldness of her language. She is the woman most loved by the miners and most feared by the operators. Her thoughts are expressed in language both picturesque and striking. She knows no fear and is as much at home in jail as on the platform. In either situation she wields a greater power over the miners than does any other agitator.

And Fred Mooney, a West Virginia miner, described her and her techniques.

> With that brand of oratorical fire that is only found in those who originate from Erin, she could permeate a group of strikers with more fight than could any living human being. She fired them with enthusiasm, she burned them with criticism, then cried with them because of their abuses. The miners loved, worshipped, and adored her. And well they might, because there was no night too dark, no danger too great for her to face, if in her judgment "her boys" needed her. She called them her boys, she chastised them for their cowardice, she criticized them for their ignorance. She said to them, "Get you some books and go into the shade

while you are striking. Sit down and read. Educate yourself for the coming conflicts."

At the state capitol meeting, Mother Jones presented a demand for the abolition of the mine guards, and she exhorted a group of miners to take the document to the governor's office. But Governor Glasscock, a frail, former school teacher and lawyer, did little to meet the miners' demands. Upon adjourning the capitol meeting, Mother Jones said she told the miners, "We will protect ourselves and buy every gun in Charleston." She later recalled that they "left the meeting peacefully and bought every gun in the hardware stores of Charleston. They took down the old hammerlocks from their cabin walls. Like the Minute Men of New England, they marched up the creeks to their homes with the grimness of the soldiers of the revolution."

The Violence Continues

By the end of August, shootings were occurring almost every night and sometimes during the day. Assaults, murders, and property destruction were common. The struggle climaxed on September 1, 1912, when union miners on the north side of the Kanawha River armed themselves and began crossing the river to help the beleaguered strikers drive out the guards and the miners who were still at work. Estimated at anywhere from 1,500 to 6,000 men, the combined armies massed near the mouth of Cabin Creek. The mine owners quickly imported more than a hundred extra guards and recruited every employee who could hold a rifle. In all, about 400 well-armed and determined defenders waited behind breastworks to repel the invaders. A monstrous war was in the making.

On September 2, Governor Glasscock declared the entire strike zone to be under martial law, and 1,200 militiamen were rushed to the creeks where they would stay for six weeks. During the first few days of military occupation, the soldiers seized 1,872 rifles, 556 pistols, 6 machine guns, 225,000 rounds of ammunition, 480 blackjacks as well as daggers, bayonets, and brass knuckles from the two sides.

Yet of the miners, "the great majority of them followed Mother Jones' advice" and hid their weapons, one observer stated. Despite the martial law, Mother Jones continued to speak with gusto throughout the Kanawha region. At Charleston on September 6, she castigated the miners as "a lot of cowards" without "enough marrow in your backbone to grease two black cats' tails. If you were men with a bit of revolutionary blood in you, you wouldn't stand for the Baldwin guards, would you?" She warned against the bad publicity that grew from destruction of Chesapeake and Ohio railroad trackage. "Don't meddle with the track, take care of it," she advised, "and if you catch sight of a Baldwin bloodhound, put a bullet through his rotten carcass (loud applause)."

Throughout the month she kept up her speeches, and during a talk at Eskdale a few days after the imposition of martial law, she was said to have been seized and detained briefly for reading the Declaration of Independence to strikers at a railway depot. On September 21, she led a protest parade in Charleston of 100 miners' children with banners and a band. Her actions, chronicled closely by socialist magazines and newspapers, won her a growing following, not only among West Virginia coal miners but the metal miners of the West as well. *Miner's Magazine*, the organ of the WFM, said, "A few years more, and 'Mother' Jones will be sleeping in the bosom of Mother Earth, but when the history of the labor movement is written and there is recorded the glad tidings of labor's emancipation, the name of 'Mother' Jones will shed a halo of lustre upon every chapter that portrays the struggle of man against the despotism of capitalism."

CHAPTER 2

Entertainment and Technology

AMERICA'S DECADES

The Hollywood Star Factory

Robin Langley Sommer

When the twentieth century opened, New York City reigned as the entertainment capital in America. Patrons had their choice of plays, operas, and concerts, and the infant film industry stirred in New York and New Jersey. Within twenty years the focus had shifted to a quiet community near Los Angeles, California. Drawn by the region's agreeable weather, which permitted film companies to shoot in the open for most of the year, movie directors and producers gathered in Hollywood to create a string of full-length motion pictures, short features, and weekly serials (on-going dramas with suspenseful endings designed to draw back the same audience in following installments). In his history of Hollywood, Robin Langley Sommer explains the rise of that California town and its reliance on the star system to record incredible profits.

By 1919 Hollywood had already become the world capital of motion-picture production. It produced four out of every five movies and constituted America's fifth largest industry, grossing over $700 million a year. Many of the early silent-movie stars are scarcely remembered now—John Bunny, for example, was an incredibly popular comedian of the 1910s in a series of one-reelers. People named their children for him. Francis X. Bushman kept his mar-

Excerpted from *Hollywood: The Glamour Years, 1919–1941*, by Robin Langley Sommer (New York: Gallery Books, 1987). Copyright ©1987 by Bison Books Corp. Reprinted with permission from the author.

riage to Beverly Bayne a secret when they played screen lovers in *Romeo and Juliet* (1916), so as not to disillusion their fans. But when the secret leaked out, along with evidence of bigamy, Bushman's career foundered. The lesson was not lost on Hollywood, which sought to present its stars as unattached (and therefore attainable if only in daydreams), no matter what their marital status. But publicists had to tread a fine line between availability and promiscuity. Any hint of scandal was box-office poison.

Some of the early silent stars became legends in their own time, like Norma Talmadge, who was a beautiful leading lady at Vitagraph in her teens. Her sister Constance was a featured player with the Griffith company. The Gish sisters, Lillian and Dorothy, came to Los Angeles in 1914 for Lillian's role as Elsie Stoneman in *The Birth of a Nation* (1915). (Later, Lillian Gish would recall that they had rented a five-room apartment on Hope Street 'because it was cheap and I could ride the streetcar back and forth to the studio.')

The Demand for More Actors

Moviemakers also turned to New York for established stage players to meet the ever-growing demands of film production. Opera star Geraldine Farrar and matinee idol Wallace Reid made a fiery couple in Cecil B. De Mille's elaborate *Carmen* (1915). Other crossovers from the legitimate theater, including Russian-born Alla Nazimova, enjoyed great popularity—provided they did not play roles that were too highbrow. However, many stage-trained actors could not meet the test of the silent screen. Deprived of their voices, they fell back on exaggerated pantomimed effects that the camera magnified to the point of laughability. Hollywood photoplayers who had dreaded the invasion of big-name Broadway professionals were relieved to find out that Adolph Zukor's series of 'Famous Players in Famous Plays' was a resounding flop. The public stoutly rejected stagey performers like opera star Mary Garden, whom they considered hams. Garden's statuesque poses and frozen reactions led one critic to describe her film debut as 'a close approach to a motionless motion picture.' Instead, audiences demanded established favorites in their familiar roles: spunky 'Little Mary' Pickford; seductive Theda Bara; Charlie Chaplin, 'the Little Fellow'; and the dashing Douglas Fairbanks. Pioneer screenwriter Anita Loos, the author of *Gentlemen Prefer Blondes,* tells the story of how Douglas Fairbanks, Sr. became a movie star in the film comedy *His Picture in the Papers,* which the Griffith studio produced as a trial balloon in 1915. It is a case study in the star system.

Fairbanks Vaults to the Top

Fairbanks had been imported from Broadway, where he was enjoying a modest success in light comedy roles. However, his first few pictures made little impression, and Griffith was preparing to drop his option, while the young actor himself was increasingly homesick for New York. Loos prepared a screenplay with humorous subtitles—much more extensive than usual—that starred Fairbanks in a spoof of the wealthy nearby community of Pasadena. She and her future husband, director John Emerson, also left in the spontaneous horseplay improvised by the high-spirited young actor on the set. When the picture reached New York, it was rushed to the Roxy Theatre, where showman S.L. 'Roxy' Rothafel complained bitterly, because Fairbanks was almost unknown. However, the Exchange had failed to deliver his scheduled feature film and he had to use *His Picture in the Papers.* Roxy puffed up to the stage and apologized to the audience, promising to pull the picture as soon as the expected feature arrived.

When the Fairbanks comedy began to roll, roars of laughter greeted the first subtitle. They increased to a gale as the film continued. Halfway through the picture, the missing feature arrived, and Roxy made his way back to the stage and lifted his hand to stop the show. '"Listen, children, the regular film just got here. Do you want me to yank Doug Fairbanks?" "No! No! No!" came a reply that sounded like thunder. The picture continued to a hilarious end, by which time Doug Fairbanks had put an entire audience permanently into his pocket.'

Later, of course, the athletic Fairbanks became even more popular as the star of such swashbucklers as *The Thief of Bagdad* (1924) and other vehicles in which he performed his own hair-raising stunts, swinging into a scene on ropes and descending the length of a velvet curtain by cutting it with his outthrust sword. (Even at home, Fairbanks' bemused guests were treated to a running exhibition of handstands, dives and broad jumps.)

The Birth of the Star System

Other personalities were in equal demand by the public, which knew what it wanted, including Mack Sennett comedies with bathing beauties, Keystone Kops and Mabel Normand, the gifted comedienne. (Sennett endeared himself to staid long-time residents of Hollywood by spreading oil at street intersections and filming the skids as part of his comedies.) The public also wanted William S. Hart playing the good bad guy in the cinematic Wild West pioneered by 'Bronco Billy' Anderson's Essanay productions. It demanded, and got, action-packed serials that bridged the awkward transition from two-reelers to features and confirmed the movie-going addiction of a nation.

The first serial was produced by the Edison Company in 1912 to satisfy the growing demand for competitive product. The popular newspaper *McClure's Ladies World* was then running an adventure-story series called 'What Happened to Mary?' and Edison used it as the basis for several short films. The success of the format, which starred Mary Fuller as the Little Orphan Annie-type heroine, was immediate, and Edison rushed additional melodramas into production: *Mary in Stageland, A Clue to Her Parentage* and *The High Tide of Misfortune*. The following year, Kathlyn Williams and Tom Santschi made the first action-oriented serial, entitled *The Adventures of Kathlyn*. The beautiful heroine was pursued by sundry villains and wild animals as she tried to lay claim to a title she had inherited in India.

This improbable scenario was a great success, and in 1914 an even more appealing heroine appeared in the form of Pearl White, who played the title role in 20 episodes of *The Perils of Pauline*. The films were amateurishly directed and full of inconsistencies, but the public took Pearl to its heart and made her the screen's major serial heroine. She was soon copied by Helen Holmes, Helen Gibson and Ruth Roland, who made hundreds of episodic cliffhangers.

By the mid-1910s, known actors and actresses were demanding and getting $250 to $500 a week—a far cry from the five to ten dollars a week (and no screen credit) offered to the first film players at the turn of the century. A few stars like Mary Pickford commanded salaries in the hundreds of thousands. The basis was what film historians Arthur Mayer and Richard Griffith have called 'something indefinable and uniquely cinematic'—a quality that audiences could identify with or admire. Personality was at the heart of it, and no amount of technique or even physical beauty could compensate for its absence.

The inevitable result of the star system was that the most popular performers increased their salary demands beyond what even the most successful studios could—or would—pay. In 1919 four of the biggest names in Hollywood formed United Artists to produce and distribute their own pictures: Douglas Fairbanks, Charlie Chaplin, Mary Pickford and D.W. Griffith. In the mid-1920s, they were joined by producer Joseph M. Schenck, who brought in Norma and Constance Talmadge, Gloria Swanson, John Barrymore and Buster Keaton.

As the prestige and popularity of the movies increased, the town of Hollywood took a brighter view of the 'gypsies' who had encamped in its midst. There was a shift away from the mood described by director Allan Dwan, who recalled that in the early days 'If we walked in the streets with our cameras, they hid their girls under the beds, closed doors and windows and shied away.' Now that the movies had become the country's leading entertainment medium, the movie-makers were regarded with more tolerance.

The $5 Day: Henry Ford Revolutionizes Industry

Mark Sullivan

In 1914, automotive industry pioneer, Henry Ford, announced that he would offer to his factory workers the then spectacular salary of $5 per day. Applicants rushed Ford headquarters in Michigan seeking employment. However, they found that with higher pay came greater expectations. The noted social historian of the first three decades of the twentieth century, Mark Sullivan, wrote of the event in a volume of his popular series, *Our Times: The United States, 1900–1925.*

For nearly ten years Henry Ford had been making the largest quantity of the new vehicle that was revolutionizing the country's life, and at a price that made it available to the largest number of people—by 1914 more than half a million Model T's were on the nation's then modest network of highways. Yet Ford as a man had attracted no attention; there were no books about him, no magazine articles. He had not been deemed eligible for "Who's Who," the national roster of the great and the near-great and the would-be-great, which in its 1913 edition contained 18,794 names, including a Henry Jones Ford, who was a university professor, and a Henry P. Ford, who was an ex-Mayor of Pittsburgh—but not *the* Henry Ford who was an automobile manufacturer. In the newspapers Ford's name appeared almost solely as a signature to advertisements, chiefly in country weeklies. A baseball player named Napoleon Lajoie was a public character, but not Henry Ford. An actor named Douglas Fairbanks was a public character, and a magician named Houdini; a moving picture actress named Mary Pickford and a reformed train robber named Al Jennings; a professional walker named George Weston and a speculator named Tom Lawson; a dancer named Vernon Castle and an Indian athlete named Jim Thorpe; a blind girl named Helen Keller and a champion swimmer named Annette Kellerman—all these and a dozen others were public characters, their personalities familiar to the country, but Henry Ford was unknown. The name "Ford" was a brand, not a man—merely a proper noun linked with an article of commerce, like Fairbanks and scales, Ingersoll and watches, Colgate and soap, Lydia Pinkham and female restoratives, Singer and sewing machines. Like all these, "Ford" was to the public merely the first half of a trade-name. He was no more thought of as having a living personality than the dog in the Victor phonograph advertisement, or the Quaker of "Quaker Oats," or the twins of "Gold Dust," or the bull in "Bull Durham."

Ford Stuns the Nation

Then, in the afternoon newspapers of January 5, 1914, Ford announced that as a way of sharing his profits with his 13,000 employees, he would pay a minimum wage of five dollars per eight-hour day.

On the first pages and in the editorial columns of the next morning's papers, Ford's announcement overshadowed the war in Mexico and every other topic of national or local interest. Sensationally, a little appalled, with a manner of believe-it-or-not, the New York *Times* exclaimed: "The lowest paid employees, the sweepers, who in New York City may claim from $1.00 to $1.50 a day, are now to receive $5 in Ford's plant." "It was," said the New York *Sun*, groping frantically for a sufficient superlative, "a bolt out of the blue sky, flashing its way across the continent and far beyond, something unheard of in the history of business." "An epoch in the world's industrial history," said the New York *Herald*.

Headlines that proclaimed the sensation were followed by teeming columns of excited discussion. Ford became the man of the hour, his plan the topic of the day. Quickly the phrase "Ford idea" became as familiar as the Ford car. The discussion had two sides, and innumerable angles. The plan was good, the plan was bad. It was a "magnificent act of generosity" (New York *Evening Post*); it was merely a cunning way of getting an advantage over competitors. It would make the workers self-respecting and independent; the workers would be robbed of their independence by Ford's paternalism. The workers would become home-owners and build up savings; the workers would—time-honored concern of the "haves" for the best good of the "have-nots"—"spend their money foolishly." Ford was "an inspired millionaire" (New York *World*); Ford was a shrewdly self-interested business man.

Spotlight on Ford

To finding out just what sort of being this strange new Crœsus was, at once Midas and Messiah, to satisfying public curiosity about him, the country's mechanisms of publicity now dedicated themselves. In seven days the press of New York City alone printed fifty-two columns.

All over the country, managing editors wired "rush" telegrams to Detroit correspondents, who hastily sent out such casual information as was in their minds about their hitherto comparatively unnoticed fellow-citizen, in despatches to which they appended "more to follow." Writers and press photographers competed at Ford's door with the crowds of applicants for jobs; newspapers which formerly had sent only their advertising solicitors to the Ford plant now sent their star reporters, who found that, as the New York *Times* put it, "there was nothing about Ford's demeanor to indicate that he thought he had done anything remarkable." Over-night the press, from taking it for granted that Ford was of no more public interest than any other citizen, now combed his present and his past for anything that would help satisfy the public hunger for information about him. Not only was Ford himself "good copy," his wife, his son, all his relatives, his neighbors, his associates in business, his former teachers, all were tracked down by ubiquitous reporters with pencils poised lance-like. That curious and numerous army of baskers in vicarious publicity, the men who "knew him when," eagerly dropped their contributions into newspaper columns that gaped like hungry birdlings, and presses that panted for more.

The public learned that Ford liked skating and did not like Wall Street; that after he had become a millionaire he had continued to live in "a plain small house which would probably rent for $50 a month"; that in hiring men he set no extra value on a college education and was tolerant of former prisoners—one of his important executives was an ex-convict; that he liked outdoor recreation and had an adage (he later inscribed it over the open fireplace of his new house) "Chop Your Own Wood and It Will Warm You Twice"; that he liked birds—once to avoid disturbing a nest of phœbes on his front porch he had used the back door of his house for a week; that he raised pheasants on his farm and fed them custard; that he did not approve of professional charity—he had a principle, "the best use I can make of my money is to make more work for more men"; that in his business he was himself impatient of routine—though devotion to rigid routine was the very heart of his factory methods; that he was rarely to be found in that part of his plant which was known as his office, and that he often held conferences out of doors under trees.

Ford's hobby and his law of life, the press reported, was to produce a good car at the lowest possible cost; to save a few cents on each car he had dropped the "stripers" who painted a slender ornamental line of yellow on the bodies. When salesmen complained that customers demanded more ornament, in a time when other makes of cars were sold largely on the basis of seductiveness of appearance, Ford's answer had been, "They can have any color they want so it's black." This, the press reported, was a basic detail of the process by which Ford had made his fortune. His formula of mass production had been: make a thoroughly good car; make few models and stick to them, thus avoiding the expense, immense in the automobile business, of equipping the factory for new models; make the car as inexpensive as possible by eliminating costly decorativeness, putting all the expenditure into serviceableness only. Sell the car at the lowest price; by that means achieve large sales; by large sales reduce the manufacturing cost of each car; use this reduction of cost to lower the price to the consumer; thereby get larger sales—and so on, in an ascending spiral of expansion, which in 1913 yielded Ford profits of about twenty million dollars. It was this twenty million dollars that Ford now announced he would divide with his workers during 1914 by paying a minimum wage of $5 a day.

The Reasons for the Raise

The question which everybody speculated about was, why had Ford decided to pay $5 a day to men he could have had for $2? Whatever may have been the motives in Ford's mind before he took the step, and whatever the relative weight of different reasons in the mixture of many motives that commonly lie behind any human action, Ford was now to learn the truth of the worldly counsel, Never give your reasons at the time of an act, because thus you preserve for yourself a mobility which enables you later to adopt any of the motives that others attribute to you, or that which best fits the unanticipatable conditions that subsequently arise. Ford, within twenty-four hours after his announcement, could accept any one of almost as many reasons as there were sources of comment. The head of the rival Chalmers automobile factory attributed Socialistic leanings to him, and the New York *Times* sent a reporter to ask him, point-blank and accusingly, whether he was a Socialist, and if it was true that his purpose was to prevent his son from inheriting a cloying fortune. At the other end of the gamut of imputed motives, a mass-meeting of five hundred Socialists denounced Ford's act as a detestable trap: "Ford," they unanimously resolved, "had purchased the brains, life and soul of his men by a raise in pay of a few dollars a week;" the Socialist New York *Call*, seeing nothing to praise in any "division of earnings between labor and capital," said it would be interested only "when the working class decides to cease dividing" with capital. Between these extremes of alleged motive ran an infinite range; Ford sought the favor of labor; Ford sought advantage over other manufacturers; Ford sought publicity for himself; Ford sought advertising for his car—and so on and so on and so on.

Ford's own statement of his motive, given to reporters—who called upon him in the spirit of demanding an explanation for having done an unheard-of thing—was that he had taken the step as "a plain act of social justice." This answer was too off-hand and simple to be acceptable as a carefully accurate statement of motives which actually must have been complex and must have sprung in part from little understood deeps of human psychology. "Social justice" was a rough-and-ready phrase, at that time much hackneyed by use as part of the creed of the Progressive party; it would come naturally to anyone's lips, but it was rather too vague to explain so startling and original an act.

Ford's action could be regarded as a kind of unconscious expression of a deep and instinctive urge not understood by Ford himself. A more exact statement of his motive than he gave, and one not at all inconsistent with what he avowed, might say that the institution which Ford had built up had developed, like any living thing, a kind of cosmic urge of its own, an instinct to survive and grow and come to fruit; that the institution sensed that if it were to expand it must have a larger quantity of purchasers of the car it produced than was provided by the number of persons then able to pay for a car; that such new purchasers could only be created by bringing into the world the notion of paying larger wages to workers; and that this urge of the institution to function expressed itself in an inner compulsion upon Ford to do the thing he did. In short, that Ford the institution took possession of Ford the man, expressing its will to live in the form of cerebration on Ford's part that he called a hunch; that the step which the institution thus took was as much an instinctive act of nature as that of a tree reaching upward for sun; and that Ford, in throwing off into the world the idea of high wages for labor, was acting as instinctively, as blindly and as inevitably, on behalf of the institution of which he was a part, as the stamen of a flower when it sheds pollen upon the wind.

This hypothesis would comport with what later came to be realized as a fundamental law of such institutions as the Ford one, namely, that mass production can only exist by being fed with a constantly increasing purchasing power on the part of labor. And if we accept the theory that mass production was a normal and logical step in the development of civilization, then this hypothesis would explain the favor with which the world received Ford and his idea.

The 1919 World Series:
A Sad Moment for Baseball

Geoffrey C. Ward

America's favorite pastime, baseball, enjoyed immense popularity as the nation approached the 1920s. The sport boasted talented individuals and remarkable teams. Few matched the credentials posted by the 1919 Chicago White Sox, but in a stunning upset, the team lost the World Series. When rumors that the Sox were paid to throw the games proved true, baseball took steps to repair its sullied image. In conjunction with noted television documentarian Ken Burns, author Geoffrey C. Ward explains why some of the Chicago White Sox so willingly agreed to lose the fall classic.

The 1919 World Series between the Chicago White Sox and Cincinnati looked to be no contest. Chicago was one of the strongest clubs in baseball history. "They were the best," said Chicago second baseman Eddie Collins, who had once played for Connie Mack's championship Athletics. "There never was a ball club like that one." The odds favored them, 5 to 1.

But things were not entirely as they seemed. On September 18, thirteen days before the series was to start, Chicago first baseman Chick Gandil summoned an old acquaintance to his Boston hotel room. Joseph "Sport" Sullivan was a small-time gambler who, over the years, had made a

Excerpted from *Baseball: An Illustrated History*, by Geoffrey C. Ward. Copyright ©1994 by Baseball Film Project, Inc. Reprinted with permission from Alfred A. Knopf, Inc.

good thing out of the little inside tips that Gandil gave him: there was money to be made in knowing that a pitcher wasn't feeling quite up to par on the day of a big game, or that a big hitter had twisted his ankle. Now, Sullivan sensed, something much bigger was in the wind.

Gandil was a rough customer, a former hobo, boiler-maker, and club-fighter, thirty-two years old, nearing the end of his career, and eager for one last shot at some really big money before he had to get out of the game. For $100,000, he told Sullivan, he and several of his teammates were willing to throw the World Series.

There was nothing new in ballplayers working closely with gamblers. Many were rumored to supplement their incomes that way, and first baseman Hal Chase, most recently of the Giants, had made something of a career of it. Handsome and skilled enough to have become one of baseball's most popular stars—his fans called him Prince Hal—he was also so unabashed about consorting with gamblers that three different managers publicly accused him of wrongdoing and the fans took to chanting, "What's the odds?," whenever he took the field.

Single games had been thrown before, too, but dumping the World Series was something else again. Still, Gandil seemed serious, and the prospects for big profits from betting on Cincinnati were staggering. Sullivan hurried off to see if he could raise the money, while the first baseman went to work on his teammates.

An Unhappy Team

The White Sox were an unhappy team. No club played better in 1919, but few were paid as poorly or got along as badly. It was torn into two factions. "I thought you couldn't win without teamwork until I joined the White Sox," said Eddie Collins, whose relatively high salary and college education were both bitterly resented by his teammates. During pregame practice no one threw the ball to Collins all season long, and Chick Gandil had not spoken to him for two years.

Their owner was "The Old Roman," Charles A. Comiskey, himself a former first baseman and Players' League rebel but now among the game's most tightfisted owners. He was too cheap even to pay to have the team's uniforms laundered, and his men had bitterly renamed themselves the Black Sox in 1918 after wearing their increasingly dirty uniforms for several weeks in protest.

Chicago's two top pitchers, Claude "Lefty" Williams and right-hander Eddie Cicotte, had won 52 games between them that season. Gandil needed the cooperation of both men if his plot was going to succeed.

Williams remembered how he was approached:

> The proposition to throw the World's Series . . . was first brought to me in New York City in front of the Ansonia Hotel. Gandil came to me and said he wanted a conference. . . . He asked me if anybody had approached me on the 1919 World's Series with the purpose of fixing [it]. . . . I told him not yet. He asked me what I thought of it. I told [him] I had nothing to say. He asked me if it was fixed, would I be willing to get in and go through with it? I told him I would refuse to answer right then.

Eventually, Williams agreed to go along.

Eddie Cicotte turned out to be interested, too. He had his own special grudge against Comiskey, who had promised him a $10,000 bonus if he ever won 30 games, then, when he'd won 29 in 1919, had ordered him benched just to keep from ever having to pay up. Cicotte wanted $10,000 up front before he'd join the conspirators: "I needed the money . . . $10,000 to pay off a mortgage on a farm and for the wife and kids. . . . I had to have the cash in advance. I didn't want any checks. I didn't want any promises, . . . I wanted the money in bills. I wanted it before I pitched a ball." Gandil promised to get it for him.

The Fix

On September 21, Gandil assembled seven players in his room in the Ansonia Hotel on Broadway at Seventy-Fourth

95

Street—Williams and Cicotte, outfielder Happy Felsch, infielders Buck Weaver and Swede Risberg, utility infielder Fred McMullin (who had overheard Gandil talking to Risberg and demanded to be let in on the fix), and the idol of schoolboys all over the Midwest, Joseph Jefferson Jackson.

He was called Shoeless Joe because it was said he was once spotted in the minors playing in his stocking feet when new shoes proved too tight. A South Carolina country boy, he had hoped to be a pitcher until he broke his catcher's arm with a wild pitch, and had been taught how to bat by a Confederate veteran who had learned his baseball from Union soldiers in a northern prison camp.

The sportswriter Joe Williams knew him fairly well:

> He was pure country, a wide-eyed, gullible yokel. It would not have surprised me in those days to learn he had made a down payment on the Brooklyn Bridge. . . . He was a drinker and a heavy one. He carried his own tonic: triple-distilled corn. And on occasions he carried a parrot, a multi-colored pest whose vocabulary was limited to screeching, "You're out!"

Jackson could neither read nor write, a fact not lost on opposing fans: Once, when he tired of hearing a drunk shouting "Hey, Jackson. Can you spell 'cat'?" again and again, Jackson finally answered, "Hey mister, can you spell 'shit'?" (Jackson broke in with Philadelphia, where, Connie Mack recalled, he had thoughtfully "arranged for a more literate boy to join the team at the same time . . . to read to him the menus and . . . reports of the games.")

But Jackson could hit—.408 in 1911, his first year in the starting nine, .356 lifetime, the third highest average in history. His home runs were called "Saturday Specials," because most of the textile workers' games in which he had got his start had been played on Saturdays. Jackson hit these homers with a special 48-ounce bat, "Black Betsy," made for him by a local lumberman from "the north side of a hickory tree," he said, and darkened with coat after coat of Jackson's tobacco juice.

Ty Cobb himself thought Joe Jackson "the greatest natural hitter I ever saw," and Babe Ruth would later say he'd modeled his own swing after Jackson's. "Blindfold me," another player remembered half a century later, "and I could tell you when Joe Jackson hit the ball. It had a special crack."

According to Jackson, when Gandil offered him $10,000 for his help in throwing the series, he turned him down flat; when Gandil then upped the ante to $20,000, and was rebuffed again, Gandil had just shrugged: the slugger could take it or leave it. The fix was on in any case, provided someone came up with the money.

Someone did, although the evidence is murky and contradictory as to just who it was. Several gamblers—including Sport Sullivan; Bill Maharg, a mysterious figure, whose real name may have been Graham ("Maharg" spelled backward); Abe Attell, the former featherweight boxing champion; and a onetime White Sox pitcher, "Sleepy Bill" Burns—served as go-betweens. However, the cash seems to have been provided mostly by New York's most celebrated gambler, Arnold Rothstein, known as "Mr. Bankroll" at the track, who was said to have been willing to bet on anything except the weather because there was no way he could fix that.

The day before the series was to open in Cincinnati, with Eddie Cicotte slated to pitch for the White Sox, rumors of wrongdoing were everywhere. For no apparent reason, the odds were steadily shifting away from Chicago. "You couldn't miss it," one New York gambler remembered. "The thing had an odor. I saw smart guys take even money on the Sox who should have been asking five to one." Another gambler cornered the Reds outfielder Edd Roush in the lobby of a hotel and urged him to get some money down on his own team before it was too late; the White Sox were not on the level. Roush thought the man was crazy.

But when Cicotte got back to his hotel room that evening he found the $10,000 he'd demanded under his pillow. He sat up into the night sewing the crisp green bills into the lining of his coat.

The Series Opens

It was to be a best-of-nine contest. Sportswriter Hugh Fullerton, who had made his name as a baseball expert by picking the White Sox "Hitless Wonders" to beat the Cubs in the 1906 series, had heard enough rumors to think something very wrong. The lobby of his hotel was filled with gamblers; he'd never seen so many big bills changing hands so fast. He sent a wire to all the papers that carried his column: ADVISE ALL NOT TO BET ON THIS SERIES. UGLY RUMORS AFLOAT.

Fullerton was joined in the press box by Christy Mathewson, who left the sanatorium where he had been fighting his losing battle against the damage poison gas had done to his lungs to cover the series for the New York *World*. Fullerton filled him in on what he'd heard, and Mathewson agreed to help him judge if everything was on the up and up. They would be among the first to see that it was not.

Cicotte was ordinarily a master of control and his first pitch to the Reds second baseman Morrie Rath was a called strike, but his second pitch hit Rath right between the shoulder blades. It was a signal to his accomplices that the fix was in.

Cicotte caught an easy double-play grounder, then seemed to throw it over Swede Risberg's head in the fourth, and fed the Cincinnati batters enough fat pitches to score six runs before he was driven from the mound. Risberg ruined a double play of his own by failing to step on the bag (though he was not charged with an error), while Joe Jackson—who had asked Comiskey if he could be excused from the game at the last minute because he was "not feeling well"—seemed to some to throw wide from the outfield and deliberately to slow down to miss balls hit near him. (Jackson would always deny he had ever done anything but play his hardest during the championships, and he cited the record book to back his claim: he batted .375, drove in 6 runs, set a series record of 12 hits, and was never charged with an official error.)

In any case, Chicago lost the first game, 9–1. Charles Comiskey was so shaken by his team's miserable showing that he knocked on the door of Ban Johnson's hotel room long after midnight to share his fear that something was funny about the series. Johnson—who heartily disliked Comiskey—ordered him to go away: "That," he shouted, "is the response of a beaten cur!"

The players did not get the $20,000 in cash Gandil had been promised for losing game one—Rothstein's agents claimed it was all out on bets—but he and several others agreed to go ahead and throw game two, anyway, so long as the money for both games was in their hands by the end of the next day.

Now, it was Lefty Williams's turn to lose. He held the Reds to only four hits, but uncharacteristically walked three men in the fourth, allowing Cincinnati to score three runs. Chicago lost again, 4–2. In the stands, Judge Kenesaw Mountain Landis was impressed enough with Cincinnati's play to tell *The New York Times* that the Reds were "the most formidable machine I have ever seen." But beneath the stands, after the game, the frustrated White Sox manager, Kid Gleason, tried to strangle Gandil, and catcher Ray Schalk had to be pulled off Williams: "Three fucking times, three times," he said, "Williams shook off my signals for curve balls.". . .

The Scheme Begins to Crumble

The conspirators weren't happy, either, for that night a bruised Gandil went to see Abe Attell and demanded the $40,000 owed him and his teammates for having thrown two games. Attell gave him just $10,000. The players felt betrayed, and began to lose interest in continuing to risk their reputations.

The third game was held in Chicago and Dickie Kerr, a White Sox rookie not in on the fix, threw a masterly three-hit shutout to win it, 3–0. Now, it was the gamblers' turn to feel betrayed. Bill Burns had lost all his winnings betting against his old team in game three. "The Sox got even with us by winning that game," Bill Maharg remembered. "Burns and I lost every cent we had in our clothes. I had to hock my diamond pin to get back to Philadelphia."

Attell now refused to advance the players another dime: they were untrustworthy, he said. But Sport Sullivan agreed to come up with $20,000 before the next game and another $20,000 if the White Sox lost it. Gandil took the money and split it evenly among four of his fellow conspirators: Risberg, Felsch, Williams, and Jackson.

Lefty Williams brought Jackson his money in a dirty envelope. When Shoeless Joe counted it and saw that it was only $5,000 he asked what had happened to his $20,000. That was all there was, Williams said; they'd all been the victims of a "jazzing" by Abe Attell. Two men—McMullin and Weaver—would never see a penny.

Still, at least some of the eight evidently continued to want to lose the next day. Cincinnati's Jimmy Ring pitched a fine game, but the Reds' 2–0 victory was at least in part due to critical fielding errors by Eddie Cicotte. For the first time, Hugh Fullerton committed his growing suspicions to paper.

There is no alibi for Cicotte. He pitched a great game, a determined game, and one that would have won nine out of ten times, but he brought the defeat crashing down upon his own head by trying to do all the defensive work. He made the wild throw that gave the Reds their opening, the only real one they had, and he followed that up by grabbing at a ball thrown from the outfield and deflecting it past Schalk [the catcher]. A high fly to left blown by the wind over the head of Jackson, who was playing close in, followed, and Chicago was beaten. . . .

There is more ugly talk and more suspicion among the fans than there ever has been in any World's Series. The rumors of crookedness, of fixed games and plots, are thick. It is not necessary to dignify them by telling what they are, but the sad part is that such suspicion of baseball is so widespread.

Chicago lost game five, too, 5–0. Lefty Williams gave up only four hits this time, but three of them came in a four-run Cincinnati sixth.

The Reds needed only one more game to take the series. Kid Gleason was stunned by how badly his boys were doing: "They aren't hitting. I don't know what's the matter, but I do know that something is wrong with my gang. The bunch I had fighting in August for the pennant would have trimmed this Cincinnati bunch without a struggle. The bunch I have now couldn't beat a high school team."

But the tide was about to turn. Still another promised $20,000 had now failed to materialize, and as the White Sox rode the train back to Cincinnati for game six, the conspirators evidently decided to abandon their plot. If there were no more money to be made by losing, they might as well win; they all had their contracts to worry about, after all and even Comiskey would provide a bonus if they took the series.

Chicago won the sixth game 5–4, thanks to critical tenth-inning hits by Jackson and Gandil. They also took the seventh, 4–1: Cicotte was back in form and Jackson and Happy Felsch drove in all the Sox runs.

The series now stood at 4–3; Chicago was just one game behind, their fans began again to hope, and most of the conspirators were now eager to pull off the victory that should have been theirs early on. "For the second day in a row," a relieved Kid Gleason told the press aboard the night train bringing the two teams back to Chicago, "my gang played the kind of baseball it has been playing all season. Even though we are still one game behind, we will win for sure."

The Gamblers Mean Business

But Gleason had not counted on Arnold Rothstein's continuing interest in the outcome. Mr. Bankroll was said to be very unhappy. He had been too shrewd to bet on individual games. His money was on Cincinnati to win the series, but now there seemed a real chance that there might be some risk even in that. Rothstein did not like risks of any kind. He is said to have arranged to have a Chicago thug known to history only as "Harry F." pay a call on Lefty Williams, who was to pitch the eighth game.

There was to be no ninth game, Harry F. told Williams; the series must end the next day. If it didn't, he continued, if Williams was still on the mound past the first inning, in fact, "something is going to happen to you." And something might happen to his wife, as well.

Williams kept the threat to himself. The next day, with all of Chicago counting on him, he gave up three runs on four consecutive hits in the first inning and was pulled from the game before he'd made two outs. Despite fine hitting by Gandil and Jackson, Chicago lost the deciding game 10–5. In the end, one frightened man had given the Series to Cincinnati. In the New York *World,* Hugh Fullerton strongly hinted the series had been fixed.

> There will be a great deal written about the World Series. There will be a lot of inside stuff that will never be printed. The truth will remain that the team which . . . had the individual ability . . . spilled the dope terribly. . . . So much so that an evil-minded person might believe the stories that have been circulated during the Series. The fact is, this Series was lost in the first game.

> Yesterday's, in all probability, is the last game that will ever be played in any World Series. If the club owners and those who have the interest of the game at heart have listened during the Series, they will call off the annual interleague contest.

None of the owners wished even to consider such a thing. Privately, many had grave doubts about the integrity of the series, but in public, they were indignant at even a hint of suspicion about it. When Fullerton later charged openly that major league baseball was "besmirched with scandal"—in a story headlined IS BIG LEAGUE BASEBALL BEING RUN FOR GAMBLERS WITH BALL PLAYERS IN THE DEAL?—

Reach's Baseball Guide spoke for most of the owners:

> Any man who insinuates that the 1919 World Series was
> not honorably played by every participant therein not only
> does not know what be is talking about, but is a menace to
> the game quite as much as the gamblers would be, if they
> had the ghost of a chance to get in their nefarious worst.

The Controversy Blows Over

Charles Comiskey just wanted the whole business to go
away. While he had himself feared the worst after the first
game, he had a big investment in protecting the reputation
of the team he'd built. When Joe Jackson, apparently conscience stricken, had tried to see him right after the series,
to ask what he should do with the $5,000 he'd been given,
Comiskey refused to let him into his office. Jackson then
sent Comiskey a letter—dictated to his wife, of course—
suggesting that some series games had been rigged, but
Comiskey did not answer it.

Instead, he stoutly defended his men:

> There is always some scandal of some kind following a big
> sporting event like the World's Series. These yarns are manu-
> factured out of whole cloth and grow out of bitterness due to
> losing wagers. I believe my boys fought the battles of the re-
> cent World's Series on the level. . . . And I would be the first
> to want information to the contrary. I would give $20,000 to
> anyone unearthing any information to that effect.

The Sporting News, too, scoffed at the rumors and
hinted darkly that they had been started by a conspiracy of
Jewish gamblers, part of an alien attempt to subvert the national pastime.

> Because a lot of dirty, long-nosed, thick-lipped and strong-
> smelling gamblers butted into the World Series—an *Ameri-
> can* event, by the way—and some of said gentlemen got
> crossed, stories were peddled that there was something
> wrong with the way the games were played. . . . There will
> be no takers [for Comiskey's offer] because there is no such

evidence, except in the mucky minds of the stinkers who—because they are crooked—think all the rest of the world can't play straight.

The controversy finally died down, the 1920 season got under way, and other players on other teams evidently began to see the advantages of getting close to gamblers. There were rumors, unsubstantiated but widespread, of games being sold by players on the Giants, Yankees, Braves, Red Sox, Indians, as well as the White Sox.

First Steps to Court

In September, a special Cook County grand jury was convened to look into allegations that the Cubs had thrown a three-game series against the Phillies. The probe soon widened to include the 1919 World Series. "Baseball is more than a national game," the jury foreman said, "it is an American institution, [our great teacher of] respect for proper authority, self-confidence, fair-mindedness, quick judgment and self-control." To tamper with baseball was to tamper with the future of the American character.

The White Sox were in close contention for the 1920 pennant when the grand jury began calling players and gamblers alike to testify about what had happened the previous autumn.

Eddie Cicotte was the first to come clean:

I did it by not putting a thing on the ball. You could have read the trademark on it, the way I lobbed it over the plate. A baby could have hit 'em. Schalk was wise the moment I started pitching. . . . It did not look crooked on my part. It is hard to tell when a game is on the square and when it is not. A player can make a crooked error that will look on the square as easy as he can make a square one. . . . All the runs scored against me [in the two games I threw] were due to my own deliberate errors.

Joe Jackson confessed, too, in a colloquy with Assistant State's Attorney Hartley Replogle:

REPLOGLE: Did anybody pay you any money to help throw that series in favor of Cincinnati?

JACKSON: They did.

REPLOGLE: How much did they pay?

JACKSON: They promised me $20,000, and paid me five.

REPLOGLE: Who promised you the twenty thousand?

JACKSON: Chick Gandil . . .

REPLOGLE: Who paid you the $5,000?

JACKSON: Lefty Williams brought it in my [hotel] room and threw it down. . . .

REPLOGLE: Does [Mrs. Jackson] know that you got $5,000 for helping throw these games?

JACKSON: She did that night, yes. . . .

REPLOGLE: What did she say about it?

JACKSON: She said she thought it was an awful thing to do. . . . She felt awful bad about it, cried about it a while.

Chick Gandil, whose idea it all had been, admitted nothing.

Arnold Rothstein, the man whom F. Scott Fitzgerald would say had tampered with "the faith of fifty million people," asked to appear before the grand jury and indignantly denied knowing anything about any fix. He loved baseball, he said; it was the national game. Why, he'd once been part-owner of a poolroom with John McGraw and was now a business partner of Charles Stoneham, the latest owner of the Giants. If anything untoward had happened, he said, it must have been Abe Attell's doing. (Rothstein, who would move on to bootlegging, drug peddling, and labor racketeering, was eventually shot to death by a rival gambler, whom he had accused of fixing a poker game.)

Attell, several other gamblers, and all eight ballplayers were indicted for conspiring to defraud the public and injure the business of Charles Comiskey and the American League. (There was no Illinois statute against throwing a game or arranging to have one fixed.) All were acquitted for want of evidence after the transcripts of Cicotte's and Jackson's testimony mysteriously vanished from the court files. When the verdict was announced, Chick Gandil, still unrepentant, shouted, "I guess that'll learn Ban Johnson he can't frame an honest bunch of ballplayers."

No one went to jail.

Enter Judge Landis

Meanwhile, the scandal had so disillusioned the public that the owners felt compelled to take drastic action. They dissolved the old three-man National Commission run by Ban Johnson that had overseen the game in favor of a single, independent commissioner, who would be vested with extraordinary powers. They considered all sorts of candidates for the new post, former president Taft, General John J. Pershing, and General Leonard Wood among them.

But in the end they picked Kenesaw Mountain Landis, a federal judge with a reputation for willful independence equaled only by his flair for self-promotion. Landis took baseball almost as seriously as he took himself. "Baseball is something more than a game to an American boy," he said. "It is his training field for life work. Destroy his faith in its squareness and honesty and you have destroyed something more; you have planted suspicion of all things in his heart."

Born in Millville, Ohio, and named for the Civil War battlefield on which his father had lost his leg, Landis had preferred bicycling to baseball as a boy. Before one race, he bought twenty miscellaneous medals and pinned them to his jersey just to intimidate those who dared pedal against him. As a jurist, he was best known for trying to extradite the Kaiser, for declaring free speech expendable in wartime, and for having hauled John D. Rockefeller into his courtroom to testify, then levying a huge fine against Standard Oil (in a decision that a higher court later overturned). He once sentenced a bank robber to fifteen years in jail. "Your honor," the man said, "I'm seventy-five years old. I can't serve that long." "Well," Landis answered, "do the best you can."

Ban Johnson opposed his appointment—"Keep non-baseball people out of baseball," he warned—but Landis had seemed to side with the American and National leagues in their struggle with the Federal League, and this time Johnson was outvoted by the frightened owners. The survival of their leagues was at stake. The *New York Times* stated the fans' case:

> Professional baseball is in a bad way, not so much because of the Chicago scandal, as because that scandal has provoked it to bring up all the rumors and suspicions of years past . . . the general effect is to wrinkle the noses of fans who will quit going to ball games if they get the impression that this sort of thing has been going on underground for years.

The day after the eight Chicago players were acquitted, Judge Landis barred them all from baseball for life. "Regardless of the verdict of juries," he decreed, "no player who throws a ball game, no player that undertakes or promises to throw a ball game, no player that sits in conference with a bunch of crooked players and gamblers where the ways and means of throwing a game are discussed and does not promptly tell his club about it, will ever play professional baseball."

Exit Eight Players

Even Buck Weaver, who had known of the plot but had neither participated in it nor profited from it, was permanently barred. Six times he begged Landis to reinstate him, but the judge was unmoved. "I had Weaver in this office," he told a delegation of the player's sympathizers.

> I asked him, "Buck, did you ever sit in on any meeting to throw the 1919 World Series?" He replied, "Yes, judge, I attended two such meetings, but I took no money and played the best ball I am capable of." So I told him anyone who sat in on such a meeting and did not report it was as

guilty as any of the others. "Buck, you can't play ball with us again."

Happy Felsch was rueful: "I got five thousand dollars," he said. "I could have got just about that much by being on the level if the Sox had won the series. And now I'm out of base-ball—the only profession I knew anything about, and a lot of gamblers have gotten rich. The joke seems to be on us."

Joe Jackson played outlaw baseball on several Southern teams under assumed names, then opened a liquor store in Greenville, South Carolina. Ty Cobb once came in for a fifth of bourbon. Jackson did not seem to recognize his old rival. Cobb finally asked, "Don't you know me, Joe?"

"Sure—I know you, Ty," Jackson answered. "I just didn't think anyone I used to know up there wanted to rec-ognize *me* again."

In appointing Judge Landis commissioner of baseball, the club owners had done their best to reassure the public that the game's honesty had been restored, but fans remained skeptical. Something—or someone—else was needed to re-vive their shattered faith.

CHAPTER 3

America Enters the World Arena

AMERICA'S DECADES

The Panama Canal Unites the Oceans

David McCullough

A marvelous engineering feat of the early 1900s was the digging and opening of the Panama Canal in Central America. With its completion, ships could more quickly pass from the Atlantic to the Pacific Ocean, and the United States could more easily assert her power in both bodies of water. Renowned historian David McCullough, who has written extensively on topics of twentieth century America, summarized the canal's completion and impact in a 1977 book.

For all practical purposes the canal was finished when the locks were. And so efficiently had construction of the locks been organized that they were finished nearly a year earlier than anticipated. Had it not been for the slides in the Cut, adding more than 25,000,000 cubic yards to the total amount of excavation, the canal might have opened in 1913.

The locks on the Pacific side were finished first, the single flight at Pedro Miguel in 1911, Miraflores in May 1913. Morale was at an all-time high. Asked by a journalist what the secret of success had been; [chief engineer George] Goethals answered, "The pride everyone feels in the work."

"Men reported to work early and stayed late, without overtime," Robert Wood remembered. ". . . I really believe that every American employed would have worked that year without pay, if only to see the first ship pass through the

---

Excerpted from *The Path Between the Seas: The Creation of the Panama Canal, 1870–1914*, by David McCullough. Copyright ©1977 by David McCullough. Reprinted with permission from Simon & Schuster, Inc.

completed Canal. That spirit went down to all the laborers."

The last concrete was laid at Gatun on May 31, 1913, eleven days after two steam shovels had met "on the bottom of the canal" in Culebra Cut. Shovel No. 222, driven by Joseph S. Kirk, and shovel No. 230, driven by D.J. Mac-Donald, had been slowly narrowing the gap all day when they at last stood nose to nose. The Cut was as deep as it would go, forty feet above sea level.

In the second week in June, it would be reported that the newly installed upper guard gates at Gatun had been "swung to a position halfway open; then shut, opened wide, closed and . . . noiselessly, without any jar or vibration, and at all times under perfect control."

On June 27 the last of the spillway gates was closed at Gatun Dam. The lake at Gatun had reached a depth of forty-eight feet; now it would rise to its full height.

Excavation Ends

Three months later all dry excavation ended. The Cucaracha slide still blocked the path, but Goethals had decided to clear it out with dredges once the Cut was flooded. So on the morning of September 10, photographers carried their gear into the Cut to record the last large rock being lifted by the last steam shovel. Locomotive No. 260 hauled out the last dirt train and the work crews moved in to tear up the last of the track. "The Cut tonight presented an unusual spectacle," cabled a correspondent for *The New York Times,* "hundreds of piles of old ties from the railroad tracks being in flames."

Then on September 26 at Gatun the first trial lockage was made.

A seagoing tug, *Gatun,* used until now for hauling mud barges in the Atlantic entrance, was cleaned up, "decorated with all the flags it owned," and came plowing up from Colón in the early-morning sunshine. By ten o'clock several thousand people were clustered along the rims of the lock walls to witness the historic ascent. There were men on the tops of the closed lock gates, leaning on the handrails. The sky was cloudless, and in midair above the lower gates, a photographer hung suspended from the cableway. He was standing in a cement bucket, his camera on a tripod, waiting for things to begin.

But it was to be a long, hot day. The water was let into the upper chamber shortly after eleven, but because the lake had still to reach its full height, there was a head of only about eight feet and so no thunderous rush ensued when the valves were opened. Indeed, the most fascinating aspect of this phase of the operation, so far as the spectators were concerned, was the quantity of frogs that came swirling in with the muddy water.

With the upper lock filled, however, the head between it and the middle lock was fifty-six feet, and so when the next set of culverts was opened, the water came boiling up from the bottom of the empty chamber in spectacular fashion.

The central control board was still not ready. All valves were being worked by local control and with extreme caution to be sure everything was just so. Nor were any of the towing locomotives in service as yet. Just filling the locks took the whole afternoon. It was nearly five by the time the water in the lowest chamber was even with the surface of the sea-level approach outside and the huge gates split apart and wheeled slowly back into their niches in the walls.

The Initial Testing

The tug steamed into the lower lock, looking, as one man recalled, "like a chip on a pond." Sibert, Schildhauer, young George Goethals, and their wives were standing on the prow. "The Colonel" and Hodges were on top of the lock wall, walking from point to point, both men in their shirt sleeves, Goethals carrying a furled umbrella, Hodges wearing glossy puttees and an enormous white hat. The gates had opened in one minute forty-eight seconds, as expected.

The tug proceeded on up through the locks, step by step. The gates to the rear of the first chamber were closed; the water in the chamber was raised until it reached the same height as the water on the other side of the gates ahead.

The entire tremendous basin swirled and churned as if being stirred by some powerful, unseen hand and the rise of the water—and of the little boat—was very apparent. Those on board could feel themselves being lifted, as if in a very slow elevator. With the water in the lower chamber equal to that in the middle chamber, the intervening gates were opened and the tug went forward. Again the gates to the stern swung shut; again, with the opening of the huge subterranean culverts, the caramel-colored water came suddenly to life and began its rise to the next level.

It was 6:45 when the last gates were opened in the third and last lock and the tug steamed out onto the surface of Gatun Lake. The day had come and gone, it was very nearly dark, and as the boat turned and pointed to shore, her whistle blowing, the crowd burst into a long cheer. The official time given for this first lockage was one hour fifty-one minutes, or not quite twice as long as would be required once everything was in working order.

The Final Touches

That an earthquake should strike just four days later seemed somehow a fitting additional touch, as if that too were essential in any thorough testing-and-proving drill. It lasted more than an hour, one violent shudder following another, and the level of magnitude appears to have been greater than that of the San Francisco quake of 1906. The needles of a seismograph at Ancon were jolted off the scale paper. Walls cracked in buildings in Panama City; there were landslides in the interior; a church fell. But the locks and Gatun Dam were untouched. "There has been no damage whatever to any part of the canal," Goethals notified Washington.

Water was let into Culebra Cut that same week, through six big drain pipes in the earth dike at Gamboa. Then on the afternoon of October 10, President Wilson pressed a button in Washington and the center of the dike was blown sky-high. The idea had been dreamed up by a newspaperman. The signal, relayed by telegraph wire from Washington to New York to Galveston to Panama, was almost instantaneous. Wilson walked from the White House to an office in the Executive Building (as the State, War, and Navy Building had been renamed) and pressed the button at one minute past two. At two minutes past two several hundred charges of dynamite opened a hole more than a hundred feet wide and the Cut, already close to full, at once became an extension of Gatun Lake.

In all the years that the work had been moving ahead in the Cut and on the locks, some twenty dredges of different kinds, assisted by numbers of tugs, barges, and crane boats, had been laboring in the sea-level approaches of the canal and in the two terminal bays, where forty-foot channels had to be dug several miles out to deep water. Much of this was equipment left behind by the French; six dredges in the Atlantic fleet, four in the Pacific fleet, a dozen self-propelled dump barges, two tugs, one drill boat, one crane boat, were all holdovers from that earlier era. Now, to clear the Cut of slides, about half this equipment was brought up through the locks, the first procession from the Pacific side passing through Miraflores and Pedro Miguel on October 25.

The great, awkward dredges took their positions in the Cut; barges shunted in and out, dumping their spoil in designated out-of-the-way corners of Gatun Lake, all in the very fashion that Philippe Bunau-Varilla [agent for the French company that had begun the canal project] had for so long championed as the only way to do the job. Floodlights were installed in the Cut and the work went on day and night. On December 10, 1913, an old French ladder dredge, the *Marmot,* made the "pioneer cut" through the Cucaracha slide, thus opening the channel for free passage.

The first complete passage of the canal took place almost incidentally, as part of the new workaday routine, on January 7, when an old crane boat, the *Alexandre La Valley,* which had been brought up from the Atlantic side sometime previously, came down through the Pacific locks without ceremony, without much attention of any kind.

That the first boat through the canal was French seemed to everyone altogether appropriate.

The Job Winds Down

The end was approaching faster than anyone had quite anticipated. Thousands of men were being let go; hundreds of buildings were being disassembled or demolished. Job applications were being written to engineering offices in New York and to factories in Detroit, where, according to the latest reports, there was great opportunity in the automobile industry. Families were packing for home. There were farewell parties somewhere along the line almost every night of the week.

William Gorgas resigned from the canal commission to go to South Africa to help fight an alarming surge of pneumonia among black workers in the gold mines. The understanding was that it would be a brief assignment, after which he was to be made surgeon general of the Army.

Joseph Bucklin Bishop left to resume his literary career in New York.

With the arrival of the new year the Isthmian Canal Commission was disbanded and President Wilson named Goethals the first Governor of the Panama Canal, as the new administrative entity was to be officially known. Goethals' salary as governor was to be $10,000 a year, which was $5,000 less than what he had been paid as chairman of the I.C.C., a decision made in the Senate, which inspired the popular "Mr. Dooley," the syndicated creation of humorist Finley Peter Dunne, to observe:

> They say republics are ongrateful, but look, will ye, what they've done f'r that fellow that chopped the continent in two at Pannyma. He's a hero, I grant ye, although I'm sorry f'r it, because I can't pronounce his name. . . . What is he goin' to git? says ye? Why, Hinnissy, th' Governmint has already app'inted him Governor iv th' Canal at a greatly rejooced salary.

In Washington after a drawn-out, often acrimonious debate, Congress determined that the clause in the Hay-Pauncefote Treaty stipulating that the canal would be open to the vessels of all nations "on terms of entire equality" meant that American ships could not use the canal toll free, as many had ardently wanted and as much of the press had argued for. American ships would pay the same as the ships of every other nation, 90 cents per cargo ton.

In Washington also, and in San Francisco, plans were being made for tremendous opening celebrations intended to surpass even those at the opening of the Suez Canal. More than a hundred warships, "the greatest international fleet ever gathered in American waters," were to assemble off Hampton Roads on New Year's Day, 1915, then proceed to San Francisco by way of Panama. At San Francisco they would arrive for the opening of the Panama-Pacific International Exposition, a mammoth world's fair in celebration of the canal. The estimate was that it would take four days for the armada to go through the locks.

Schoolchildren in Oregon wrote to President Wilson to urge that the old battleship *Oregon* lead the flotilla through the canal. The idea was taken up by the press and by the Navy Department. The officer who had commanded the ship on her famous "race around the Horn" in 1898, retired Admiral Charles Clark, hale and fit at age seventy, agreed to command her once again and the President was to be his honored guest.

The First Ship Passes Through

But there was to be no such pageant. The first oceangoing ship to go through the canal was a lowly cement boat, the *Cristobal,* and on August 15 the "grand opening" was performed almost perfunctorily by the *Ancon.* There were no world luminaries on her prow. Goethals again watched from shore, traveling from point to point on the railroad. The only impressive aspect of the event was "the ease and system with which everything worked," as wrote one man on board. "So quietly did she pursue her way that . . . a strange observer coming suddenly upon the scene would have thought that the canal had always been in operation, and that the *Ancon* was only doing what thousands of other vessels must have done before her."

Though the San Francisco exposition went ahead as planned, all but the most modest festivities surrounding the canal itself had been canceled.

For by ironic, tragic coincidence the long effort at Panama and Europe's long reign of peace drew to a close at precisely the same time. It was as if two powerful and related but vastly different impulses, having swung in huge arcs in the forty some years since Sedan, had converged with eerie precision in August 1914. The storm that had been gathering over Europe since June broke on August 3, the same day the *Cristobal* made the first ocean-to-ocean transit. On the evening of the third, the French premier, [René] Viviani, received a telephone call from the American ambassador who, with tears in his voice, warned that the Germans would declare war within the hour. The American ambassador was Myron T. Herrick, who had once been so helpful to Philippe Bunau-Varilla, and at the same moment in Panama, where it was still six hours earlier in the day, Philippe Bunau-Varilla was standing at the rail of the *Cristobal* as she entered the lock at Pedro Miguel, at the start of her descent to the Pacific, he being one of the very few who had come especially for the occasion.

Across Europe and the United States, world war filled the newspapers and everyone's thoughts. The voyage of the *Cristobal,* the *Ancon*'s crossing to the Pacific on August 15, the official declaration that the canal was open to the world, were buried in the back pages.

There were editorials hailing the victory of the canal builders, but the great crescendo of popular interest had passed; a new heroic effort commanded world attention. The triumph at Panama suddenly belonged to another and very different era.

The Canal Exacts Its Toll

Of the American employees in Panama at the time the canal was opened only about sixty had been there since the

A marvelous feat of engineering, the Panama Canal permitted quicker travel between the Atlantic and Pacific Oceans.

beginning in 1904. How many black workers remained from the start of the American effort, or from an earlier time, is not recorded. But one engineer on the staff, a Frenchman named Arthur Raggi, had been first hired by the Compagnie Nouvelle in 1894.

Goethals, Sibert, Hodges, Schildhauer, Goldmark, and the others had been on the job for seven years and the work they performed was of a quality seldom ever known.

Its cost had been enormous. No single construction effort in American history had exacted such a price in dollars or in human life. Dollar expenditures since 1904 totaled $352,000,000 (including the $10,000,000 paid to Panama and the $40,000,000 paid to the French company). By present standards this does not seem a great deal, but it was more than four times what Suez had cost, without even considering the sums spent by the two preceding French companies, and so much more than the cost of anything ever before built by the United States government as to be beyond compare. Taken together, the French and American expenditures came to about $639,000,000.

The other cost since 1904, according to the hospital records, was 5,609 lives from disease and accidents. No fewer than 4,500 of these had been black employees. The number of white Americans who died was about 350.

If the deaths incurred during the French era are included, the total price in human life may have been as high as twenty-five thousand, or five hundred lives for every mile of the canal.

Yet amazingly, unlike any such project on record, unlike almost any major construction of any kind, the canal designed and built by the American engineers had cost less in dollars than it was supposed to. The final price was actually $23,000,000 below what had been estimated in 1907, and this despite the slides, the change in the width of the canal, and an additional $11,000,000 for fortifications, all factors not reckoned in the earlier estimate. The volume of additional excavation resulting from slides (something over 25,000,000 cubic yards) was almost equal to all the useful excavation accomplished by the French. The digging of Culebra Cut ultimately cost $90,000,000 (or $10,000,000 a mile). Had such a figure been anticipated at the start, it is questionable whether Congress would have ever approved the plan.

The total volume of excavation accomplished since 1904 was 232,440,945 cubic yards and this added to the approximately 30,000,000 cubic yards of useful excavation by the French gave a grand total, in round numbers, of 262,000,000 cubic yards, or more than four times the volume originally estimated by Ferdinand de Lesseps for a canal at sea level and nearly three times the excavation at Suez.

The canal had also been opened six months ahead of schedule, and this too in the face of all those difficulties and changes unforeseen seven years before.

The Canal's Benefits

Without question, the credit for such a record belongs chiefly to George Goethals, whose ability, whose courage and tenacity, were of the highest order.

That so vast and costly an undertaking could also be done without graft, kickbacks, payroll padding, any of the hundred and one forms of corruption endemic to such works, seemed almost inconceivable at the start, nor does it seem any less remarkable in retrospect. Yet the canal was, among so many other things, a clean project. No excessive profits were made by any of the several thousand different firms dealt with by the I.C.C. There had not been the least hint of scandal from the time Goethals was given command, nor has evidence of corruption of any kind come to light in all the years since.

Technically the canal itself was a masterpiece in design and construction. From the time they were first put in use the locks performed perfectly.

Because of the First World War, traffic remained comparatively light until 1918, only four or five ships a day, less than two thousand ships a year on the average. And not until July of 1919 was there a transit of an American armada to the Pacific, that spectacle Theodore Roosevelt had envisioned so long before. Thirty-three ships returning from the war zone, including seven destroyers and nine battleships, were locked through the canal, all but three in just two days.

Ten years after it opened, the canal was handling more than five thousand ships a year; traffic was approximately equal to that of Suez. The British battle cruiser *Hood* and the U.S. carriers *Saratoga* and *Lexington* squeezed through the locks with only feet to spare on their way to the Pacific in the 1920's. By 1939 annual traffic exceeded seven thousand ships.

Pershing Proves His Mettle:
The Raid into Mexico

Gene Smith

The United States would soon become involved in World War I's fighting, but who would command such an enormous force? One leader jumped to the front. John J. Pershing showed both organizational genius and superb field guidance when he commanded a punitive expedition into Mexico to capture the bandit leader Pancho Villa. Gene Smith, who has written numerous histories and biographies of the events and people of 1900–1940, explains Pershing's raid into Mexico in his biography of the leader.

In March 1916 the former mayor of Cleveland was appointed as new secretary of war. President Wilson's choice was esteemed an odd one, for so ardent a pacifist was Newton D. Baker that it was said he once declined the leadership of Ohio's Boy Scouts on the basis that he would have nothing to do with so militaristic a body. He was jockey-sized, an eyeglass-wearing and mild-mannered soul who when first seen with the weather-beaten horsemen comprising the army's officer corps was often taken for an attending clerk or stenographer. Baker was given little time to get acquainted with his new duties, for on the day he accepted his post the United States was thrown into a crisis involving his area of responsibility, the military. Pancho

Excerpted from *Until the Last Trumpet Sounds: The Life of General of the Armies John J. Pershing,* by Gene Smith. Copyright ©1998 by Gene Smith. Reprinted with permission from John Wiley & Sons, Inc.

Villa had taken it into his head to go rampaging into American territory and into the tiny hamlet of Columbus, New Mexico, there to shoot up the town, set fires, and send a great "*¡Viva!*" into the desert air. Two months earlier he had yanked more than a dozen Americans off a Chihuahua train, stripped them naked, shot them dead, and run off with all they had.

The Last Straw

Why the Columbus raid? The reason was never fully explained. It was Pancho Villa's way. The marauders galloped off, bodies left in the sandy streets of the little settlement set in the flat and dusty and bleached, unshadowed land of shimmeringly hot and dry winds, sagebush and rattlesnakes. It was the last straw for the Americans. For years *pronunciamentos* of *presidente* and *caudillo* were followed by constant fighting, confiscations, irregular armies battling each other, bullet-pocked walls, expropriation of American property in Mexico—and now this. President Wilson dreaded getting involved in Mexico's problems. But the Columbus matter could not be let go. A long-standing treaty permitting troops of both Mexico and the United States to enter one another's territories in pursuit of "barbarians"—Indians—would be utilized: America would pursue the band or bands that had so disturbed its peace. "I suppose," Secretary of War Baker said to a group of officers whose acquaintance he had made only hours before, "if we are going to send an expedition, the first thing to be decided is who is to command it." He himself had no suggestions, hardly knowing the names of any officers save the ones just introduced to him. One of them was Assistant Chief of Staff Tasker H. Bliss, who spoke of the Eighth Brigade leader. Pershing would be a logical choice, Bliss told Baker. Baker said, "If there is no difference of opinion on that subject, we will consider it settled." Orders went out from Washington. Above all things, Pershing must not get involved in a real war with Mexico. Across the Atlantic, Europe was in flames, with the great Battle of Verdun just under way. America could not get bogged down south of its border. Pershing must walk on eggs.

Pershing Organizes an Expedition

He gathered cavalry, infantry, and field artillery to be formed into two parallel columns seeking Pancho Villa. Trains filled with troops, hustlers, adventurers, prostitutes, some traveling on flatcars, poured into a Columbus that previously was innocent even of electricity but that now suddenly possessed newspapers, hotels, saloons, gambling halls, bordellos, keno parlors, acres of tents on rocky areas amid prickly pear cactus and thorny mesquite by the railroad tracks running through what passed for the center of town. The Old West gathered for its final moment in the sun, old-time trappers and prospectors hiring out to the army as guides through uncharted Chihuahua, Apaches who knew the area, gunfighters looking to sign on, muleteers and college boys and taxi drivers, assorted hands who wanted to exchange a seat on a cow pony for one behind a steering wheel on one of thirty trucks swiftly purchased. An officer of field artillery was put in charge of the trucks. He had never driven anything in his life. He got hold of an automobile, took three lessons, learned more or less how to move the machine from one point to another. He likened gas, oil, and water to oats, hay, and water, held "stables" every evening with "feed" for his trucks. The First Aero Squadron, Aviation Section, Signal Corps, arrived, canvas-and-wood-covered Curtis JN-2's, Jennies, their pilots equipped with yokes to rest on their shoulders for use in banking a plane into a turn. The pilots carried pistols. There were no other armaments.

Pershing's traveling headquarters would consist of two clerks, an orderly, a cook, a couple of officer-aides, and a few trailing journalists from the Sheldon Hotel bar in El Paso. One officer not detailed to accompany the group camped outside of Pershing's Fort Bliss quarters and never permitted him to pass without begging for assignment. "Everyone wants to go," Pershing said. "Why should I favor you?"

"Because I want to go more than anyone else," replied Lt. George S. Patton, Jr. One morning Patton's phone rang and Pershing asked when he could report for duty. Patton replied that his things were already packed. "I'll be goddamned," Pershing said. He had been reminded of himself as a lieutenant when, told he must stay at his West Point assignment while others went off to the invasion of Cuba, he desperately pulled strings to join them. And he was fond of Patton. Even more so was he of Patton's sister Anne, always addressed as "Nita." They had gotten to know one another at Fort Bliss when she made a protracted visit from California to her brother and her brother's wife. She was twenty-nine. Previously something of a wallflower, and all her life in the shadow of Georgie, as her brother was called, Nita Patton suddenly blossomed at Fort Bliss. "Beaus galore," she wrote her mother. Of General Pershing: "He is awfully good-looking."

Pershing Heads to Mexico

A week after the Villa raid, the two columns moved, Pershing leading on horseback. It was March 15, 1916. All Columbus turned out to cheer. All spit and polish, Pershing offered salutes. His health had sadly declined in the wake of [his wife] Frankie's death, and he had thought of resigning his commission, but the sudden call to duty invigorated him. He was certainly presented with a challenge. Trapping Villa in the limitless deserts or in the mountains of the Sierra Madre was as likely a prospect, he said privately, as locating a rat in a cornfield or a needle in a haystack. The Mexicans met on his way, he knew, would be as anxious for him to capture Pancho as had been the denizens of Sherwood Forest that the sheriff of Nottingham do the same for Robin Hood. Villa was unpredictable and really not normal in his casual manner of taking life and taking women—but at least he was Mexican, and few countrymen of his preferred the gringos. And everyone knew that the last time the Yankees came to Mexico, in 1846, the result was that Mexican territories were taken to make up four American states.

Pershing headed south through great plumes of dust raised by the hooves of the horses from ground that had not seen a drop of rain in months, equipment thumping and thudding and squeaking, sabers and pistols and pennons and the horse-drawn artillery pieces, the trucks and a few touring sedans groaning in the rear, laden as they were with forage for the horses and rations and ammunition for the men, great slabs of bacon strapped side by side with drums of gasoline, tins of hardtack, bedding, rifles, and bags of water for the steaming radiators. Men wore goggles and tied bandanas over their mouths. The heat during the day could rise to 110° or 115°F; it was freezing at night.

He pushed his men 140 miles in the first thirty-six hours. Villa was somewhere to the south. Perhaps the Americans could get behind him. Vague desert trails ran out, and the men negotiated by compass or by the purple mountains in the distance. Pershing did not sleep under cover, but lay on the ground in a bedroll. Wearing a four-dented campaign hat, he bathed naked when he could in half-dried trickling streams or water holes, the region's intensely alkaline water making lathering up difficult and sometimes blistering the skin. No one ever saw him anything but clean-shaven and usually wearing a tie. He split his leading elements to fan out seeking Pancho, men going up into mountain fastnesses while leading their horses for hours and pack trains following, the trails inaccessible to wheeled transport. Even on the flat, trucks came to rocky points where wheels hopelessly spun and soldiers massed together to shove. Rattlesnakes seeking warmth came to your sleeping bag in hopes of making you, it was said, a snake-warmer. Lieutenant Patton killed two one morning with a pistol as people asked why he hadn't used a saber—he had been named Master of the Sword at Fort Riley and detailed to teach his specialty there. (Georgie replied that an officer should be proficient in all arms, and additionally sabers were for use when mounted.)

Overhead the Jennys took pictures while taking rifle fire from the ground, the shooters Mexicans who might be allied with Villa, or an independent band, or freelancers, or very likely identified with what was called the de facto government. The Americans came across men in varied uniforms, some in the blue with red piping of Porfirio Diaz's old *federales*, some in the now-tattered white of his *rurales*, others with nothing but belts filled with cartridges and bandoliers slung across their chests to identify them as military adherents of one group or another adding their bit to Mexico's chaos. Those who definitely followed Pancho Villa wore hair-woven hatbands with a little silver buckle. Every Mexican save for those actually firing at the gringos was by Pershing's orders to be treated with patience and restraint. Under no conditions must the Punitive Expedition incite such feelings as might bring on a general uprising of the people.

Deeper into Mexico

General Pershing had spent years negotiating with Moros, and now his diplomatic skills were needed for dealing with Mexicans. Once as he sat with a tiny group detached from other elements of his spread-out command, a couple of dozen men, a band of some two hundred armed Mexicans appeared. They circled the little camp. Pershing rubbed his chin. The situation wasn't very good, the reporter Frank Elser of the *New York Times* unnecessarily told himself. The Mexicans' leader, General Luis Herrera, who had fought with, and then against, Pancho Villa, came up. A Pershing orderly ceremoniously took charge of Herrera's horse; Pershing's cook swept an area clean of litter and offered empty gas tins for the two generals to sit on. Herrera had fine white teeth and spoke in a low voice, Elser noted. He wanted to know how many Americans there were in Mexico, how far south they thought to go, and how long they would be staying. Pershing in turn asked how many Mexican troops were hunting Villa, and where they were. Herrera bowed with Latin courtesy and took his departure. The next time Americans ran into his men, there was shooting.

The cavalry of the Punitive Expedition performed some

of the most extraordinary marching feats in the world's history of mounted operations as it sped into Mexico. Soon the army's line of communication and supply back to Columbus was longer than that of Sherman on his Georgia–South Carolina March to the Sea, five hundred miles past wrecked railroad stations shot up during the years of irregular warfare, and blown bridges, through little one-street towns where the troops negotiated purchases of frijoles, tortillas, goat brains, soft drinks, half-candied bananas in thin wood boxes, *huevos rancheros*, cactus candy, cinnamon-flavored chocolate, cane sugar, enchiladas and tamales sold from trays women carried on their heads or displayed on little three-legged tables in rutted roads before adobe houses by tinkling fountains. The fact that the Americans paid with good money was astonishing to vendors often forced to accept cheap-paper bills printed by bands carrying their printing presses along with them. Pershing looked wonderful, reporters thought, the inspiring picture of how a cavalryman looks and acts. He got along on little sleep, often rising before his men to sit with maps and papers or to censor the dispatches reporters got the Jenny pilots to fly out to a telegraph station. He munched soda crackers, went back to smoking after a decade of doing without. He was easy with the newspapermen, one of them remembering how he asked the general where Villa was, anyway. "Your guess is as good as mine," Pershing answered, taking a swig of tequila.

Once in the little ranch settlement of San Geronimo, nearly three hundred miles from Columbus and seventy-five hundred feet up in the sierras, cold murderous, snow falling, his little group stretched a bull hide between two poles and built a fire in its lee. There they crouched, grimy, pestered by the blowing sand. There were thirty of them, hired scouts and guides whose directions were always questionable in the light of what Pancho would do if he ever got hold of them, reporters, a handful of soldiers. There was no tent for the general commanding, no table, no folding chair. Dinner was hardtack fried in bacon grease—some fish taken from a stream had proved not to be trout, as hoped, but suckers. Dusk approached. Pershing was sitting on an empty box. A rickety wagon came into sight carrying four peons with musical instruments and a woman with children. The musicians got out, a fiddler, a guitar player, a cornetist, and a man with a huge bass viola. No one said anything. The men began to play and sing, very sweet and very sad Mexican love songs. Then they played rollicking dance tunes, and couldn't resist "La Cucaracha," the unofficial anthem of Villa's people. The listeners all applauded and yelled, *"¡Más!"* With a battered sombrero American silver was collected and for an encore the players offered "Adeleta," singing it in the high, wailing, falsetto Mexican manner. Pershing got up and moved away to stand by himself. The Mexicans stood shuffling, fearful, the Americans saw, that the *jefe* was somehow offended. Reassuring looks were offered and they strummed their instruments, awaiting a suggestion. "Play 'La Paloma,'" someone said, and they began and then halted suddenly, for Capt. James Collins had raised a hand commanding them to stop. "That was a favorite tune of Mrs. Pershing," he told the other Americans in a low tone.

Everyone looked at the general, standing apart. He came closer. "I liked that," he said. "Why did they stop? Tell them to play 'La Paloma,' please, for me." They did and then went on their way, the Americans standing by the fire and watching as they vanished into the darkness of the valley.

Where Is Villa?

Villa was dead, assassinated, cremated, he was dying, he was gone, he was going, Pershing was assured. In fact he lived on, and the Americans never got him. But the Punitive Expedition had been sent south, its orders read, to break up the band or bands that had plagued the border, Villa's name not mentioned for fear that if he ran away to the ends of the earth the U.S. Army would have to pursue him there. At least what was required had been accomplished. The days of the Villistas firing in the air from moving trains as they sat dangling their legs out of boxcar sides, their goats and chickens tethered on the tops, shouts for Villa aides rising—"¡*Viva la brigada Francisco Portillo!*" or "¡*Viva la brigada José Ortiz!*"—were over. Many of his people had in the day's shifting-loyalty manner of Mexico gone over to Pancho's enemies, or were dead. The important Villista colonel Julio Cardenas was dead, for Georgie Patton killed him with a pistol at a shoot-out in a walled hacienda along with another man. A third was killed by Patton's soldiers. The bodies were strapped onto the fenders of a Dodge touring car like deer bagged during a hunting expedition and brought back to camp. After that Pershing referred to Georgie as The Bandit.

But it was evident that Villa was beyond reach and that to continue aggressively to seek him might end the complicated family fights of the Mexicans and unite them all in violent opposition to the Punitive Expedition and so involve the United States in an all-out war. Frank Elser handed Pershing a dispatch to the *New York Times* for the commander's censorship: "General Pershing from a military standpoint for the time being has come to the end of his line" it began.

"Is that your deduction?" Pershing asked. The reporter nodded. "All right, send it." He knew Elser was right. The Americans settled down in isolated way station outposts and in the main camp at Colonia Dublán, some two hundred miles south of Columbus. The summer of 1916 came and went. In September Brigadier General Pershing was given a second star. His West Point classmate T. Bentley Mott sent congratulations from his military attaché post in Paris, and in reply the new major general referred in sad, oblique fashion to what had happened back at the Presidio: "All the promotion in the world would make no difference now." In California at her parents' home Nita Patton did not see it that way: "Dear Major General Pershing: Do you feel horribly dignified now, or can you still smile occasionally?"

Pershing Heads Home

November came and with it the presidential election back home to the north. [Pershing's son] Warren was very interested in the Wilson-Hughes contest, Aunt May wrote her brother in Colonia Dublán, and had set up a box so that all the household could cast ballots, and then found out where the real polling places were and went about and observed what went on and came back to tell all about it. Christmas was coming and the general asked May to do his shopping, mostly candy to be sent to the children of friends, and boxes of fruit candy for their wives. She was to get a tree for Warren and in the boy's name send presents to Frankie's father and step-mother, and the children of Frankie's brother Fred and Fred's wife, Bessie. Would she please send cards in the general's name to some one hundred people on a list from the preceding year? He had left it with her. And please append his name to any presents she gave their mutual relatives? For himself, he was busy with preparations for a Christmas celebration with his soldiers.

By his orders a great tree was constructed out of small firs. It towered sixty-five feet in the air and had hundreds of lights which flicked on after fireworks shot up into the sky. In the glare of massed truck headlights the American flag was seen to be floating from the top of the tree. A soldiers' chorus of four hundred that had practiced for weeks burst into "Joy to the World." For each of the ten thousand men in Mexico there was a gift. NONE IS OVERLOOKED IN DISTRIBUTION OF PRESENTS, headlined the *Washington Post*. Christmas dinner was a feast, with the men singing "The Battle Hymn of the Republic" and "America." Pershing's army by then, after nine months in Mexico, had worked out methods for improving truck performance and the use of tractors for pulling guns, trained drivers and wireless operators, created air photography experts, and was completely drilled in unit exercises that its commander devised and whose results he rigorously studied. It was a brilliant little army so strongly disciplined in health matters that its incidence of disease was as nothing to what afflicted the troops of the Civil and Spanish Wars.

Pershing knew by name every scout, knew after a lightning storm how many horses were hit, the limit a wagon could be expected to carry; accepted that regulars were tough, hard-bitten, rootless save for the service, and required prostitutes, whose housing he arranged. He was approachable, made up his mind quickly, gave completely clear orders. He could be reasoned with by his subordinate officers. For reporters he always had questions about what was going on and was himself able to tell them what was fact and what was only the nosebag gossip of the picket line, or latrine rumor. When papers arrived from the States he scanned them quickly and kept up with what was happening in the outside world and in the European war. In later years, when Pancho Villa turned into a folk hero, Mexican legend had it that Pershing ran away dressed in woman's clothing; in actuality the commander and his columns crossed over the international border barbed-wire fence at Columbus on February 5, 1917, bands playing "When Johnny Comes Marching Home," Chinese who had served the troops as launderers and cooks coming along for fear of what Mexicans might do to them if they stayed. The Punitive Expedition passed into history. Columbus lapsed into the somnolent place it had always been save for its brief moment of excitement. Pancho Villa was shot to death from ambush six years later.

The United States Exerts Its Influence: The U.S. Marines in Haiti

Allan R. Millett

Since the United States joined the ranks of world powers with an overwhelming victory in the Spanish-American War, the nation had taken other steps to gain influence around the globe. A stronger Navy had been constructed. The Panama Canal had been dug. Politicians rose to prominence who believed that the nation's rightful place lay at the forefront of nations.

One of the important ways of gaining influence was the use of the military to both exert authority over unstable governments, and to protect America's interests in different nations. One location illustrating this phenomenon was Haiti, a republic situated on the Caribbean island of Hispaniola. Haiti was considered of strategic importance to the United States because of its proximity to the Panama Canal. Esteemed military historian Allan R. Millett, the author of numerous books and articles on American military forces, describes the events on Hispaniola and the role played by the United States Marines in taming the dissident elements that threatened Haitian security.

Excerpted from *Semper Fidelis: The History of the United States Marine Corps,* by Allan R. Millett. Copyright ©1980, 1991 by Allan R. Millett. Reprinted with permission from The Free Press, a division of Simon & Schuster, Inc.

A merican interest in Hispaniola dated back to the early nineteenth century, but the United States government took a more active interest in Haiti and the Dominican Republic after the War with Spain and the creation of the Canal Zone. The forces that shaped American policy were complex. Initially, the Roosevelt and Taft administrations were most concerned with the traditional tasks of protecting American lives and property, but as the State and Navy departments practiced gunboat diplomacy, they became increasingly concerned with strategic and economic concerns. Navy planners recognized the utility of naval bases at Mole St. Nicolas on Haiti's north coast and the Dominican Republic's Samana Bay. Naval forces operating from either could control the Windward and Mona Passages into the Caribbean Sea and access to the Panama Canal. The possibility that either France or Germany might attempt to establish bases was tied to the question of foreign loans. These European nations had already demonstrated that they might collect their debts with naval gunfire and might conceivably extend their influence into the internal management of weak Latin republics, so the American government might preempt European intervention with intervention of its own. Whether the policy was described as the Roosevelt Corollary to the Monroe Doctrine, "preventive intervention," or "dollar diplomacy," the purpose was the same. To deter European intervention in an American sphere of interest and to protect foreign investment in both the investors' and hosts' economic interest, the United States would protect Haiti and the Dominican Republic. This policy was applied to both countries between 1905 and 1913 as Navy warships and embarked Marines hovered offshore to protect foreigners and support American negotiators.

Dollar Diplomacy

The policy was developed most completely first in the Dominican Republic. At the request of a provisional president, the State Department between 1905 and 1907 worked out a set of agreements that gave the United States control of the Dominican customs service. Under American management the revenues would go to foreign bondholders and claimants and to the incumbent regime; to assist the Dominican government the State Department also helped negotiate a new $20 million loan in the United States. Although this agreement angered many Dominicans and failed to curb civil war, it pacified the foreign creditors and their governments. It also committed the United States to protecting Dominican sovereignty and made the United States in Dominican and European eyes the decisive actor in Dominican domestic politics.

The State Department took a similar approach in 1910 when the Haitian government began new loan negotiations with French and German agents. Although there were few American investments in Haiti, the State Department objected to a plan to reorganize the National Bank of Haiti and to finance a new foreign bond issue without American participation. After intrigue that involved the mulatto *élite*, European businessmen in Haiti, and a few American entrepreneurs, the State Department allowed American and European financiers to reorganize the national bank and the railways with increased American interest and further loans to the Haitian government. The American government, however, would not accept responsibility for another customs receivership, a proposal even more unattractive to the Haitian government. But the concept of American involvement in managing Haiti's finances was still alive in 1913.

While the State Department was exploring the possibility of managing Haiti's finances, it was learning about the drawbacks of such responsibilities in the Dominican Republic. After the assassination of another president in late 1911, the Dominican *politicos* again went to war to decide upon a successor. Sporadic fighting dragged on into 1913, with no single faction able to consolidate its power. American naval officers and legation officials negotiated truces and urged compromise, while the State Department wondered whether it would have to defend the customs houses with Marines. The American role in dampening the rebellion consisted mostly in pouring money on the fires of in-surgency; since the Dominican government could neither pay its bills nor borrow money without American ap-proval, the State Department was able to influence the se-lection of a new provisional president and negotiate for greater control of Dominican fiscal policy. Early in 1913 the National City Bank of New York loaned the Domini-can government $1.5 million dollars to pay its ragtag army and accommodate its opponents.

The Wilson Plan

Into the diplomatic quagmire stepped President Woodrow Wilson. Convinced that American foreign policy was the in-strument of greedy capitalists, Wilson promised that foreign-owned banks and railroads would no longer exploit either the State Department or Hispaniola. The United States would refuse to deal with governments that took power through violence or other unconstitutional means. In-stead, it would negotiate the end of civil wars, the establish-ment of acceptable provisional governments, and free elec-tions—under American supervision if necessary. The United States might also reorganize the island's armed forces in order to bolster the legitimate government against rebels. As the President told a visitor: "I am going to teach the South American Republics to elect good men!" The substance of the "Wilson Plan" was communicated to the governments of Haiti and the Dominican Republic during 1913.

The nations of Hispaniola ignored the sermon from Washington and continued to change governments with dispatch and bloodshed. In the Dominican Republic civil war simmered on until an American-supervised election produced a new president, the aging *caudillo* Juan Isidro Jiménez, in 1914. Jiménez immediately complained that the customs receivership was not providing him with enough money to buy off his enemies or to prevent his fol-lowers from joining a new coalition of oppositionists. . . .

The situation was no more promising in Haiti. From 1913 to 1915 the Haitians rotated presidents through civil war and conspiracy. Whoever was president now bore the additional burden of being tagged a tool of foreign imperialism, as the State Department continued to urge an American-managed financial protectorate. In 1914 and 1915 the State Department offered to protect incumbent presidents with Marines if they and the Haitian congress would accept a treaty like the one in effect with the Dominican Republic. Before the negotiations could progress, rebels led by General Vilbrun Guillaume Sam occupied Port-au-Prince with a *caco* army and sent the *élite* politicians scurrying. In the meantime, the State Department concluded that French and German financiers were subsidizing the rebels in order to curb American economic penetration; some Americans, like Secretary of State Robert Lansing, were convinced that the Europeans were seriously interested in a Mole St. Nicolas naval base. The Sam government, however, would not negotiate either the Mole St. Nicolas issue or the question of making the National Bank of Haiti a completely American-managed institution. The government would accept American troops on a temporary basis to restore order but would not accept long-term foreign intervention.

The Navy's Increased Role

The Navy Department, an active participant in the effort to pacify Hispaniola, had little inkling that its role would soon expand beyond providing landing parties to protect foreign lives and property or to bolster some administration the State Department thought worth saving. By 1913 American landing parties had been ashore thirteen times in Haiti alone. In 1914 Marine ships guards had landed three times, once to escort a National Bank gold shipment to a waiting gunboat. Twice between August 1914 and January 1915, Marine expeditionary regiments had sailed into Port-au-Prince harbor in response to State Department fears that a *caco* army was threatening the capital. Neither regiment landed, but their officers reconnoitered the city, knowing that their mission someday might be to occupy the capital. . . .

In the spring of 1915 another uprising in Haiti gave President Wilson and the State Department a dramatic opportunity to put their reform plans into operation. Protesting that President Sam was about to sell the customs service to the United States, Ronsalvo Bobo raised a *caco* army along the northern border and took Cap Haïtien. A Marine guard landed on July 9 to guard foreign property, which was not harmed. The war simmered on until July 27, when a sudden coup in Port-au-Prince sent Sam and his henchmen running for sanctuary in the foreign legations. In the chaos the local military prison commander ordered all political prisoners executed; 167 members of the *élite* died in the eleventh-hour massacre. Outraged, the *élite* and a mob of urban workers stormed the French and Dominican legations and slaughtered Sam and the erring prison commander. Shredding Sam for a bloody torchlight parade, the Port-au-Prince mob made the Bobo rebels victors.

Learning of the rising, the State Department requested that the Navy protect all foreign lives and property. On July 28, 1915, the afternoon after Sam's death, Rear Admiral William B. Caperton landed a party from the battleship *Washington* to patrol the city. Believing that the intervention was temporary, the Port-au-Prince officials agreed to disarm the Haitian soldiers in the city, but the Americans were met with scattered shots. During the first night ashore two sailors were killed, probably shot accidentally by other members of the landing party.

The Marines Enter the Picture

In reality, President Wilson worried about the wisdom and legality of extending the intervention to bring peace to Haiti. While the administration debated, Secretary of State Lansing asked the Navy to send sufficient troops to control Port-au-Prince and the surrounding countryside. One Marine company from Guantanamo Bay was joined on August 15 by the 1st Marine Brigade, composed of the 1st and 2d Marines Regiments, which had been organized in the United States. The brigade commander was that expeditionary veteran Colonel L.W.T. Waller, assisted by the irrepressible Major Smedley D. Butler.

In the meantime, the Wilson administration had decided to apply its reform program to Haiti, but not directly through an American military government. Instead, the Navy Department ordered Admiral Caperton to encourage the Haitian congress to elect a new president, preferably senate president Sudre Dartiguenave, who agreed to cooperate with the Americans. The chief obstacle to the plan was Ronsalvo Bobo and his *caco* force of perhaps 1,500 in the Port-au-Prince area. As the Haitian congress tried to avoid an election and persuade the Americans to leave, Marine patrols occupied key points around the city and disarmed the Haitian militia. During the sweeps two Haitians were killed, but there was no serious resistance to the occupation. With the Bobo forces neutralized and Caperton uncompromising, the Haitian congress elected Dartiguenave on August 12. The same day the American chargé d'affaires in Port-au-Prince presented the new president with a draft treaty that in effect made Haiti an American protectorate. The treaty provided for American control of Haiti's finances, the creation of an American-officered national constabulary, and the use of American engineers and public health officials to reform the public works and sanitation systems. The treaty also provided that Haiti would not sell any land to any other foreign power except the United States, but foreigners as individuals could buy Haitian land. More important, it provided for American intervention to preserve Haitian independence, to enforce the treaty's other provisions, and to maintain a Haitian government "adequate for the protection of life, property, and individual liberty." Designed to be in force ten years, with the possibility of a ten-year extension, the treaty was accepted by the Dartiguenave government on September 12 and later was ratified by the Haitan and American congresses. The great American reform of Haiti had officially begun.

For the Marine expeditionary brigade, the first phase of the intervention had gone fairly smoothly. As Admiral Caperton and the State Department reconstructed the Haitian government, the Marines held Port-au-Prince and Cap Haïtien without difficulty. The greatest danger came from wild shots at night, slipping on street garbage, or a chamberpot bath from a hostile Haitian housewife. As Colonel Waller recognized, the Wilson administration did not want any open fighting, especially not before the occupation treaty was arranged. Waller's principal duty, in fact, was to negotiate for Haitian firearms, for which his officers could pay between $6 and $10. His other responsibility was to send small detachments to the other coastal towns to keep the peace and prepare for American control of the customs houses. . . .

With a force of more than two thousand Marines, Waller felt confident that his brigade could pacify northern Haiti, break up the *caco* roadblocks that were hindering rural commerce, and disarm the Haitian peasantry. With his bases secure, he ordered company-size patrols into the interior in October. He was satisfied with the results, for he found most *caco* leaders willing to accept amnesty and money rather than face death or imprisonment with manual labor. In dealing with the Haitians, Waller developed sympathy for the impoverished peasantry and contempt for the *caco* leaders. . . . Executed primarily by the 2d Regiment, the pacification of northern Haiti proceeded with little bloodshed and quick results. Marine losses in 1915–1916 were three killed, eighteen wounded; Haitian losses were larger but probably numbered only two hundred. As the Marine patrols converged on the mountain areas, they worked primarily to destroy *caco* camps, supplies, and arms. The most difficult task was finding the *caco* bases, but by the end of the year the Marines had dispersed most of *caco* bands and killed or captured the chiefs.

The Amazing Smedley Butler

The most dramatic combat patrols against the *cacos* were led by Smedley Butler. Working from the inland town of Grande Rivière, Butler's patrols repeatedly clashed with the *cacos* as they pushed into the mountains. Locating the supposedly impregnable *caco* camp in the ruins of ancient Fort Rivière, Butler surrounded the camp with four companies and assaulted it on November 17. In a dawn brawl, Butler and a handful of Marines plunged into the fort and took it in close fighting. As the *cacos* fled, the Marines slaughtered them with rifle and automatic rifle fire, later counting fifty-one dead Haitians. There were no Marine casualties. Butler's force then blew up the fort and withdrew. The destruction of Fort Rivière and nearby Fort Capois brought an end to *caco* resistance. In December there were only six skirmishes with small bands, and the first months of 1916 produced no greater action. . . .

Secretary of the Navy Josephus Daniel's horror at the number of Haitian casualties in the 1915 *caco* campaign accelerated Waller's interest in creating a Haitian constabulary. The treaty of 1915 provided that a native constabulary would be one of the five "treaty services" that the United States would organize and manage. Although the Marine Corps had no prior experience in forming a native police force, it drew upon the Army's experience with the Philippine Constabulary, the Cuban *Guardia Rural,* and the Puerto Rican insular police. As early as September 1915, Headquarters provided organizational plans and cost estimates for a Haitian constabulary, and within Haiti the Marines had already begun to organize local police. The protocol establishing the *Gendarmerie d'Haiti* was not to be signed until 1916, but Waller assigned Smedley Butler as the *Gendarmerie* commandant in December 1915 and told him to move rapidly in organizing his force. Taking the rank of Haitian major general (which his fellow Marine officers ridiculed), Butler tackled the problem of abolishing the inefficient Haitian army and consolidating the five Haitian police forces into a single national constabulary.

Butler threw himself into the assignment with characteristic enthusiasm. From an initial force of fewer than 500 local policemen, Butler started raising a constabulary of 120 American officers and 2,600 Haitian enlisted men. To attract dependable Marine officers and enlisted men (especially ones who spoke French), the Navy Department arranged for the Americans to draw both Marine Corps and Haitian pay. By becoming a *Gendarmerie* officer, a Marine noncommissioned officer could double his annual pay; on the other hand, the frustrations and squalor the officer faced probably discouraged many qualified Marines. It was also difficult to find Americans free of substantial prejudice against blacks, although the *Gendarmerie's* officers tried to find such Marines. The problem of finding promising Haitian enlisted men was no less distressing. Members of the *élite* refused to join the *Gendarmerie*. Most of the gendarmes, therefore, were recruited from the urban unskilled masses; as a group the recruits were illiterate, undisciplined, irresponsible, and infected with a number of diseases, predominantly hookworm and syphillis. The basic appeal of the *Gendarmerie* was the steady pay, food, and clothes.

Using Local Forces

Using "monkey see, monkey do" instruction, the *Gendarmerie* officers first taught their recruits drills and found arms, equipment, and uniforms for them. The gendarmes were equipped first with obsolete French rifles and then American Krags and were outfitted in Marine uniforms with Haitian buttons and rank insignia. The gendarmes performed routine city police patrols and garrison housekeeping but received little field training, law enforcement education, or rifle instruction until their American instructors learned some Creole (or found a dependable interpreter) and trusted their dependability. In 1916, however, the gendarmes proved their willingness to fight *cacos* in a few scattered skirmishes, and Butler increased the pace of training and deployment to interior posts. He also placed *Gendarmerie* detachments in charge of the national penitentiary as well as local jails and linked the posts with telephone lines. As the *Gendarmerie* improved, it assumed many of the patrol routes that had been handled by the Marines and created its own administrative and logistical organization.

As the *Gendarmerie* grew, Waller and Butler increasingly

saw it as a viable political force in Haiti and the chief in-strument of American reform. So did the Haitian govern-ment, and for that reason the *Gendarmerie* was soon the target of *élite* critics of the occupation. Waller wanted the gendarmes to remember that "they are to preserve order, protect the rich and poor alike, fear God, and serve their Government and country," but the brigade commander was irritated at the uncooperative attitude of the *élite* and its criticism of the *Gendarmerie's* incorruptibility. He and But-ler wanted to use the *Gendarmerie* free of Haitian influence and State Department supervision. They also believed that the *Gendarmerie* should assume not only police functions but also those of supervising sanitation, communications, and public works programs. In the absence of definitive guidance from either the State Department or their nominal Navy superior, they gradually expanded the *Gendarmerie's* functions into all phases of occupation administration ex-cept the customs service. By the time Butler left Haiti in 1918, the *Gendarmerie* was the principal agent of the oc-cupation in its routine contact with the Haitian people.

The *Gendarmerie's* rise to political influence was more rapid than the growth of its professionalism, and its ascent was soon to cause problems for the occupation. The *Gen-darmerie* continued to have internal personnel problems. Especially after the Dominican intervention of 1916 and American entry in World War I the next year, it was diffi-cult to find promising American officers, and the supervi-sion of those who remained declined. Since *Gendarmerie* officers were recruited from the 1st Brigade, and since the brigade's strength fell after 1916, there were fewer Marines to choose from. Despite indoctrination, some of the Hai-tian gendarmes could not resist using their status to exploit the common people or settle personal scores by arrest or even murder. Relations with the *élite* remained especially strained. Few Haitians appreciated the *Gendarmerie* en-forcement of laws governing gambling, tax collection, li-censing practices, firearms control, and criminal activities. Haitian politicians continued to badger the *Gendarmerie* for favors. In addition, the *Gendarmerie* became responsible for supervising sanitation and public works projects, because the Navy provided few officers for the "treaty services," and Haitian revenues were not large enough to provide an adequate civil service even if the talent had been available in the Haitian population—which it was not. For roadbuilding, for example, the American officials invoked the ancient French law of the *corvée*, which required all Haitians to donate their labor in lieu of taxes. Supervised by the *Gendarmerie*, the *corvée* worked well enough when the laborers were well cared for and not used outside their own communes and when local Haitian officials did not misuse local funds. But the *Gendarmerie* also bore the onus when the *corvée* law was violated. In some cases this was deserved, for some *Gendarmerie* officers thought that their careers depended upon the number of miles of road they built and sometimes drove their workers beyond the time and geographic limits set by the law.

In fact, the *Gendarmerie* became the occupation, for both the State Department and the Navy did little to supervise the occupation, leaving this task largely to the Marine brigade commander and the commandant of the *Gendarmerie*. Without a greater infusion of American money and skilled specialists, the occupation became a pale imitation of the great reform promises of the treaty of 1915. The Marines were left to explain why the dream of modernizing Haiti did not become reality.

The Navy Steps into the Future: The First Attempt to Launch Aircraft from a Ship

George van Deurs

In the 1910s, little was known of the aircraft's capabilities, particularly when applied to the United States Navy. Could aircraft be profitably used by that branch? If so, how would it be developed? These questions received a partial answer in 1910, when Eugene Ely took off from the deck of the USS *Birmingham*. The naval weapon of the future, air power, had been born, setting in place one of the main instruments with which the United States would rise to military and political dominance. Rear Admiral George van Deurs writes of the moment in his history of naval aviation in the 1910s.

On 3 November 1910, another air show opened at Halethorpe Field near Baltimore. Again, Chambers [aviation pioneer, Washington] left his desk in Washington to attend. Many of the Belmont pilots sent their planes to the Baltimore show, but an expressmen's strike held up delivery of most of the planes and, on opening afternoon, only two Curtiss planes flew. One of these was flown by Eugene Ely. Ely was feeling pretty confident. He liked to fly. He was making big money and a good name in an exciting business, which promised an unlimited future. His wife, Mabel, was also an aviation fan.

A rain storm stopped the show; by evening tent hangars were blown down and Ely's planes were smashed. Since nothing could be done at the field in such weather, Gene and Mabel went shopping in Baltimore. When they returned to the hotel at the end of the wet afternoon, they met Captain Chambers.

Ely Steps Forward

During their conversation, Chambers mentioned he had just asked Wilbur Wright for a pilot and a plane to fly from a ship. Wright had flatly refused all help, saying it was too dangerous. He would not even meet Chambers to talk it over. Chambers was taken aback because it was Orville's suggestion in 1908 that had given him the idea. "I had hoped it would get the Navy interested in planes," he said.

Gene Ely quickly asked for the job. "I've wanted to do that for some time," he told the surprised captain. Ely would furnish his own plane and he asked for no fee. He had three reasons for his eagerness. He had argued shipboard takeoffs with other fliers and he wanted to show them it could be done, he wanted the publicity, and he wanted to do a patriotic service.

Chambers wanted to get [aircraft manufacturer Glenn H.] Curtiss' consent. "Not necessary," Ely assured him. "I make my own dates under our contract." That was a happy chance. As a matter of fact, Curtiss did his best to talk Ely out of it. Maybe he agreed with Wilbur Wright and thought it too dangerous. He argued that a failure would hurt plane sales. Mabel Ely believed he feared success even more. It might detract from the naval value of his hydroaeroplane.

Back in Washington, [Politician John D.] Wainwright turned down Chambers' proposal to let Ely fly from a cruiser. Chambers' boss, Captain Fletcher, told reporters the Navy had no money for such things. Meyer returned to Washington; in Baltimore that same day, Chambers asked Curtiss and Ely to back his appeal with technical arguments. Only Ely went to Washington with him to confer with Meyer.

The Navy Hesitates

Secretary Meyer was back at his desk after his long inspection trip. Undoubtedly Wainwright had coached him before the conference. Ely never forgot how the Secretary covered his technical ignorance of aircraft and ships with an imperious coldness, and he never forgave him for calling Ely's plane a mere carnival toy when he turned down the proposed shipboard takeoff.

Then John Barry Ryan, a millionaire publisher and politician, got into the act. Two months earlier he had organized financiers, investors, and scientists, interested in aeronautics, with a few pilots, as the U.S. Aeronautical Reserve. He furnished this organization with a Fifth Avenue clubhouse, provided several cash prizes for aeronautical achievements by its members, and made himself commodore of the organization. One of these prizes was $1,000 for the first ship-to-shore flight of a mile or more. Ryan was in Washington to pledge the club's pilots and their planes to the Army and Navy in case of war, when he heard of the Chambers-Ely plan and reopened the subject with Secretary Meyer.

When Ryan urged Chambers' proposal, Secretary Meyer responded that the Navy had no funds for such experiments. Ryan then offered to withdraw the $1,000 prize, which the non-member Ely could not win anyway, and use it to pay the costs of the test. Meyer had little interest in planes, but he was an accomplished politician, and he knew Ryan could swing votes in both Baltimore and New York. After consulting the White House, he agreed that the Navy would furnish a ship, but no money. Thereupon he left town.

Winthrop, "acting," acted in a hurry. He rushed the *Birmingham*, commanded by Captain W.B. Fletcher, to the Norfolk Navy Yard and told the yard commandant to help equip her with the ramp which Constructor McEntee had designed. The ship was a scout cruiser, with four tall stacks. Her open bridge was but one level above the flush main deck. On her forecastle, sailors sawed and nailed until they finished an 83-foot ramp, which sloped at five degrees from the bridge rail to the main deck at the bow. The forward edge was 37 feet above water.

Meanwhile, Henning and Callen, Ely's mechanics, worked at Piny Beach, where later the Hampton Roads Naval Base would be built. Using bits shipped from Hammondsport and pieces salvaged in Baltimore, they built a plane. Ely got there on a Sunday in foul weather. He added cigar-shaped aluminum floats under the wings and a splashboard on the landing gear. Late in the day he saw the plane—without its engine—aboard the Navy tug *Alice*, headed for the Navy Yard. The engine had been shipped; no one knew when it might arrive.

Gene Ely was not a worrying man. But the storm at Baltimore had cost him money. Shortly before Belmont, a speck of paint in a gas tank vent had robbed him of fame and a $50,000 prize. In previous months other crack-ups had bruised his body and damaged his pocketbook. These mishaps taught him how tiny, unexpected flaws could foul up a flight. Each time he charged it off to experience and tried again. Since his interview with Mr. Meyer, the cruiser flight had become a must. To his original motives, Ely had added an intense desire to show Secretary Meyer the error of his ways. At the same time he knew that, if he failed in his first try, Meyer would never give him another chance. And so Ely was worried when he joined his wife and Chambers.

At the old Monticello Hotel in Norfolk, Ely told reporters, "Everything is ready. If the weather is favorable, I expect to make the flight tomorrow without difficulty." Mabel knew that her husband was whistling in the dark. He had not seen the platform. The plane was untested. He hoped his engine would come on the night boat. But she had complete confidence in Gene, so she enjoyed a seafood dinner and untroubled sleep. Ely ate little, turned in early, and slept poorly.

In the morning, as he worried into his clothes, the clouds looked level with the hotel roof. He skipped breakfast and took the Portsmouth ferry.

Ely Takes Off

Callen and Henning had hoisted the plane aboard the *Birmingham,* pushed it to the after end of the platform, and secured it with its tail nearly over the ship's wheel. Only 57 feet of ramp remained in front of the plane. Henning was worried. But Callen reassured him. "Old Gene can fly anywhere," he said. Then Ely's chief mechanic, Harrington, arrived with the engine. The three were getting it out of the crate when Ely and Chambers boarded the ship.

At 1130, sooty, black coal smoke rolled from the *Birmingham*'s stacks as she backed clear and headed down river. Two destroyers cleared the next dock. One followed the cruiser; the other headed for Norfolk to pick up Mabel Ely and the Norfolk reporters.

Going down river, Ely helped his men install the engine. He wanted to double check everything to avoid another failure; besides, the familiar work eased his tensions. He blew out the gas tank vent twice. In spite of squalls, they had the plane ready before the ship rounded the last buoy off Piny Beach. They had almost reached the destroyers *Bailey* and *Stringham,* waiting with Winthrop and other Washington officials, when another squall closed in. A quarter mile off Old Point Comfort, Captain Fletcher anchored the *Birmingham.* Hail blotted out the Chamberlain Hotel.

It was nearly two o'clock when that squall moved off to the north. Ely climbed to his plane's seat. Henning spun the propeller. Under the bridge the wireless operator tapped out a play-by-play account of the engine testing. When the warm-up came to an end, nobody liked the looks of the weather. Black clouds scudded just above the topmast. The cruiser *Washington* radioed that it was thick up the bay, and the Weather Bureau reported it would be worse the next day. Chambers nodded toward the torpedo boats. "If this weather holds till dark," he said, "a lot of those guys will go back to Washington shouting 'I told you so.'"

By 1430 the sky looked lighter to the south. Captains Fletcher and Chambers decided to get under way. Iowa-born Ely could not swim, feared the water, got seasick on ferryboats, and knew nothing about ships. He thought the cruiser would get under way as quickly as a San Francisco Bay ferry. He had no idea that the windlass he heard wheezing and clanking under the aeroplane platform might take half an hour to heave 90 fathoms of chain out of the mud. So he paced first the bridge, then the launching platform. Then he climbed into his seat and tried the controls. Sixty fathoms of chain were still out. Henning spun the propeller. Ely opened the throttle and listened approvingly to the steady beat. Under the plane's tail, the helmsman at the wheel took the full force of the blast.

Ely was ready. He idled the engine and waited. Then he gunned the engine to clear it, twisted the wheel for the feel of the rudder, rechecked the setting of the elevator, and looked back at the captains on the bridge wing. They looked completely unhurried.

Then Ely noticed the horizon darkening with another squall and he began to wonder why the *Birmingham* did not start. He looked at Chambers, pointed at the approaching blackness. The captain nodded. He knew it would be close, but he could do nothing. Thirty fathoms of chain were still in the water.

Gene Ely checked everything again, and stared at the squall ahead. He seemed about to lose his chance because the Navy was too slow. At 1516 he decided he would wait no longer for the ship to start steaming into the wind. If ever he was going to fly off that ship, it had to be now. He gave the release signal.

Harrington, who knew the plan, hesitated. Ely emphatically repeated his signal. The mechanic yanked the toggle, watched the plane roll down the ramp and drop out of sight. Water splashed high in front of the ship. Then the plane came into sight, climbing slowly toward the dark clouds. Men on the platform and bridge let out the breath they had held. One of them spoke into a voice tube, and the wireless operator tapped out, "Ely just gone."

In 1910, Curtiss pilots steered with their rudder, balanced with their ailerons and kept the elevator set, by marks on its bamboo pushrod, either at a climb, level, or a glide position. In order to dip and pick up a bit more speed, Ely took off with his elevator set for glide. Off the bow he waited the fraction of an instant too long to shift to climb. The machine pointed up, but squashed down through the air.

Gene felt a sudden drag. Salt water whipped his face. A rattle, like hail on a tin roof, was louder than his engine. He tried to wipe the spray from his goggles but his gloved hand only smeared them, so he was blinded. Then the splashboard pulled the wheels free of the water. The rattle stopped. He snatched off his goggles and saw dirty, brown water just beyond his shoes.

The seat shook. The engine seemed to be trying to jump out of the plane. Ely's sense of direction left him. There were no landmarks, only shadows in the mist, and that terrifying dirty water below. He swung left toward the darkest misty shadow. He had to land quickly. On the ground he might stop the vibration, take off again, and find the Navy Yard. He wondered if the bulky life jacket that fouled his arms would keep him afloat if the plane splashed.

A strip of land bordered by gray, weathered beach houses loomed ahead. Five minutes after the mechanic had pulled the toggle, Ely landed on the beach at Willoughby Spit. "Where am I?" he asked Julia Smith, who had dashed out of the nearest house.

"Right between my house and the yacht club," she said.

It sounded funny but it wasn't. He knew the splintered propeller would not take him to the Navy Yard. He had failed. He blamed himself bitterly for the split second delay in shifting the elevator. Now he knew how to do it without hitting the water, but would he ever get another chance?

A Plane Could Fly from a Ship

Boats full of people converged on the yacht club dock. Their enthusiastic congratulations confused him. "I'm glad you did not head for the Navy Yard," Chambers told him. "Nobody could find it in this weather." Captain Fletcher agreed. John Barry Ryan offered him $500 for the broken propeller. "A souvenir of this historic flight," he explained.

Ely figured that in not making the Navy Yard, he had failed, and Chambers and Ryan spent the evening trying to convince him that he had succeeded. His particular landing place was unimportant. It would soon be forgotten. The world would remember that he had shown that a plane could fly from a ship, and that navies could no longer ignore aeroplanes. Ely did not cheer up until Chambers promised to try to arrange a chance for him to do it again. "I could land aboard, too," was Ely's comment.

The next morning Ryan's valet wrapped the splintered propeller in a bathrobe and carried it into his pullman drawing room. There Ryan gave a champagne party until train time, presented Ely with a check for the propeller, and made him a lieutenant in his U.S. Aeronautical Reserve. After the train pulled out, Gene spent the check on a diamond for Mabel.

The morning of 15 November 1910, the *Birmingham* flight filled front pages all over the United States and Europe. Foreign editors speculated that the United States would probably build special aviation ships immediately. American editors, more familiar with naval conservatism, said the flight should at least lead Secretary Meyer to ask for appropriations for aviation. But Wainwright's friends belittled the performance. A ship could not fight with its guns boxed by a platform. A masthead lookout, they said, could see farther than Ely had flown.

And so it went and so it would go for a long time, this argument between the Navy's black shoe conservatives and the brown shoe visionaries.

CHAPTER 4

World War I

The Sinking of the *Lusitania* Nudges America Toward War

John M. Taylor

Citizens of the United States watched European events with concern, but mainly they hoped that World War I would remain overseas. Some Americans supported England and her allies, others favored Germany, but most went about their business as if nothing unusual had happened. That changed with the 1915 sinking of the passenger ship, *Lusitania*. Torpedoed by a German submarine, the ship took 1,198 people, including 128 Americans, to their deaths. Anti-German sentiment gained momentum in the United States, which would be at war within two years. Historian John M. Taylor, a specialist in military history, examines the role of the *Lusitania* in turning public opinion in the United States against Germany.

Shortly after noon on a drizzly spring day in 1915, the Cunard liner *Lusitania* backed slowly away from Pier 54 on New York's Lower West Side. It was *Lusitania*'s 202nd Atlantic crossing, and as usual the luxury liner's sailing attracted a crowd, for the 32,500-ton vessel was one of the fastest and most glamorous ships afloat. In the words of the London *Times*, she was "a veritable greyhound of the seas."

Passengers, not yet settled in their accommodations, marveled at the ship's size and splendor. With a length of

Excerpted from "Fateful Voyage of the *Lusitania*," by John M. Taylor, *MHQ: The Quarterly Journal of Military History*, vol. 11, no. 3, Spring 1999. Reprinted with permission from the author.

745 feet, she was one of the largest man-made objects in the world. First-class passengers could eat in a two-story Edwardian-style dining salon that featured a plasterwork dome arching some thirty feet above the floor. Those who traveled first class also occupied regal suites, consisting of twin bedrooms with a parlor, bathroom, and private dining area, for which they paid four thousand dollars one way. Second-class accommodations on *Lusitania* compared favorably with first-class staterooms on many other ships.

People strolling through nearby Battery Park watched as three tugs worked to point the liner's prow downriver toward the Narrows and the great ocean beyond. While well-wishers on the pier waved handkerchiefs and straw hats, ribbons of smoke began to stream from three of the liner's four tall funnels. Seagulls hovered astern as the liner slowly began to pick up speed.

The Era of the Ocean Liner

The early years of the twentieth century belonged to the great ocean liners, and *Lusitania* was one of the elite. A Scotsman who was present at her launching in 1907 recalled his awe at the sight:

> Was it the size of her, that great cliff of upperworks? . . . Was it her majesty, the manifest fitness of her to rule the waves? I think what brought the lump to the boy's throat was just her beauty, by which I mean her fitness in every way; for this was a vessel at once large and gracious, elegant and manifestly efficient. That men could fashion such a thing by their hands out of metal and wood was a happy realization.

In 1908, on one of her first Atlantic crossings, *Lusitania* broke the existing transatlantic speed record, making the run from Liverpool to New York in four and one-half days, traveling at slightly more than twenty-five knots. Like her sister ship, *Mauritania,* she could generate sixty-eight thousand horsepower in her twenty-five boilers. *Lusitania* was also versatile, for the government subsidy that helped pay for her construction required her to have features that would facilitate her conversion to an armed cruiser if necessary. The liner's engine rooms were under the waterline, and she incorporated deck supports sufficient to permit the installation of six-inch guns.

The *Lusitania* Sails

It was May 1, 1915, and *Lusitania,* with 1,257 passengers and a crew of 702, was beginning a slightly nervous crossing. War was raging in Europe, and although no major passenger liner had ever been sunk by a submarine, some passengers were uneasy. The German embassy had inserted advertisements in a number of American newspapers warning of dangers in the waters around the British Isles.

Because this warning appeared only on the day of sailing, not all of those who boarded *Lusitania* saw it. Yet for travelers with an apprehensive turn of mind, there were alternatives to the Cunarder. The American Line's *New York,* with space available, sailed the same day as *Lusitania,* but she required eight days to cross the Atlantic as opposed to *Lusitania*'s six.

Despite the warning posted by the German embassy, *Lusitania*'s captain was not nervous. When Captain William Turner was asked about the U-boat threat he reportedly laughed, remarking that "by the look of the pier and the passenger list," the Germans had not scared away many people.

By the spring of 1915 the land war in Europe had settled into a bloody stalemate, but one in which the Central Powers held the advantage. A decisive German victory at Tannenberg had all but taken czarist Russia out of the war. The initial German thrust for Paris had been repulsed, but even as *Lusitania* sailed, the British were being mauled in the month-long Second Battle of Ypres.

The war at sea, however, was a different matter. The Royal Navy's numerical superiority made it perilous for the German fleet to venture out of port and enabled the Allies to move troops and materiel by sea. Most important of all, Allied control of the sea had cut the Central Powers off from overseas supplies of food and raw materials. When the increased range of shore-based guns prevented the British from maintaining a traditional offshore blockade of German ports, the Royal Navy mounted a long-range blockade instead. British cruisers patrolled choke points well away from German ports, halting all vessels suspected of carrying supplies to Germany and enlarging the traditional definition of contraband to include even raw materials and food.

Not all contraband was headed for Germany. *Lusitania* carried some forty-two hundred cases of Remington rifle cartridges destined for the Western Front. Her cargo also included fuses and 1,250 cases of empty shrapnel shells. Although the Germans had no knowledge of this cargo, it is clear that British authorities were prepared to compromise *Lusitania*'s nonbelligerent status as a passenger liner for a small amount of war materiel.

The growing effectiveness of the Allied blockade had forced Germany to take drastic measures. Germany's most promising offensive weapon at sea was the submarine, but international law of the time prohibited its most effective employment. If a submarine encountered a vessel that might belong to an enemy or might be carrying contraband, the U-boat had to surface, warn her intended victim, and "remove crew, ship papers, and, if possible, the cargo" before destroying her prey.

In response to Britain's unilateral redefinition of a naval blockade, Germany issued a proclamation of its own, declaring the waters surrounding Great Britain and Ireland to be a war zone. From February 18, 1915, on, Berlin had declared, enemy merchant vessels found within the zone would be subject to destruction without warning.

A Submarine Prowls the Seas

The day before *Lusitania* sailed from Pier 54, *U-20*, skippered by thirty-two-year-old *Kapitänleutnant* (Lt. Cmdr.) Walther Schwieger, left the German naval base at Emden on the North Sea. Schwieger's orders were to take *U-20* around Scotland and Ireland to the Irish Sea. There he was to operate in the approaches to Liverpool for as long as his supplies permitted. His orders allowed him to sink, with or without warning, all enemy ships and any other vessels whose appearance or behavior suggested that they might be disguised enemy vessels. The British were known to dispatch ships under neutral flags.

Submarine warfare was still in its infancy, and Germany had only eighteen seagoing subs, of which only about one-third could be on station at any one time. Schwieger's *U-20* displaced just 650 tons, making it about half the size of a fleet submarine in World War II. The boats were crowded and damp, and the eight torpedoes they carried were often unreliable. But the men who commanded the U-boats included some of the boldest officers of an elite service, and *U-20* had a reputation as a "happy" ship. The scion of a prominent Berlin family, Schwieger was popular with his officers and crew. One of his colleagues recalled him as "tall, broad-shouldered, and of a distinguished bearing, with well-cut features, blue eyes and blond hair—a particularly fine-looking fellow."

On May 3, *U-20*'s fourth day at sea, Schwieger spotted a small steamer just north of the Hebrides. Although the vessel was flying Danish colors, Schwieger concluded that she was British and fired a torpedo at her from three hundred meters. The torpedo misfired and his quarry escaped, but the incident said much about Schwieger's interpretation of his orders. He would not risk his boat by questioning possible neutrals. Rather, he would make full use of his authorization to sink ships without warning.

On the sixth day of his patrol, Schwieger rounded the southern tip of Ireland and entered the Irish Channel. There he encountered a small schooner, *Earl of Lathom,* under sail. Schwieger considered her so minimal a threat that he surfaced, allowed the schooner's five-man crew to abandon ship, and destroyed the vessel with shellfire. Later the same day he attacked a three-thousand-ton steamer flying Norwegian colors, but the single torpedo he fired missed.

The next day, May 6, brought better fortune. That morning *U-20* surfaced and pursued a medium-sized freighter, bringing her to a halt with gunfire. Schwieger believed in shooting first and identifying later, but in this case he was vindicated, for his prey turned out to be a British merchantman, *Candidate*, out of Liverpool. Schwieger dispatched her with a torpedo. That same afternoon *U-20* sighted another ship of undetermined nationality. Schwieger stopped her with one torpedo and watched as her crew took to the boats. He then sent her to the bottom with a second torpedo. This victim was *Centurion*, sister ship to the fifty-nine-hundred-ton *Candidate*.

After sinking *Centurion*, Schwieger made a critical decision. Although his orders called for him to press on to Liverpool, he had only three torpedoes left and was near the end of his cruising range. Schwieger would expend one more torpedo in his current operational area and then begin the return voyage, confident of finding targets en route for his remaining two torpedoes.

The *Lusitania* Nears Europe

Although *Lusitania* had left New York City with much of the pomp of a peacetime crossing, not all was well aboard the liner. To conserve coal, six of the ship's twenty-five boilers had been shut down, effectively reducing her top speed from twenty-five to twenty-one knots. Perhaps most important, there was a shortage of experienced seamen on *Lusitania*. The Royal Navy had called up most reservists, leaving Cunard to recruit crewmen as best it could.

Nevertheless, the ship was in the hands of one of the most experienced skippers on the Atlantic run. Captain Turner, sixty-three, had been assigned to *Lusitania* just before her previous crossing, but he was a veteran commander. One of his officers, Albert Worley, saw his skipper as a typical British merchant captain, "jovial yet with an air of authority." The son of a sea captain, Turner had signed aboard a clipper as a cabin boy at age thirteen and had served as a junior officer on a variety of sailing vessels.

Some believed that Turner's blunt speech and unpolitic manner were liabilities, but no one questioned his seamanship. In 1912, while captain of *Mauritania*, he had won the Humane Society's medal for rescuing the crew of the burning steamer *West Point*.

Much would later be made of Turner's seeming lack of concern about the submarine menace. But the skipper knew that no ship the size and speed of *Lusitania* had ever fallen victim to a U-boat. Even steaming at a reduced speed, *Lusitania* could outrun any submarine, underwater or on the surface.

The liner plowed ahead on its northeasterly course, averaging about twenty knots. The normally festive atmosphere on board had been dampened somewhat by the war; indeed, Cunard had obtained a full passenger list only by reducing some fares. The only gilt-edged celebrity on board was multimillionaire Alfred Gwynne Vanderbilt, en route to Britain for a meeting of horse breeders. Vanderbilt was fortunate in more than his inherited wealth; three years earlier he had booked passage on *Titanic*'s maiden voyage but had missed the fatal cruise because of a change in plans. Other first-class passengers included Broadway impresario Charles Frohman, scouting for new theatrical offerings, and Elbert Hubbard, the homespun writer of inspirational essays such as "A Message to Garcia."

On Sunday, May 2, the first day out, Captain Turner conducted church services in the main lounge. The following day found the liner off Newfoundland's Grand Banks. On May 4, *Lusitania* was halfway to her destination. The weather was fine, and Turner had reason to anticipate an easy crossing. Even so, the war was never entirely forgotten. On the morning of May 6, as the ship prepared to enter Berlin's proclaimed war zone, some passengers were startled by the creak of lifeboat davits. Early risers on B deck saw the Cunard liner's lifeboats being uncovered and swung out over the sides of the ship, where they would remain during the final, most dangerous portion of the voyage.

That evening Turner was called away from dinner to receive a radio message from the British Admiralty that warned of submarine activity off the southern coast of Ireland. There was no elaboration; the Admiralty did not mention the recent losses of *Candidate* and *Centurion*. Forty minutes later, however, came an explicit order to all British ships: "Take Liverpool pilot at bar, and avoid headlands. Pass harbors at full speed. Steer midchannel course. Submarines off Fastnet."

Lusitania acknowledged the message and continued on course. She was now about 375 miles from Liverpool, making twenty-one knots. Turner ordered all watertight doors closed except those providing access to essential machinery, and he doubled the watch. Stewards were instructed to see that portholes were secured and blacked out.

May 7 began with a heavy fog, and *Lusitania*'s passengers awakened to the deep blasts of the liner's foghorn. Turner maintained a course of eighty-seven degrees east but because of the fog ordered a reduction in speed to eighteen knots. The skipper was timing his arrival at the Liverpool bar for high tide so that, if no pilot was immediately available, he could enter the Mersey River without stopping.

Some 130 miles east, in his surfaced boat, Schwieger was wondering whether, given the poor visibility, he should continue on station. He recalled:

We had started back for Wilhelmshaven and were drawing near the Channel. There was a heavy sea and a thick fog, with small chance of sinking anything. At the same time, a destroyer steaming through the fog might stumble over us before we knew anything about it. So I submerged to twenty meters, below periscope depth.

About an hour and a half later . . . I noticed that the fog was lifting. . . . I brought the boat to the surface, and we continued our course above water. A few minutes after we emerged I sighted on the horizon a forest of masts and stacks. At first I thought they must belong to several ships. Then I saw it was a great steamer coming over the horizon. It was coming our way. I dived at once, hoping to get a shot at it.

The Torpedo Finds Its Mark

Until midday, Turner had taken most of the measures that a prudent captain would be expected to take during wartime. On the fateful afternoon of May 7, however, he reverted to peacetime procedures. The coast of Ireland was in clear view at 1 P.M., but Turner was uncertain of his exact position. Ignoring Admiralty orders to zigzag in dangerous waters, to maintain top speed, and to avoid headlands, Turner changed *Lusitania*'s course toward land to fix his position. At 1:40 P.M. he recognized the Old Head of Kinsale, one of the most familiar headlands of the Irish coast. With cottages on the coast clearly visible to her passengers, *Lusitania* swung back toward her earlier course of eighty-seven degrees east and headed toward her reckoning.

The change of course involved two turns. In Schwieger's recollection:

> When the steamer was two miles away it changed its course. I had no hope now, even if we hurried at our best speed, of getting near enough to attack her. . . . [Then] I saw the steamer change her course again. She was coming directly at us. She could not have steered a more perfect course if she had deliberately tried to give us a dead shot. . . .
>
> I had already shot away my best torpedoes and had left only two bronze ones—not so good. The steamer was four hundred yards away when I gave an order to fire. The torpedo hit, and there was a rather small detonation and instantly after a much heavier one. The pilot was beside me. I told him to have a look at close range. He put his eye to the periscope and after a brief scrutiny yelled: "*My* God, it's the *Lusitania*."

U-20's torpedo, carrying three hundred pounds of explosives in its warhead, struck between the first and second funnels, throwing a huge cloud of debris into the air. Turner, who had been in his cabin when the torpedo wake was spotted, rushed to the bridge. Survivors later testified almost unanimously that a second, heavier explosion followed. Power was cut off throughout the ship, preventing Turner from communicating with the engine room and trapping some people below decks. Passenger Margaret Mackworth and her father were about to step into an elevator when they felt the ship tremble from Schwieger's detonating torpedo. Both stepped back, an action that undoubtedly saved their lives.

Above, confusion was rampant. Passengers rushed to the boat deck, only to be told that the ship was safe and that no boats need be launched. Most life rafts were still lashed to the decks. Passengers and crewmen alike milled about; although *Lusitania* carried ample lifeboats, passengers had never been informed to which boat they were assigned in case of an emergency. Charles Lauriat, a Boston bookseller, later noted that as many as half the passengers had put on their life jackets improperly.

The ship immediately took on a heavy list to starboard that made it impossible to lower boats from the port side. The inexperienced crew could not cope. When Third Officer Albert Bestic reached the No. 2 lifeboat on the port side, he found it filled with women—most in full-length skirts—but only one crewman was available to man the davits. When Bestic, the crewman, and a male passenger attempted to lower the boat, there was a sharp crack. One of the guys had snapped, dropping the bow of the lifeboat and spilling its passengers against the rail and into the sea.

Three years earlier, those aboard *Titanic* for whom there were not enough lifeboats had had some two hours in which to stare into their icy grave. Aboard *Lusitania,* the imminence of the disaster left little time for contemplation. For instance, shortly after the torpedo struck, second-class passenger Allan Beatty slid across the entire width of the deck, caught the side of a collapsible raft, and still almost drowned as water poured over the rail.

Although Turner never gave an order to abandon ship, individual officers began loading boats on their own initiative. But the fact that the liner was still under way made it difficult to launch even the starboard boats. Several capsized, spilling their occupants into the water. Only eighteen minutes after Schwieger's torpedo struck, *Lusitania* sank with a roar that reminded one passenger of the collapse of a great building during a fire. Hundreds of passengers went down with her, trapped in elevators or between decks. Hundreds of others were swept off the ship and drowned in the roiled waters. Because *Lusitania* was nearly eight hundred feet long, her black-painted stern and four great screws were still visible to horrified onlookers on shore at Kinsale when the liner's bow struck bottom at 360 feet.

Not a ship was in sight when the liner went down; other skippers appear to have taken the submarine warnings more seriously than had Turner. But a stream of fishing boats from nearby Queenstown collected the living and the dead during the afternoon and evening of May 7. More than 60 percent of the people on board died—a total of 1,198—of whom 128 were Americans. About 140 unidentified victims were buried at Queenstown, but the remains of nine hundred others were never found. Of the American celebrities, all three—Frohman, Hubbard, and Vanderbilt—went down with the ship. One survivor recalled, "Actuated by a less acute fear or by a higher degree of bravery which the well-bred man seems to feel in moments of danger, the men of wealth and position for the most part hung back while others rushed for the boats."

The World Reacts

Whatever *Lusitania* may have been carrying as cargo, the death toll aboard the liner ensured that the sinking would become a public relations disaster for Germany. Instead of issuing an apology, however, or at least holding out the promise of an investigation, Berlin first sought to deflect responsibility. Adding insult to injury, thousands of Germans purchased postcards that portrayed Schwieger's torpedo striking *Lusitania,* with an inset of Admiral Alfred von Tirpitz. The newspaper of one of the centrist political parties, *Kolniche Volkszeilung,* editorialized:

The sinking of the *Lusitania* is a success of our submarines which must be placed beside the greatest achievements of this naval war. . . . It will not be the last. The English wish to abandon the German people to death by starvation. We are more human. We simply sank an English ship with passengers who, at their own risk and responsibility entered the zone of operations.

In Britain, reaction to the sinking was immediate and violent. British officials denied German suspicions that *Lusitania* was carrying contraband, and in London and Liverpool, mobs attacked German-owned shops. The reaction in the United States was less destructive but more ominous. Former President Theodore Roosevelt denounced the sinking as piracy; to Roosevelt, it was inconceivable that the United States could fail to respond. The press reaction outside the German-American community was almost uniformly condemning. The *New York Tribune* warned that "the nation which remembered the *Maine* will not forget the civilians of the *Lusitania.*" A cartoon in the *New York Sun* depicted the kaiser fastening a medal around the neck of a mad dog.

The United States was not yet ready for war, however, and amid the indignation there were calls for restraint. But the *Lusitania* tragedy caused thousands of Americans, heretofore indifferent to the war in Europe, to side with the Allies. On May 12 the British government released a report on German atrocities in Belgium. The report exaggerated the extent of German depredations, but in the aftermath of *Lusitania*'s sinking most Americans were a receptive audience. The German ambassador in Washington reported that the *Lusitania* affair had dealt a fatal blow to his efforts to enhance his country's image.

The foreign reaction was sufficiently disturbing to the German government that Schwieger, on his return to Germany, met with a cool reception. Then *U-20*'s log mysteriously disappeared. Typewritten versions of Schwieger's log, made available after *Lusitania* survivors had reported a second explosion, included this sentence: "It would have been impossible for me . . . to fire a second torpedo into this crowd of people struggling to save their lives."

In the diplomatic exchanges that followed the sinking, Germany was for a time intransigent and then issued a statement expressing regret for the loss of American lives. President Woodrow Wilson's secretary of state, William Jennings Bryan, resigned his post over the stern tone of Wilson's notes protesting the German action, arguing that Germany had a right to prevent contraband from going to the Allies and that a ship carrying contraband could not rely on passengers to protect her from attack. But Germany had lost the propaganda war.

On August 19, 1915, while diplomatic notes on the *Lusitania* affair were still being exchanged, another British liner, *Arabic,* was torpedoed, with the loss of two American lives. This time the German Foreign Ministry impressed upon the kaiser the seriousness of any rupture with the United States, and Germany promised that no more merchant ships would be torpedoed without warning. The threat of American intervention receded until, more than a year later, the beleaguered Germans believed it was necessary to resume unrestricted submarine warfare to break the British blockade. Berlin's announcement, on January 31, 1917, that its submarines would "sink on sight" brought the United States into the war.

Nearly two years had passed between the sinking of *Lusitania* and President Wilson's call for a declaration of war. But when Germany resumed unrestricted submarine warfare in 1917, the picture that came to American minds was of the women and children aboard the legendary Cunard liner. Indeed, much of the world seemed prepared to accept the judgment of a British court that responsibility for *Lusitania* rested exclusively with the Germans, "those who plotted and . . . committed the crime."

Turner, who survived the sinking of his ship, was roundly criticized for having failed to maintain top speed and for having ignored Admiralty orders to avoid headlands such as the Old Head of Kinsale. He never again took a Cunard liner to sea. As for Schwieger, he went on to become one of Germany's top U-boat aces, receiving his country's highest decoration for having destroyed 190,000 tons of Allied shipping. About five weeks after receiving his decoration, however, Schwieger took *U-88* on what proved to be his last cruise. The submarine never returned; she apparently struck a mine and went down with all hands. . . .

By the standards of his day, however, Schwieger's action was reprehensible. Although the U-boat commanders' orders permitted them to attack without warning, many of his colleagues chose to warn their victims when possible, and most of them probably would have done so in the case of a passenger liner. By his own admission, Schwieger torpedoed *Lusitania* before he had even identified her. The one point in Schwieger's defense is that he certainly did not expect his target to go down in eighteen minutes. As in the case of *Centurion* the day before, Schwieger probably expected his first torpedo to stop *Lusitania*. Then, after those aboard had abandoned ship, he would sink his victim at leisure. But this is not what happened, and *Lusitania*'s victims were not the only ones who paid a price. Winston Churchill, British first lord of the Admiralty when *Lusitania* went down, wrote in 1931:

> The Germans never understood, and never will understand, the horror and indignation with which their opponents and the neutral world regarded their attack. . . . To seize even an enemy merchant ship at sea was an act which imposed strict obligations on the captor. To make a neutral ship a prize of war stirred whole histories of international law. But between taking a ship and sinking a ship was a gulf.

The Road to War

Ernest R. May

Europe erupted into war on June 28, 1914, with the assassination of Archduke Franz Ferdinand of Austria-Hungary. For the next three years the American president, Woodrow Wilson, steered a tortuous path around and through international incidents in an effort to keep his nation out of the conflict. Eventually German measures, especially with regard to submarine warfare and a possible alliance with Mexico, pushed Wilson's hand and made war inevitable. A former Harvard University professor and a distinguished historian who specialized in United States foreign policy during the century's first decades, Ernest R. May describes the three hectic years from 1914–1917, which brought the United States to war and helped end the Progressive Era.

On June 28, 1914, Archduke Franz Ferdinand of Austria-Hungary had been assassinated in Sarajevo. This event had set off a chain of events that within a few months engulfed all Europe in what was to become known as the Great War or the World War.

At the outset American reactions were mixed. Some people, mostly German-Americans, took the side of Austria and Germany. Probably a majority favored the alliance of Russia, France and Britain. Although cultural ties with England undoubtedly accounted for some of this sympathy, Germany's violation of Belgian neutrality to strike at

France had profoundly shocked and alienated American opinion. German Chancellor Theobald von Bethmann-Hollweg's contemptuous description of the solemn treaty of neutrality as a mere "scrap of paper" was widely quoted with disapproval. German atrocities in Belgium horrified Americans. Many agreed with Allied propagandists that the war was one between civilization and barbarism.

Nearly everyone had assumed that the war would be short. But after the near miracle on the Marne that checked the German drive against Paris in September 1914, a stalemate developed on the Western Front. It became clear that fighting might go on for months (perhaps even years), and the passions of most Americans cooled. Cases arose in which the Allies, too, paid scant attention to international law. Invoking dubious rules, the British stopped American ships on the high seas and took them into their ports to be searched for contraband; as in the past, Americans were touchy about freedom of the seas. Nevertheless, most Americans regarded the Allies as morally the better. The commonest attitude, however, was a mixture of relief at not being involved and conviction that none of the issues in the conflict concerned America. At the outbreak of the war, President Wilson had felt it necessary to exhort his countrymen to remain "impartial in thought as well as in action."

The Administration made it its business to see that nothing disturbed this mood of noninvolvement. At first the chief threat to continuing American neutrality seemed to be that of disputes with the British over neutral rights—disputes that might get out of hand as they had in 1812. To avoid this possibility became the chief business of certain key advisers. Walter Hines Page, the American ambassador in London, who wanted the United States to support England in the war, on more than one occasion actually helped the British government reply to complaints from Washington. . . .

Submarine Warfare Threatens the Peace

On February 4, 1915, however, the Germans suddenly announced that submarines would sink without warning any

Allied ships found in the waters around the British Isles. Pointing out that submarines would not necessarily be able to distinguish between Allied and neutral vessels, the German government urged neutral states to keep their ships out of the zone.

Wilson was incredulous. The submarine was a relatively new weapon, whose use in enforcing a blockade had hardly been thought of. Undersea raiders first showed they could execute independent missions when two German U-boats sank four British ships in the North Sea in September 1914. To young German naval officers, frustrated by the glory won by the army, the sinkings suggested a concerted campaign against merchantmen. Admiral Alfred von Tirpitz, the grand old man of the German navy, publicly endorsed this idea and thus gave it some publicity. But if Wilson had read of it, it is likely that he had dismissed it as Allied propaganda. Accepted practice permitted belligerents to stop enemy merchantmen and inspect their papers and, in exceptional circumstances, to sink them after first insuring the safety of crew and passengers. In the case of neutral vessels, the rule was that contraband could be removed, after which the ship could proceed. To Wilson it seemed absolutely unthinkable that the German government should now discard this tradition and threaten neutral shipping and lives.

[State Department legal officer Robert] Lansing felt that the Germans had to be reproached in strong language, and he and the President quickly drew up a note warning that if an American were killed or an American ship sunk, the United States would consider it "an indefensible violation of neutral rights." In such an event, "the United States would be constrained to hold the Imperial German Government to a strict accountability . . . and to take any steps it might be necessary to take." This was the toughest language that diplomacy permitted.

The Germans replied at length, promising that they would try to keep neutral ships from harm. Without formal notification to Washington, the submarine offensive against Allied shipping was postponed and then recommenced under such stringent restrictions that its initial results were unspectacular.

But if Wilson felt elation, as he was perhaps entitled to, it was short-lived. April brought reports of increasing submarine activity. An American citizen had died in the torpedoing of a British passenger liner, the *Falaba*. Since he had been on a belligerent ship in a war zone, the case was somewhat ambiguous. Lansing and most of Wilson's advisers felt it violated American rights. Since [Secretary of State William Jennings] Bryan thought otherwise, the President—who was of two minds—deferred action. On May 1 an American ship, the *Gulflight,* was torpedoed, though not sunk. In the panic that followed, three Americans died. This was a very serious incident, but the events of the next week quickly turned attention from the *Gulflight.*

On May 7 at 3 in the afternoon, a cablegram reached Washington from the United States embassy in London: "The *Lusitania* was torpedoed off the Irish Coast and sunk in half an hour." One of the largest and most luxurious liners afloat, the *Lusitania* had sailed from New York on May 1. Among its 1,257 passengers were many prominent Americans. Despite the war, and regardless of the German embassy's warning in New York papers that the British ship was sailing into a war zone, social life aboard ship had been as gay as ever. Although the captain of the *Lusitania* had instructions to steer a zigzag course in the war zone as protection against submarines, he disregarded them, partly because he could not believe that his ship would be attacked.

The torpedo struck the starboard bow and apparently blew up a boiler. The giant vessel at once began to heel and sink. In the quarter hour before it went under, there was a frantic rush to the lifeboats. Some 700 got away. But 1,198 passengers and crewmen died, 128 of them Americans.

Wilson's Diplomatic Triumphs

In Washington almost everyone felt the time had come to hold Germany to the "strict accountability" promised by

Wilson. But Bryan, now desperately fearful of war, saw points on the German side. The *Lusitania* had carried munitions; the dead passengers had knowingly taken a risk that they could have avoided. But few others in the Administration sympathized with this reasoning. The Germans, most agreed, had committed a barbarous crime and would have to pay for it.

Wilson went into almost complete seclusion to decide what he should do. Three days later, in a speech before a group of newly naturalized citizens, he declared: "There is such a thing as a man being too proud to fight. There is such a thing as a nation being so right that it does not need to convince others by force that it is right."

These words provoked fierce criticism from segments of the press, Congress and the public. However the note that Wilson sent to Berlin on May 13 was firmer than might have been expected. It demanded an apology, reparations and assurances that no such incident would recur. To comply, Germany would have to abandon any undersea warfare against merchant shipping.

When Berlin's answer arrived, 18 days later, it was unsatisfactory, for it practically justified the sinking on grounds similar to those argued by Bryan. Countering the American demands, Germany proposed that the United States enter into prolonged investigation of and debate about whether the *Lusitania* had carried munitions, had orders to sink submarines on sight and other matters. Wilson was in a quandary. He had meant every word in his first *Lusitania* note. On the other hand, he had a horror of the obvious alternatives to acceptance of the German position—the severance of diplomatic relations or a message to Congress proposing a declaration of war. Feeling in the country was obviously calmer than it had been immediately after the sinking, and Bryan and a few others in the Administration, citing the more moderate climate of public and congressional opinion, were frantically pleading for retreat.

Wilson concluded that the best course was merely to reiterate what he had said earlier and, while offering the Germans further time for consideration, to make clear to them that he insisted on action. . . .

On the following day the second *Lusitania* note went off by cable to Germany. Reiterating earlier demands, it warned: "The Government of the United States is contending for something much greater than mere rights of property or privileges of commerce. It is contending for nothing less high and sacred than the rights of humanity."

The Germans again delayed answering, and when their response finally came it was once more disputatious and inconclusive. But meanwhile secret orders went out to submarine commanders to refrain from attacking passenger-carrying vessels. Wilson saw that his essential demand had, in effect, been met, and he was content not to insist upon more. "Apparently the Germans *are* modifying their methods," he wrote to Colonel [Edward] House [the president's friend and adviser]. "They must be made to feel that they must continue in their new way unless they deliberately wish to prove to us that they are unfriendly and wish war."

This was the line Wilson followed consistently. In August 1915, after there had been some revival of submarine activity, another passenger liner, the *Arabic,* was sunk. Wilson protested again. Despite the impatience of the press and some of his closest advisers, he gave the German government time to consider, and he won from it a public admission that, since the *Lusitania* exchanges, submarine commanders had been given secret orders not to attack large passenger-carrying vessels without warning.

There was another lull. Then in the spring of 1916, a French steamer, the *Sussex,* was torpedoed. This time Wilson dispatched a virtual ultimatum. He went before Congress to declare solemnly that diplomatic relations would be severed unless Germany abandoned submarine attacks on passenger and freight vessels. From Berlin came a pledge that ships would not be sunk without warning or without provision for the safety of passengers and crew. Out of these crises Wilson had pulled one diplomatic triumph after another. . . .

He was so sure that the American position was morally right, and so hopeful that on reflection the Germans would accept it, that he set before them the choice between doing as he asked and inviting war. For some time to come, this policy was successful. But the choice was still Germany's. As the fighting in Europe settled into an interminable pattern of butchery, as weary anger grew, the danger mounted that the Germans might decide for war. . . .

The Nation Edges Toward War

From the end of 1914 on, there had been widespread German subversion and sabotage in America—enough to justify several sensational trials and official requests by the American government for recall of a number of German and Austrian diplomats implicated in these incidents. People in Eastern cities who remained pro-German were likely to be regarded as unpatriotic. But even among people who thought of Germany as an enemy, there were few who felt that immediate action was called for. As for the submarine issue, the most widespread attitude appeared to be a mixture of approval for Wilson's stand, delight that the American government could make Germany back down and doubt that attacks on passenger liners flying Allied flags actually constituted adequate justification for war. The spectrum of opinion included many different views, ranging from those of devout pacifists at one extreme to outright interventionists at the other. In the middle was a large group described by Wilson as demanding "two inconsistent things, firmness and the avoidance of war."

This was a confusing situation for a President who liked to be at the head of public opinion. Early in 1916, at the height of the spy and sabotage revelations. Wilson feared a swing toward chauvinism that would make it hard for him, in the next submarine crisis, to be as patient as in the past. He exclaimed to his private secretary, Joseph P. Tumulty: "If my reelection as President depends upon my getting into war, I don't want to be President. . . . I intend to stand by the record I have made in all these cases, and take whatever action may be necessary, but I will not be rushed into war . . ."

Only a few weeks later the pendulum had swung to the other extreme, at least in Congress. Thomas P. Gore, the blind senator from Oklahoma, and Representative Jeff McLemore of Texas proposed that American citizens be required to stay off armed belligerent ships. Wilson fought these resolutions on the ground that their passage would undermine him in his dealings with Germany. After a bitter fight with members of his own party, he was able to whip enough votes into line to defeat the resolutions.

Again there was a shift in public opinion. During the *Sussex* crisis, which followed hard on the heels of the legislative fight, the loudest voices Wilson heard were advocating a tougher policy toward Germany. Loudest of all was that of the man whom he had beaten for the presidency in 1912, Theodore Roosevelt. . . .

Facing the grim prospects that confronted him after reelection, Wilson knew there was little hope of arranging acceptable peace proposals with the Allies. Robert Lansing, who had succeeded Bryan as Secretary of State, warned that overtures for peace carried the risk of an unacceptable answer from the Allies—one that might end with the United States on the side of the Germans. This risk became all the more apparent when, on December 12, 1916, Chancellor Bethmann-Hollweg surprised the world by declaring that Germany was ready to discuss terms with the Allies. Nevertheless Wilson strove to make peace, for he saw no other way to avoid the imminent danger of war over the submarine issue.

On December 18 he sent a note to all the belligerents asking them to reveal, in confidence, their conditions for peace. Despite their chancellor's recent speech, the Germans gave him a vague and disappointing answer. The Allies, on the other hand, returned a full and seemingly precise statement.

In an effort to secure greater co-operation by Germany, Wilson went before Congress on January 22, 1917, and delivered a speech addressed as much to Germany as to

America. He called for a settlement of all international issues, limitation of armaments, the opening of the seas to all
nations and a world in which justice and friendly relations
would prevail. And he promised that the United States
would join other nations in guaranteeing peace if it were "a
peace without victory."

Victory, however, was precisely what both sets of com-
batants still wanted. Allied statesmen privately expressed
scorn of Wilson for not realizing that the defeat and humil-
iation of Germany must precede lasting peace. On January
31 the Germans disclosed their minimum terms. These included annexation of parts of France and Russia, a protectorate over Belgium, colonial gains and reparations. On the
same day Germany also stated that, in pursuing victory, unrestricted submarine warfare would be launched.

Shock Waves from Germany and Mexico

For nearly two years Bethmann-Hollweg had been able to
restrain those who insisted that the submarine could win
the war regardless of American intervention. But in the late
summer of 1916 the kaiser, despairing of victory, had summoned Field Marshal Paul von Hindenburg and his chief of
staff, General Erich Ludendorff, to take the supreme command. Equally at the end of its rope, the Reichstag helped
to vest the two officers with virtually dictatorial powers,
including explicitly that of deciding whether or not to em-
bark on an all-out submarine campaign. In early January
1917 Hindenburg and Ludendorff decided to take this step
and to let the United States decide whether or not this
meant war. The kaiser and the parliamentary leaders
backed them up, and Bethmann-Hollweg was helpless.

By the last day of the month the submarines were on station, ready to begin the new campaign, and on that day the
American government was notified that within 24 hours
any and all shipping in the war zone, neutral vessels included, would be treated as fair game. Wilson felt he had
to carry out the threat he had made during the *Sussex* crisis. On February 3 he announced to Congress that he had

severed diplomatic relations. He added, however, that he could not believe Germany would actually carry out such a ruthless and reckless campaign: "Only actual overt acts on their part can make me believe it even now."

During succeeding weeks he tried, and failed, to persuade the German government that it should back down as it had in the past. On February 25 the British passenger liner *Laconia* was sunk with three Americans among those lost. On March 12 an American merchantman, the *Algonquin,* went down, followed within days by three other American vessels, *City of Memphis, Illinois* and *Vigilancia.* The Germans had supplied the overt acts.

Compounding the shock was the revelation that the German government had opened negotiations for an alliance with Mexico. A message from German Foreign Minister Arthur Zimmermann to the German minister in Mexico City had been intercepted and deciphered by the British and passed on via Ambassador Page to Washington. Dated January 16, it proposed that if the United States entered the war, Mexico should ally itself with Germany "on the following basis: make war together, make peace together, generous financial support and an understanding on our part that Mexico is to reconquer the lost territory in Texas, New Mexico, and Arizona."

When Wilson saw this text, his first reaction was indignation. When he learned that it had been sent through Washington over cable facilities which the State Department had specially opened to the German Embassy for possible communications about peace negotiations, he exclaimed, "Good Lord! Good Lord!" After the message was given to the press and its authenticity confirmed, war seemed to become a certainty.

Wilson was still not sure. And, as Winston Churchill was to recall when writing his history of World War I, the "action of the United States . . . depended . . . upon the workings of this man's mind and spirit to the exclusion of almost every other factor." On the day after he received the Zimmermann text, Wilson proposed to Congress that American merchantmen be armed and authorized to fight submarines and that he be given broad authority to respond to Germany's challenge. Wilson hoped this measure might preserve America's honor without resort to all-out war.

But this was not to be. Pacifists and isolationists led by Senator La Follette blocked action with a filibuster. Although 75 of the 96 senators announced that they would vote for the bill if they could, La Follette's ranks held and the measure died. Then Wilson cried that a "little group of willful men, representing no opinion but their own, have rendered the great Government of the United States helpless and contemptible." He soon took matters in his own hands and by executive order authorized the arming of merchantmen.

What went through his mind in the next few weeks no one knows. The actual divisions in public opinion were still sharp. Fervor for war was confined to a vocal and growing minority, but sentiment for peace remained powerful. The large majority of the people appeared willing simply to trust that the President would make the right decision; they were ready to follow him. Public opinion did not guide Wilson; he had to guide it.

"What Else Can I Do?"

Frank Cobb, a newspaperman who talked with Wilson when his travail was nearing its end, recorded: "For nights, he said, he'd been lying awake going over the whole situation; over the provocation given by Germany, over the probable feeling in the United States, over the consequences to the settlement and the world at large if we entered the mêlée. . . . He said . . . that he had tried every way he knew to avoid war . . . that if there were any possibility of avoiding war he wanted to try it. 'What else can I do? he asked. 'Is there anything else I can do?'"

On April 2 Wilson asked a joint session of Congress to declare war. He had feared that war might put an end to the ideals voiced in his "peace without victory" address. In his war message, however, he still talked with the fervor of a missionary; he rose above a mere demand for revenge to the vision of a world made "safe for democracy."

When Congress voted on April 6, six senators and 50 representatives stood out against war. Among them were not only men with German-American constituencies but also La Follette, George Norris of Nebraska and others who represented major elements in the progressivism of the preceding decade. They stood out as spokesmen for the idea that America should keep to itself, perfect its own institutions, and have as little as possible to do with the world in which it lived. But they were few.

The large majority in both houses voted enthusiastically for war, and when they did so, an epoch in American history came to a close. In the 1890s the United States had broken with its self-imposed isolation. Then, for a while, America had concentrated on its national concerns. But now it was isolated no more. Though men would later try once again to recapture the illusion of innocence and non-entanglement, the nation would from that day forward be a force, or at least a presence, in the affairs of all nations everywhere, and the presence of other nations would be felt in American affairs. The burden of power was on the country and could not be shaken loose. The Progressive Era had been the last in which the nation lived unto itself.

America Enters the Fray:
The Fight for Belleau Wood

John Toland

The United States entered World War I relatively late, but
her forces fought in many battles. One of the first occurred
in June 1918 at Belleau Wood, where the U.S. Marines performed superbly. The author of many books on military history and one of the most famous historians, John Toland,
published an account of the fighting in Europe. Titled *No
Man's Land*, the book includes the action at Belleau Wood.

The vaunted principle of unity of command was totter-
ing and would probably fall unless the Marne line
held. The hinge was a pretty little wooded area some five
miles northwest of Château-Thierry. It was known as Belleau Wood. Germans infested most of it and were driving
south to take the rest so they could reach the village of
Lucy-le-Bocage. From there they would only be forty-five
air miles from the Eiffel Tower.

It was not a large wood. The trees were about six inches
thick and so densely planted that one could scarcely see
twenty feet ahead except where ax or shell had cut a swath.
Unlike American forests it had been constantly under care
of a forester who cleared out the underbrush and those
trees ready for timbering. Despite the lack of undergrowth
there was ample shelter in the high rocky ground which
was scarred with gullies and crags. It was an irregular area

Excerpted from *No Man's Land: 1918, the Last Year of the Great War*, by John
Toland (New York: Doubleday, 1980). Copyright ©1980 by John Toland.
Reprinted with permission from John Hawkins & Associates, Inc.

not much more than a square mile that from the air reminded some of a sea horse, some of a twisted kidney. It had once been the hunting preserve for the ancient Château of Belleau, which was a half mile north of the wood and was connected to Lucy-le-Bocage by a farm road. At the southeast corner of the wood was another small village, Bouresches. This was held by the Germans and had to be retaken before the Allies could clear the wood.

Eager Yanks

By June 5, the U.S. 2nd Division was stretched out below Belleau Wood, eager to show the world that Americans could fight as well as talk. It was a hybrid division with 1,063 officers and 25,602 men in two brigades, one Army and one Marine The Leathernecks were commanded by a Regular Army officer, Brigadier General James Harbord, former chief of staff to Pershing, who had told him that he was getting the best troops in France and if he failed he'd know whom to blame. . . .

The French cheered these outlandish, boisterous young men from overseas who stuck their legs out of the trucks and acted as if they were going to a party. The sight of their cheery, cocky faces gave new spirit to the people. The Yanks were finally coming and now there was hope that the Boche [German] could be stopped. "Striking was the contrast in appearance between the Americans and the French regiments, whose men, in torn uniforms, hungry and hollow-eyed, were scarcely able to hold themselves erect," recalled Jean de Pierrefeu. "New life had come to bring a fresh, surging vigor to the body of France, bled almost to death. Thus it came to pass that in those crucial days when the enemy stood for a second time on the Marne, thinking us disheartened, then, contrary to all expectation, an ineffable confidence filled the hearts of all Frenchmen.". . .

An enterprising correspondent was on the way to the scene of the action. Floyd Gibbons of the Chicago *Tribune* had motored down from Paris that morning with Lieutenant Oscar Hartzell, formerly of the New York *Times*, in hopes of seeing the Americans in their first major engagement. Gibbons reached Fifth Marine headquarters at 4 P.M. [June 6] and told its commander, Colonel [Wendell C.] Neville, that he wanted to get out to the front line.

"Go wherever you like," said Neville. "Go as far as you like but I want to tell you it's damn hot up there."

It took Gibbons and Hartzell almost an hour to reach Lucy-le-Bocage. Shells were falling. Farmhouses were in flames. The ground under the trees was covered with tiny bits of paper. Gibbons examined several and saw that they were letters from American mothers and wives which the weary Marines had removed from their packs and destroyed so the enemy could make no use of them. He came upon a pit containing two machine guns and their crews. Out front was a field sloping gently down two hundred yards to another cluster of trees. Part of it, apparently, was held by the enemy.

At 4:55 a young platoon commander arrived with the order to advance. "What are you doing here?" he asked Gibbons, looking at the green brassard and red "C" on Gibbons' left arm.

"Looking for the big story."

"If I were you I'd be about forty miles south of this place," said the officer, "but if you want to see the fun stick around. We are going forward in five minutes."

The Marines waited, stripped for action—no extra clothes or blankets and only twenty pounds in their packs. Colonel Albertus Catlin, commander of the Sixth Marine Regiment, came up to find his men cool and in good spirits. "Give 'em hell, boys!" he told several of them.

At exactly five o'clock everyone leaped up simultaneously and started forward. There was a sickening rattle of machine-gun fire. German artillery increased the fury of its attack. The 3rd Battalion of Major [Benjamin S.] Berry faced a large open field of wheat, still green but about two feet tall. It was swept by machine-gun bullets. The wheat bowed and waved in the metal storm. The advancing lines wavered until someone shouted, "Come on, you sons of bitches! Do you want to live forever?" It was the legendary Gunnery Sergeant Dan Daly, recipient of the Medal of Honor, whose voice had been striking terror in recruits for the past twenty-five years. The line moved forward, but a hundred yards from the wood the enemy fire was so brutal that the men had to fling themselves down. Many died trying to crawl back. A few got safely into the woods. The rest hugged the ground and waited for dark.

Floyd Gibbons and Hartzell were just behind Major Berry when he turned and shouted, "Get down, everybody!" They fell on their faces. Withering volleys of lead scissored the top of the wheat. It was not coming from the woods but from the left. Up ahead came a shout. Gibbons lifted his head cautiously and saw the major trying to struggle to his feet. He was grasping his left wrist in pain. "My hand's gone!" he exclaimed. "Get down. Flatten out, Major!" shouted Gibbons. "We've got to get out of here," said Berry. "They'll start shelling this open field in a few minutes."

Gibbons looked around cautiously. "You're about twenty yards from the trees," he called to Berry, and said he was coming to help. The correspondent crawled forward, keeping as flat as possible. Suddenly, it felt as if a lighted edge of a cigarette touched his upper left arm. It felt like a minor burn. There was no pain. A bullet had gone clean through his bicep muscle without even leaving a hole in his sleeve. Then something nicked the top of his left shoulder. Again the burning sensation, but he was surprised to find he could still move his arm.

It wasn't anywhere near as painful as a dentist's drill. He continued moving, occasionally shouting words of encouragement. As he swung his chin to the right to keep close to the ground, he moved his helmet over. Then came a crash like a bottle dropped in a bathtub. Sergeant M.K. McHenry was so close he saw Gibbons get hit in the face. To Gibbons it seemed as if a barrel of white-wash had tipped over and everything in the world turned white. He didn't know where he had been hit but surely not the head; if so, everything was supposed to turn black. He began taking mental notes. "Am I dead?" It wasn't a joke. He wanted to know. He tried to move the fingers of his left hand. They moved. Now the left foot moved. He knew he was alive. He brought his hand to his nose. Something soft and wet. He found his hand covered with blood. There was a pain in the entire left side of his face so he closed his right eye. Dark! He tried to open his left eye. Still dark. Something must have struck him in the eye and closed it. He didn't guess that a bullet had gone through his eye and crashed through his forehead. He could not reach the major now. But moments later he saw Berry rise and, in a hail of lead, rush forward and out of his vision.

Merwin Silverthorn, a rather small, energetic, and bright sergeant, was just to the left with his platoon commander, an Army lieutenant named Coppinger. They had set off in approved trench warfare formation, holding rifles at high port and moving at a slow steady cadence. They started down a ravine and near the bottom were raked by machine-gun fire. They hid behind a pile of wood. After five minutes Coppinger shouted, "Follow me!" and ran bent over up the other side of the ravine. At the top he looked back and said in wonder, "Where the hell is my platoon?" They had started with fifty-two and now there were six. "I'm going back," he told Silverthorn, who thought, "Here's where you and I part company, because we just got across that place, and that's the last thing I'm going to do— go back."

Silverthorn figured that in the military no one ever got into trouble for advancing toward the enemy, so he kept going until he found the remnants of another platoon, led by Sergeant Gay. They finally reached the wheat field. And there Silverthorn saw one of the most magnificent sights of his life—Major Sibley's battalion marching across the field in slow cadence under terrific fire. As Gay's platoon started up toward the field, he was hit in the back. Silverthorn bound the wound; told him it wasn't too bad. "You stay here and I'll come back after dark to get you." He took charge of the few men left and they all went forward in rushes. The din was deafening. As Silverthorn hit the ground on the second rush, he thought he'd struck a rock. He looked down. There was no rock. It felt as if someone had swung a baseball bat across the knee cap. Yet there was no pain. He told the only man left, an automatic rifleman, to move on into woods where they probably needed him. "I'm going to stay right where I am until it's dark and can get out under cover." He thought of his father, who had been shot in the lung at Gettysburg, yet lived to be ninety-six.

A Beautiful Sight

On the right, Major Berton Sibley's battalion was having better luck and Colonel Catlin watched with admiration as the battalion pivoted on its right with the left sweeping the open field in four waves, as steadily as though on parade. It was "one of the most beautiful sights I have ever witnessed." There was no yell or rush but a deliberate march with lines at right dress. Catlin's hands were clenched, all his muscles taut as he watched the Marines march in the face of machine-gun sweeps. Men fell but fortunately Sibley's men had slightly better cover than Berry's and the rest plodded on stolidly, listening for orders. Closer and closer they came to the wood and it must have been a terrifying sight to those holding it.

Catlin had no field telephone. He hurried to a little rise so he could see what was going on ahead. Through his glasses he watched Sibley's men plunge into the wood. Captain Tribot-Laspierre, a French liaison officer, begged Catlin to get to a safer place, but the colonel ignored the bullets whipping around him until one hit him in the chest. "It felt exactly as though someone had struck me heavily with a sledge. It swung me clear around and toppled me over on the ground." When he tried to get up he realized his right side was paralyzed. Captain Tribot-Laspierre rushed to Catlin's side, and dragged the big man to a shelter trench—no simple matter since he was so small. The bullet had gone through Catlin's lung, but he felt little pain and never lost consciousness. The bleeding was internal and there was little to be done for him as he lay in the trench, waiting for first-aid treatment.

In the meantime Major Thomas Holcomb of the 2nd Battalion had instructed Sergeant Don Paradise of the 80th Company to take Private Slack across the wheat field. They were to locate the 80th Company commander, Captain Coffenberg, as well as Major Sibley, the adjoining battalion commander, and get their map locations and any other information. Paradise, followed by Slack, safely crossed the deadly field and soon found Sibley. "For God's sake," said Sibley, "tell Major Holcomb not to take Captain Coffenberg and the 80th Company away from me! We've lost at least half our battalion."

"Come on, Slack, let's get back," said Paradise, but the other man was horrified. "You aren't going the same way we came?" It was the shortest route, said Paradise, and headed back alone. Sometimes the shell smoke was so thick he couldn't see where he was going; and wounded men kept calling for help, but a runner couldn't stop to be a medic. He finally found Holcomb on the side of a hill and lay down beside his hole to give him the message. He then asked permission to go back to help the wounded, but Holcomb said he'd have to carry more messages, so he crawled into a nearby hole until needed. He could see Bouresches and, figuring that the Germans could see him, crawled over to a hedge where other runners were digging in. A moment later a shell exploded directly in his evacuated hole.

Sergeant Silverthorn was still lying in the wheat field. It felt as though machine-gun bullets were passing only an inch or two over him. Every so often a speck of dirt flicked up nearby. He guessed a sniper was zeroing in on him. Then shells began falling and he decided to get up and run whether he had one leg or not. It was about two hundred yards to the woods. He dashed across plowed ground into tall grass hip high. Here be found a friend named Pilcher, who was weeping and moaning. He had been hit in the stomach. Silverthorn repeated what he had told Gay—"I'll come back after dark and get you"—then he crept through the grass, which hid him until he could lunge safely into Belleau Wood. Here it was quiet, peaceful, deserted. It was eerie and for the first time he was frightened. He was alone yet he knew that the Germans were near. He limped along and was lucky enough to find a dressing station where he was tagged to go to a hospital. But he located a stretcher and convinced someone to go back to the wheat field with him. On the way he looked for Sergeant Gay but couldn't find him, so he started for Pilcher. He looked for the wheat field in the dark, at last finding it by instinct. He softly began calling Pilcher's name. "Of all the screwy situations," he told himself. "Here you get out of this thing once and you're right back where you started from." He felt his way until he stumbled upon Pilcher. He was motionless. "Pilcher, we're here," he said, shaking his friend. "I've got a stretcher. We're going to take care of you now." But he was dead. Silverthorn was a religious man and finding the stiff body of Pilcher intensified his Christianity. "It convinced me that the Lord had something for me to do."

Gibbons was still waiting in the field for a medic. Lieutenant Hartzell, hiding nearby, called, "I don't think they can see us now. Let's start to crawl back." Gibbons had no idea where he was and crept toward the voice. They met halfway. "Hold your head up a little," said Hartzell. "I want to see where it hit you."

Gibbons lifted his head, painfully opened his right eye, and looked directly into Hartzell's face. "I saw the look of horror in it as he looked into mine." Twenty minutes later they reached the edge of the woods and safety.

In the meantime, Lieutenant Clifton Cates of Holcomb's 2nd Battalion was leading his platoon across the wheat field toward Bouresches. Men were falling on both sides. A machine-gun bullet knocked off Cates's helmet. He dropped, stunned. A few minutes later Cates came to. He tried to don his helmet, but it wouldn't go on at first because of a dent the size of a fist. "The machine gun bullets were hitting around and it looked like hail. My first thought was to run to the rear. I hate to admit it, but that was it." Glimpsing four Marines in a ravine, he staggered toward them and fell at their feet. One took off the dented helmet and poured wine from his canteen over the lump on Cates's head. "God damn it," said the lieutenant, "don't pour that wine over my head, give me a drink of it." This revived him. He then grabbed a French rifle and led the quartet into Bouresches.

Between the Devil and the Deep Sea

Several miles to the west, Major Wise's battalion was in reserve. About midnight a runner from General Harbord brought an order to go into the line to the left of Berry. "This was the damnedest order I ever got in my life—or anyone else ever got," Wise wrote. "It went on the calm assumption that all the objectives of the First and Third Battalion had been secured . . . I was between the devil and the deep sea. If I didn't move, I knew I'd catch hell. If I did move, I knew I was going right down into Germany."

They set out at 2 A.M., June 7. It was "black as pitch—impossible to see even one foot ahead"—as Wise led the battalion in single file along a road which led to "sloping grain fields like a bottleneck opening into a bottle." Wise had a hunch and stopped the column. It was too deadly quiet. He led several squads forward about two hundred yards until sharp rifle fire burst out on the left. Wise recognized the sharp bark of Springfield rifles and shouted out to hold fire. From the dark someone shouted, "Look out. The Germans are on your right in the Bois de Belleau."

Wise went back, shouted to his men, "About face to the rear—on the double!" Like everyone else Lieutenant Lemuel Shepherd was confused. He had been taught never to obey such an order without saying, "By whose command?" This word went back up the line and was answered with, "By orders of Major Wise—we're in the wrong spot."

Those in the rear decided that if a major said it was time to run it was time to move fast. "We picked up our feet," recalled Lieutenant E.D. Cooke, "and galloped back in the direction from which we had been going." Those behind could not go as fast. They would take a few steps, then halt before taking a few more. This continued until the first light of day as they were emerging from woods into an open field at the point where the road made a sharp curve to the left. Wise gave orders to take cover on both sides of the road and dig in. The 55th Company of Captain Blanchfield was in the lead and Lieutenant Lemuel C. Shepherd, Jr., led his platoon to the left, distributing them along the edge of the woods facing the clearing. All at once firing broke out.

In the light of dawn Shepherd could see Germans moving in the clump of woods up ahead and on the right. What Major Wise had unwittingly done was lead his battalion into an open field at the left of Belleau Wood—and this was heavily defended by the enemy. A fierce fire fight erupted. Mortar shells began falling on all sides, landing with dull thuds and then exploding "with a tremendous concussion which was truly frightening."

A breathless runner told Shepherd that Captain Blanchfield had been seriously wounded and ordered him to command the company. As Shepherd headed along the edge of the wood, his orderly went down. While trying to help him, something struck Shepherd in his left thigh. It felt like the kick of a mule. He crumpled in a heap, not realizing in the excitement of the moment that he had been hit. "As I lay there unable to move, I glanced down and what should I see on the ground beside me but the bullet which had struck me." Blood was oozing from his britches. Close beside him with his head on Shepherd's leg was his little dog, Ki-Ki, who had tagged along behind him all night. He was so quiet Shepherd thought be was dead. "Damn it, they shot little Ki-Ki too," he said, and pushed him to one side. But Ki-Ki jumped up and placed his head again on Shepherd's leg, apparently sensing something had happened to his master.

Later that day newspapers throughout the United States

headlined the attack, OUR MARINES ATTACK, GAIN MILE AT VEUILLY, RESUME DRIVE AT NIGHT, FOE LOSING HEAVILY announced the New York *Times*. And in Chicago the *Daily Tribune*: MARINES WIN HOT BATTLE SWEEP ENEMY FROM HEIGHTS NEAR THIERRY.

At last America had something to cheer about and the Marines were lauded incessantly. "Everywhere one went in the cars, on the streets, in hotels or skyscrapers, the one topic was the Marines who are fighting with such glorious success in France." So commented the New York *Times*. Reports received at their recruiting headquarters in New York indicated that applications had increased more than a hundred per cent.

To read these papers, one would have thought it was the most important battle of the war. The wounding of Floyd Gibbons had much to do with the spate of publicity. Before the attack he had sent to the censor in Paris a skeleton dispatch, intending to fill in the details afterward. When it was rumored that he had been killed, the Paris censor, a friend, said, "This is the last thing I can ever do for poor old Floyd," and released the dispatch. Later Gibbons' detailed story added more luster, not only to himself but to the Marines. All this was to the detriment of doughboys who were fighting in the same division, as well as those in the 3rd Division holding the Marne River line west of Château-Thierry. Everything accomplished near that city was now assumed to be done by the Marines.

Small as the action was at Belleau Wood, it put new spirit in the French and deeply impressed the German soldiers who had faced the Americans. The dash and raw courage of the Leathernecks struck terror in those defending the wood and word was passed to beware the wild Americans. To their officers, the reckless display at Belleau was even more ominous. They saw the charge over the wheat fields multiplied many times. There were already almost 700,000 Americans in France and more than a million others were on the way. And these were not worn and dispirited but strong, young and brazenly confident.

Eddie Rickenbacker: America's Extraordinary Ace

Eddie Rickenbacker

One style of warfare introduced during World War I produced warriors who in many ways compared to the knights of chivalric times. Rather than battle from a horse, these men vaulted to the skies in flimsy aircraft. Above the mud and horror in the trenches below, these daring pilots faced death from the enemy and from their own imperfect machines, but they acted according to an unwritten code of honor which bound both sides.

Eddie Rickenbacker emerged as America's foremost aviator. After shooting down his first enemy aircraft on April 29, 1918, Rickenbacker tallied 21 additional aircraft and 4 observation balloons in six months. For his valor, Rickenbacker received the nation's highest military honor, the Congressional Medal of Honor. In 1967 Rickenbacker wrote his autobiography. In the following selection, he explains what aerial warfare was like during World War I.

When the big German spring offensive of 1918 began, we were moved back to a safer location at Épiez. It was a gloomy period, but the arrival of two experienced pilots from the Lafayette Escadrille, Captains David Peterson and James Norman Hall, revived us again. Both were

---

aces, with more than five victories each, and their very presence inspired us.

Even more wonderful was the sudden arrival of our equipment, guns, ammunition, instruments, flying clothing, spare parts and spare planes. We were moved up to Toul. Once again we were only eighteen miles from the lines, but this time we were armed. Surely we would now be the first American squadron to go into action against the enemy.

The honor deserved a distinctive insignia. One of the pilots, Lieutenant Johnny Wentworth, was an architect, and he was asked to design it. We all threw out ideas. Major Huffer, the CO [commanding officer], suggested Uncle Sam's stovepipe hat with the stars and stripes for a hatband. Our flight surgeon, Lieutenant Walters from Pittsburgh, mentioned the old American custom of throwing a hat into the ring as an invitation to battle. And thus one of the world's most famous military insignia, the Hat-in-the-Ring, which became a part of my entire life from then on, was born.

The First American Air Combat Mission

The Hat-in-the-Ring was proudly emblazoned on my Nieuport on the morning of April 14, 1918, when Captain Peterson, Lieutenant Reed Chambers and I took off for a patrol of the lines in our sector. It was the first combat mission ever ordered by an American commander of an American squadron of American pilots.

It nearly turned into the first fiasco. The fog was so heavy that Peterson returned to the field. I thought he had turned back because of engine trouble, and Reed and I continued on. We became separated in the fog and were nearly lost. Two German planes pursued us, and they really became lost. Hearing them over the field, Doug Campbell and Allan Winslow took off to attack them. Winslow shot down his plane, and Campbell forced the other one to crash. On our first day of operations, the 94th had brought down two German planes. The people of Toul, who had been bombed nightly by the Germans, feted us in a great celebration. News of the 94th's double victory was flashed to the States, and cablegrams and letters poured in on our two heroes. There was even a happy ending for the two German pilots, for neither was seriously injured.

During the next few days I learned many lessons. On my second flight I trusted my judgment instead of my compass and wound up flying in the wrong direction. Then I jumped a French Spad and had to put my little ship through some tricky maneuvers, in order to show its pilot my United States markings before he could shoot me down. In the air one shot first and identified later.

On my next flight, just over Saint-Mihiel, I sighted an enemy plane and came in on him apparently unnoticed, even though shell bursts followed my path across the sky. At the last moment I remembered what Raoul Lufbery had told me a dozen times—*look out for a trap*. Coming in on top of me was an Albatros fighter. My little Nieuport could outclimb the heavier German ship, and I maneuvered away from him and came back down on his tail.

That time I had him, but again I thought of Lufbery's admonition. I looked around, and two more planes were coming at me. I banked and headed for home. The two planes stuck on my tail. I put my ship through every maneuver; they came on relentlessly, which was somewhat discouraging, as our planes were supposed to be faster than the German planes. The whole idea of aerial combat was to get on the other fellow's tail so that you could pour bullets into plane and pilot. I hunched over in dread expectation of the heavy slugs ripping into my back. Ahead was the most beautiful cloud in the world. I held my breath. Closer, closer—then I entered it. I was safe. I stayed in the cloud protection for several minutes, then poked my nose out for a look around. The planes had gone, and I proceeded on to the field.

There Doug Campbell and Charley Chapman, who had just landed, wanted to know why I had run away from them. I had been fleeing from two of my own buddies. Not only had they scared me to death, but because of my failure to identify them, I had lost what might well have been my first victory in the air. . . .

Rickenbacker Records His First Kill

For several days it rained, and then came a double blessing. The sun came out, and I was ordered to go on a mission with Captain Hall, one of the greatest fliers and finest men I have ever known. Word had come that an enemy two-seater plane was flying south over the lines. We took off and went up to look for him. Once aloft, I saw a plane far off on the horizon and sped in its direction. Jimmy Hall ignored the whole thing and with good reason, for the plane turned out to be a French two-seater.

Looking around the sky for Hall, I saw a lot of German antiaircraft activity in the direction of Saint-Mihiel. I knew it was German because the shell bursts emitted black smoke; allied Archie was white. I hurried to the area, and, sure enough, there was Jimmy amusing himself with the gunners on the ground. He was baiting them with his entire repertory of stunts, having a wonderful time while the Germans below expended ammunition. When he saw me, he wiggled his wings and headed toward Pont-à-Mousson. I followed him.

From the German lines came a single plane, a new Pfalz. Hall was climbing into the sun, with me close behind, and the German was totally unaware of us as we kept between him and the sun. We had a thousand feet of altitude on him, and we were two to one. If he saw us coming, his only hope was to put his plane into a dive. The Pfalz, a sturdy ship, could outdive a Nieuport any day, for the main weakness of the Nieuport was a tendency to shed the fabric of its upper wing in a dive. If I had been that German pilot, I would have put my nose down and headed for Germany. I decided to get in position to cut off that form of retreat. I knew that Hall would attack when he was ready.

In a second I would go into my first combat. My heart started pounding. The image of a Liberty Bond poster popped into my mind. It was of a beautiful girl with outstretched arms. In big black letters were the words "Fight or Buy Bonds." Well, I did not have much choice.

As I came out of the sun to get in position to cut him off, the German pilot saw me. He stuck up his nose and started climbing. Jimmy came into range and let go a burst of bullets. The German instantly banked his Pfalz to the right and put it into a dive, heading homeward as fast as he could go. That was what I was ready for, and I was on his tail in an instant. The Boche ran like a scared rabbit, but I was gaining. I had my sights trained on the back of his seat. I pressed both triggers.

Every fourth shell was a tracer, and I could see two streaks of fire pouring into the Pfalz's tail assembly. I held the triggers down and pulled back on the stick slightly, lifting the nose of the plane. It was like raising a garden hose. I could see the stream of fire climbing up the fuselage and into the pilot's seat. The plane swerved. It was no longer being flown. I pulled out of the dive and watched the Pfalz curve down and crash. I had brought down my first enemy airplane. . . .

I had no regrets over killing a fellow human being. I do not believe that at that moment I even considered the matter. Like nearly all air fighters, I was an automaton behind the gun barrels of my plane. I never thought of killing an individual but of shooting down an enemy plane.

As for the method, that was how we fought. All pilots, German and Allied alike, strove to gain an advantage over the adversary. The advantage could have been in superior flying ability and marksmanship, in equipment, in numbers. When the sides were even and neither could gain the advantage, then there was no battle. Frequently two pilots of equal skill would spend an hour or more fencing in the sky, each seeking to obtain the superior position over the other. When one or both ran low on gas, they would simply give each other a wave and fly back to their respective aerodromes. Though we were out to shoot down planes and the best way to shoot down a plane was to put a burst of bullets in the pilot's back, there was never, at least in my case, any personal animosity. I would have been delighted to learn that the pilot of the Pfalz or any other pilot I shot down had escaped with his life. . . .

The Specter of Fire

Death by burning was the death we dreaded more than any other. Our planes were constructed of wooden frameworks covered with fabric. The fabric was treated with "dope," a highly combustible fluid that drew up the cloth and stretched it tight. We Americans had no parachutes. Some German pilots and all their balloon observers were equipped with parachutes, and often I was pleased to see an enemy bail out of his burning plane or balloon and escape being burned alive.

We often discussed the question of whether we would jump to certain death or stay with the ship. Raoul Lufbery, whose every word I respected, was positive in his advice.

"I'd stay with the machine," he said. "If you jump you haven't got a chance. If you stay, you may be able to side-slip your plane down so that you fan the flames away from yourself. Perhaps you can even put the fire out before you reach the ground.". . .

Four days later, on a lovely morning in May, puffs of white smoke in the air announced that an Allied battery was firing at an enemy plane. It was an observation plane, and the German flew it right over our field. Lufbery was in the barracks at the time. He ran out, jumped on a motorcycle and raced to the hangar. His own plane was being worked on, and he grabbed another. It was doubtful that either plane or guns were up to Lufbery's demanding specifications. In any event, he was unfamiliar with the machine.

At two thousand feet above the field, in plain sight of everyone below, Lufbery attacked the Albatros. He fired several bursts, then zoomed up and came in again for another attack. His guns jammed. Somehow he put them back in working order, then came around again. By that time he must have realized that this particular Albatros was heavily armored. His bullets bounced off the plane. Still he came on. He flew so close that the gunner in the Albatros could not possibly have missed him. Lufbery's plane burst into flames.

He held the plane on a straight course for about five seconds. Then, from the ground, eyewitnesses saw him squirm out of the blazing cockpit and climb onto the fuselage. Straddling it, he pushed himself back toward the tail. He rode in this position for several seconds as the flames fanned back over him. Then he jumped.

I returned from patrol to hear this shocking story. A phone call came in with the exact location of the spot where he had landed. A group of us jumped into a car and drove to the spot. He had fallen in a lovely little garden in a small town near Nancy. Nearby was a small stream; he may have been trying to land in the water. Instead his body had been impaled on a picket fence. Death must have been instantaneous.

Rickenbacker Narrowly Avoids Death

After Jimmy Hall's crash, I had taken his place as commander of Number One flight in our squadron. I was honored, but I must admit it occurred to me that another pilot might soon be taking my place. For with leadership came responsibility.

In addition to leading my flight on routine patrols, I emulated Lufbery's example and flew my own lone-wolf missions over the lines. He always said that it was impossible to shoot down German planes sitting in the billet with your feet before the fire. I heeded his advice so well that I had more hours in the air than any other American flier. . . .

I flew over Metz several times, paying special attention to the aerodrome, but the Germans simply were not flying that day. Not much gas remained, but I decided to make one last check at a field near Thiaucourt. Still at twenty thousand feet, I cut off my engine to save gas. As I silently circled the field, like a great bird of prey, I saw, far beneath me, three graceful German Albatroses taxi out onto the field and take off, one by one. They headed straight southward, climbing steadily, obviously unaware of my presence above them.

I continued circling, afraid even to breathe, until the last of the three was well on his way, with his back toward me. I put the little Nieuport into a shallow dive to start the propeller going and turned on the ignition. The engine caught, and I gunned my plane after the three Germans. I hoped to time it so that I would make my attack over the lines, rather than over German territory.

Closer, closer. My eyes were glued on the leather-jacketed shoulders of the German flying the rearmost Albatros. That is where my bullets were going to go. I was so intent on the pursuit that I completely forgot about a German stratagem. In front of the planes ahead, but higher, a black puff appeared in the sky, then another and another. The German batteries had seen me, and it was their way of warning the three planes in front of me. They were setting the fuse so that the shell would burst at approximately my altitude.

The pilot in front of me turned his head to look behind him. I saw the sun glint off his glasses. All three pilots immediately put their planes into a dive. I was now within two hundred yards of the last plane, and I had no intention of letting him get away. I knew the Nieuport's fatal weakness of shedding its wing covering in a dive, but in the excitement I did not think of it at all. I gunned the plane up to a speed of at least 150 miles an hour and closed in on the man in front of me.

At fifty yards I gave him a 10-second burst of machine gunfire. I saw the bullets hit the back of his seat. I felt no sympathy. He had made a stupid mistake in diving rather than trying to outmaneuver me.

By then the other two pilots had had an excellent opportunity to pull up and get on my tail. At that moment either of them could be sighting down my back. But I still wanted to make sure that I had killed my man. Not until I saw his plane go out of control did I try to pull my own out of the dive. I had to come out of it in a hurry, put the ship into a sharp climb and have it out with the other two. I pulled the stick back into my lap.

A ripping, tearing crash shook the plane. The entire spread of linen over the right upper wing was stripped off by the force of the wind. I manipulated the controls, but it did no good. The plane turned over on her right side. The tail was forced up. The left wing came around. The ship was in a tailspin. With the nose down, the tail began revolving to the right, faster and faster. It was death. I had not lost my willingness to fight to live, but in that situation there was not much that I could do. Even birds need two wings to fly.

The two remaining Albatroses began diving at me, one after the other, pumping bullets into my helpless Nieuport. I was not angry at the two men for trying to kill me; I simply thought that they were stupid. Why waste ammunition? Did they think I was playing possum, with the framework of one wing hanging in the breeze?

A crippled plane can take a long time to flutter to earth. I wondered exactly how I would die. Would the plane shake itself to pieces? In that case, I would go whistling down to hit the ground and splatter. If the plane stayed in one piece, it might crash in the trees beneath me, and I might only break a few bones. Which announcement would my mother prefer to read in the telegram from the War Department—that I was dead or that I was injured behind the lines?

I began remembering all the major episodes of my life, the good things I had done and the bad things. The bad seemed to outnumber the good. And then I remembered the Lord above.

"Oh, God," I prayed, "help me get out of this."

The earth was coming up fast. Without thinking, almost as though I were moved by something bigger than myself, I pulled open the throttle. The sudden extra speed lifted the nose of the plane. For a second there, I was horizontal. I pulled on the joystick and reversed the rudder. I must have hit the one combination in a million that would work. The fuselage remained almost horizontal. The nose was heading for the American lines only a couple of miles away. If I could only hold her like that, I might make it.

I was at less than two thousand feet, and every antiaircraft battery, every machine gunner and practically every rifleman began sending a curtain of lead into the sky. I flew right on through it. I had no choice.

I talked to that little plane all the way home. Losing altitude, with the engine going full blast and the controls jammed in the only position that enabled it to stay aloft, my little plane and I crossed the lines. When I reached the field, I was flying at treetop height. I could not cut back the engine, for then I'd go straight down. I came in for my landing with the engine running wide open. Everybody dashed out to see what fool was coming in at full throttle. I grazed the top of the hangar, pancaked down on the ground and slid to a stop in a cloud of dust. I swung out of the bullet-riddled, battered little crate and tried to saunter nonchalantly toward the hangar as though I came in like that every day.

Eugene V. Debs's Antiwar Activism

Edward Robb Ellis

Labor leader and socialist activist, Eugene V. Debs accumulated a following among the poor and downtrodden. After years of battling for workers and equal rights, Debs turned his attention to war. Some of his most eloquent statements came during his crusade to oppose America's role in World War I. Edward Robb Ellis, a historian of turn-of-the-century America, wrote of Debs's stance against war, the government's reaction, and Debs's subsequent imprisonment.

In the spring of 1918 Eugene V. Debs was sixty-two years old and ill and angry. A veteran labor leader and America's prime apostle of Socialism, he had been the Socialists' Presidential candidate in 1900, 1904, 1908 and 1912. In thorough agreement with the party's "St. Louis Proclamation," he said, "I abhor war. I would oppose war if I stood alone. When I think of a cold, glittering steel bayonet being plunged into the white, quivering flesh of a human being, I recoil with horror."

Now federal agents were raiding Socialist headquarters across the country. Socialist periodicals were being banned from the mails, uniformed soldiers were attacking civilians on streets and disrupting meetings they considered unpatriotic. In Tulsa, Oklahoma, hooded men snatched seventeen Wobblies [members of the Industrial Workers of the World, a socialist labor organization] from the police, then whipped and tarred and feathered them. In Newport, Kentucky, a peace-loving minister, the Reverend Herbert S. Bigelow, was seized by a mob, thrown into a car, driven to a forest, stripped and lashed with a blacksnake whip. His hair was doused with gasoline, and his attackers were about to set it on fire when they were frightened away. They had snarled that they were acting "in the name of the women and children of Belgium [a nation occupied by the German army]."

Debs, in a memorable phrase, said that civilization needed to be civilized. He had heart trouble and drank too much, but his frail body and anguished heart were still capable of expressing outrage. In speeches and articles he protested against these atrocities and seethed with resentment at what he felt were Wilson's pretensions of democracy. He lived in Terre Haute, Indiana, and early in June, 1918, he was visited by his former campaign manager, Noble C. Wilson. Debs said he thought the time had come for him to make an all-out remonstrance against the war and its ugly echoes in America.

"Of course," he said with a chuckle, "I'll take about two jumps and they'll nail me—but that's all right!"

Debs Criticizes the War

On June 16 Debs arrived in Canton, Ohio, an industrial center and the home of former President William McKinley. He was scheduled to speak at the Ohio convention of the Socialist party. The rally was to be held in Nimisilla park, but while being driven there, Debs insisted upon stopping at the Stark county workhouse, across the street from the park, to visit three Socialists imprisoned for opposing the war. The warden had strung them up by their wrists for two days.

It was a hot day, but Debs wore a tweed jacket and vest. He looked a little like Lincoln, for he was tall and slender and gawky, had a high forehead, big ears and a long neck. Despite the sweetness of his smile, his blue eyes were veiled with sadness. James Whitcomb Riley, the Hoosier poet, wrote that "God was feeling mighty good the day He created Gene Debs." Self-educated and well read, Debs had developed an oratorical style that was masterful in its simplicity. Whenever he became intoxicated with the passion of his theme, the melancholy faded from his eyes, which then seemed to burst into flame, and he would lean over the edge of the platform, his right arm extended and his long forefinger jabbing here and there as he denounced capitalism.

Twelve hundred people stood in front of a plain wooden bandstand devoid of any American flag. A local Socialist opened the rally by reading the Declaration of Independence and then introduced Debs. Smiling, he moved to the front of the platform while the prisoners in the nearby jail pressed against their bars to try to hear him. Debs began by saying, "I have just returned from a visit over yonder, where three of our most loyal comrades are paying the penalty for their devotion to the cause of the working class. . . ."

As he spoke, federal agents and members of the American Protective League moved through the crowd checking draft cards. The United States attorney for the northern district of Ohio had hired a young man to record Debs' speech in shorthand, but the youth was so inept and Debs spoke so fast that he got only patches of the remarks. The local Socialists, aware of the significance of this meeting, had employed a local attorney as their own stenographic reporter.

Sweat laced Debs' face as he paced the platform, every now and then wheeling around and ramming his finger toward someone in the audience. "It felt," a man said later, "exactly as if that forefinger was hitting you in the nose." Debs said, "I realize that in speaking to you this afternoon there are certain limitations placed upon the right of free speech. I must be exceedingly careful, prudent, as to what I say, and even more careful and prudent as to how I say it—"

Laughter.

"I may not be able to say all I think—"

More laughter, followed by applause.

"But I am not going to say anything that I do not think.

I would rather a thousand times be a free soul in jail than to be a sycophant and coward in the streets! They may put those boys in jail—and some of the rest of us in jail—but they cannot put the Socialist movement in jail. . . ."

Debs spoke for two hours, the stenographers scribbling. He denounced "Wall Street Junkers" and "the gentry who are today wrapped up in the American flag." He said that "in every age it has been the tyrant, the oppressor and the exploiter, who had wrapped himself in the cloak of patriotism or religion or both, to deceive and over-awe the people." He said that each of the 121 federal judges in the land held "his position, his tenure, through the influence and power of corporate capital." He declared that "the purpose of the Allies is exactly the purpose of the Central Powers."

The Government Responds

A transcript of Debs' speech was sent to the federal office in Cleveland, and thirteen days later a grand jury indicted him for alleged violations of the Espionage Act. He was arrested on June 30, 1918, as he was about to enter the Bohemian Gardens in Cleveland to speak at a Socialist picnic. This was a Sunday, most offices were closed, and the authorities refused to let him arrange bail, so that night he slept in a cell. The next day a Cleveland Socialist put up the $10,000 bail and when he was released, he told friends, "I had a hunch that speech was likely to settle the matter."

He remained free until his trial began September 9 in federal district court in Cleveland. He retained four Socialist lawyers but hardly used them because he admitted he had made that Canton speech, while denying there was anything criminal about it. His attorneys made the sole argument that the Espionage Act violated the guarantee of freedom of speech as set forth in the First Amendment of the Constitution. The case was heard by David C. Westenhaver, judge of the United States court of the northern district of Ohio and once a law partner of Secretary of War Baker. The twelve jurors were all retired, averaged seventy-two years of age, and each was worth from $50,000 to $60,000.

Sure he would lose the case, Debs began to do some heavy drinking. His lawyers decided that one of them would have to devote all his time to keeping Gene sober. For two days the prosecution proved what Debs had already conceded—that he indeed had made that speech in Canton. When the government rested, the defense rested, for it had no witnesses to present. Then the judge agreed to let Debs speak in his own behalf.

At 2 P.M. on September 11, 1918, the courtroom darkened by a passing thundershower, Debs, dressed in a worn gray suit, rose and began speaking quietly. He went on talking for almost two hours, and when he finished, some jurors were weeping. A federal agent leaned across a table and whispered to a reporter, "You've got to hand it to the old man—he came through clean." When court adjourned, Debs walked into a corridor where a girl handed him roses and fainted at his feet.

The next day the judge told the jurors to find the defendant not guilty on those counts dealing with ridicule of the federal government. He instructed them to deliberate on other counts charging that Debs willfully and knowingly tried to obstruct the draft act. The jury was out six hours, and Debs spent this time regaling friends with anecdotes about Abraham Lincoln. About 5 P.M. the jurymen filed back inside, and one read the verdict: guilty as charged on two counts of the indictment. The judge said he would impose sentence on September 14.

Debs Moves a Nation

When court reconvened on that date, the clerk asked whether the defendant cared to make a final statement. He did. Rising from his chair and beginning to speak as he approached the bench, talking without notes. Eugene Debs delivered a speech that was to become an American classic and be printed and reprinted in anthologies; Heywood Broun called it "one of the most beautiful and moving passages in the English language."

Your honor, [Debs began] years ago I recognized my kinship with all living things, and I made up my mind that I was not one whit better than the meanest on earth. I said then, and I say now, that while there is a lower class, I am in it, while there is a criminal element I am of it, and while there is a soul in prison, I am not free. . . . I look upon the Espionage law as a despotic enactment in flagrant conflict with democratic principles and with the spirit of free institutions. . . . I am opposed to the social system in which we live. . . . I believe in fundamental change, but if possible by peaceful and orderly means. . . .

I am thinking this morning of the men in the mills and factories, of the men in the mines and on the railroads. I am thinking of the women who for a paltry wage are compelled to work out their barren lives; of the little children who in this system are robbed of their childhood and in their tender years are seized in the remorseless grasp of Mammon and forced into industrial dungeons, there to feed the monster machines while they themselves are being starved and stunted, body and soul. I see them dwarfed and diseased and their little lives broken and blasted because in this high noon of our twentieth century Christian civilization, money is still so much more important than the flesh and blood of childhood. In very truth, gold is god. . . .

When Debs finished, the judge said he considered himself second to none in his sympathy for the poor and suffering, but he was amazed by "the remarkable self-delusion and self-deception of Mr. Debs, who assumes that he is serving humanity and the downtrodden." Calling himself "a conservator of the peace and a defender of the Constitution of the United States," the judge then imposed sentence: ten years' imprisonment.

Debs' attorneys said they would appeal to the United States Supreme Court and challenge the constitutionality of the Espionage Act. During the appeal Debs could live at home in Terre Haute, but he was forbidden to leave the northern federal district of Ohio. He was at once amused and irritated when federal agents raided the home of his for-

mer campaign manager, Nobel C. Wilson, confiscated Socialist literature and letters and never returned any of these
documents. The agents also found a box they thought might
contain dynamite and began opening it gingerly. Debs'
friend laughingly warned them to be careful lest they get
their noses blown off. The box was full of charcoal tablets.

A Sentence Passed

Not until March 10, 1919, when the war had been over for
four months did the Supreme Court pass on the Debs case.
All nine justices sustained the verdict of the lower court.
Their unanimous opinion was written by Justice Oliver
Wendell Holmes. In another opinion only a week earlier
Holmes had said free speech could be abridged only in case
of "a clear and present danger" to public safety, but he did
not cite his own doctrine in this decision. Regarded as a
champion of free speech, Holmes told a friend he guessed
Chief Justice White had asked him to write the opinion in
the Debs case as a strategic move. "I hated to have to write
the Debs case," Holmes confessed. Still, this New England
aristocrat had little in common with the Midwestern pro-
letariat. He felt contemptuous of the "poor fools whom I
should have been inclined to pass over. The greatest bores
in the world are the come-outers who are cock-sure of a
dozen nostrums."

Holmes thought Debs, a noted agitator, was rightly convicted of obstructing the recruiting service, held that the
jury had acted properly and declared the Espionage Act
constitutional. But when Holmes began to receive "stupid
letters of protest," he wrote a friend, "Now I hope the
President will pardon him and some other poor devils with
whom I have more sympathy."

As for Debs, he told the press, "Great issues are not decided by courts, but by the people. I have no concern in
what the coterie of begowned corporation lawyers in Washington may decide in my case. The court of final resort is the
people, and that court will be heard from in due time."

According to Claude Bowers—journalist, historian,

diplomat—when the President heard Debs had been arrested, he said, "I never meant my law to be used like that." *My* law, Wilson's words. But when outraged telegrams and letters poured into the White House, he vowed never to pardon him.

Many disagreed with Wilson. Bowers said of Debs, "He was not a traitor. He was not a revolutionist. He was, rather, an evolutionist." The New York *Times* editorialized, "Mr. Debs was convicted for making a socialist speech. No sane person considers him a criminal," Harold J. Laski, an

I Love My Flag

One of the most strident publications on behalf of workers in the nation was a newspaper called the Industrial Worker. *In 1917 the paper printed a poem presenting its view of war.*

I love my flag, I do, I do,
Which floats upon the breeze,
I also love my arms and legs,
And neck, and nose and knees.
One little shell might spoil them all
Or give them such a twist,
They would be of no use to me;
    I guess I won't enlist.

I love my country, yes, I do
I hope her folks do well.
Without our arms, and legs and things,
I think we'd look like hell.
Young men with faces half shot off
Are unfit to be kissed,
I've read in books it spoils their looks,
    I guess I won't enlist.

William Preston Jr., *Aliens and Dissenters: Federal Suppression of Radicals, 1903–1933*. Cambridge, Massachusetts: Harvard University Press, 1963.

English political scientist who corresponded with Holmes, said of Wilson. "I must get off my chest my sense of passionate indignation at his refusal to pardon Debs."

In April, 1919, sick and old, at a time when federal prisons still overflowed with people convicted under the Espionage and Sedition acts, Debs entered the penitentiary at Moundsville, West Virginia. Two months later he was transferred to the federal penitentiary in Atlanta, Georgia. In 1920 he ran a fifth time as the Socialist candidate for President, the first man to seek this highest office while behind bars. Although he was defeated by the Republican candidate, Warren G. Harding, he polled 919,779 popular votes.

On January 31, 1921, only about a month before the end of his second term, Wilson received from his attorney general a recommendation that he commute Debs' sentence. On this sheet of paper Wilson scrawled one word, "Denied." Then he turned to his secretary and said explosively:

> I will never consent to the pardon of this man! While the flower of American youth was pouring out its blood to vindicate the cause of civilization, this man, Debs, stood behind the lines, sniping, attacking, and denouncing them. Before the war he had a perfect right to exercise his freedom of speech and to express his own opinion, but once the Congress of the United States declared war, silence on his part would have been the proper course to pursue. I know there will be a great deal of denunciation of me for refusing this pardon. They will say I am cold-blooded and indifferent, but it will make no impression on me. This man was a traitor to his country and he will never be pardoned during my administration!

On December 25, 1921, President Harding commuted Debs' sentence, but did not restore his citizenship.

The League of Nations: Triumph and Tragedy for a President

Sean Dennis Cashman

Woodrow Wilson hoped that once the bitter fighting ended on Europe's battlefields, he and other leaders could create a better way to settle disputes among nations. He thought he had the solution by proposing the creation of a League of Nations, a legislative body composed of the world's countries. Many European leaders supported the idea, but in the United States, Wilson faced strong opposition. A historian of the war, Sean Dennis Cashman, relates the struggles faced by Wilson to gain acceptance for his world organization.

A t the peak of his fame Woodrow Wilson enjoyed a prestige throughout the world unknown to any other American president. During his two visits to Paris in the winter of 1918–19 and the summer of 1919, Europeans looked to Wilson as a deliverer and redeemer. Everywhere he went he was feted on a scale unknown since Napoleon. Delegations of Swedes, Poles, Albanians, Iraquis, and Ukrainians, among others, waited for him at his house in Paris or in the Crillon Hotel, where he held court, to plead their cause. "The mass of European peasantry, shopkeepers, and day laborers looked forward to his arrival as men looked in mediaeval times to the second coming of Christ," observed William E. Dodd. Yet the hero of 1918 was to

Excerpted from *America in the Age of the Titans,* by Sean Dennis Cashman. Copyright ©1988 by New York University. Reprinted with permission from New York University Press.

leave office in 1921, his health broken, his party crushed, and his great dream in fragments.

Wilson made the achievement of world peace by [making] collective security the cornerstone of his foreign policy. Though he failed in his lifetime to convince the United States, his ideal shaped the perception of two generations across the world as to what was necessary, possible, and desirable for the concert of nations. . . .

The Peace Conference Opens

The Peace Conference at Paris had first opened on January 12, 1919, with delegates from twenty-seven countries. The chief task of negotiations was undertaken by a Council of Ten and, when this proved too cumbersome, by a Council of Four: David Lloyd George of Britain; Georges Clemenceau of France; Vittorio Orlando of Italy; and Woodrow Wilson.

Against advice and precedent Wilson had gone to Paris himself at the head of the American delegation. He was accompanied by Secretary of State Robert Lansing; his personal adviser, Colonel Edward House; the permanent military representative on the Supreme War Council, General Tasker Bliss; and a retired diplomat, Henry White. The only Republican, White, was of no significance in his party. Although the Senate would have to ratify the treaty, Wilson had not asked it to endorse the Fourteen Points [Wilson's list of war aims and what he hoped would be achieved by peace] and did not appoint a senator to the delegation. The exclusion of leading senators affronted prominent Republicans and stored up trouble for the future.

At the end of October 1918 Wilson had made an unnecessary appeal to the American electorate for a vote of confidence on his foreign policy in the midterm elections. Republicans across the country, who had supported the administration loyally in the war, were cut by Wilson's request which was interpreted as downright ingratitude and this made it easy for Republican leaders to foment public distaste. On November 5 the polls returned a Republican majority in Congress of 240 to 190 in the House and of 49 to 47 in the Senate. Theodore Roosevelt could, therefore, claim with much justification on November 26, 1918. "Our allies and our enemies and Mr. Wilson himself should all understand that Mr. Wilson has no authority whatever to speak for the American people at this time. His leadership has just been emphatically repudiated by them."

Yet in Europe, at the height of his international reputation, Wilson convinced himself he could bring peace without victory. But the crowds acclaiming him in London, Paris, and elsewhere, wanted a settlement in the interests of their own nations. Those who hated Germany forced their leaders into extreme positions. David Lloyd George had just won a British general election with the greatest majority of seats ever after a campaign of vicious slogans, including, albeit against his will, "Hang the Kaiser" and "Make Germany pay until the pips squeak." Georges Clemenceau, the French premier, had won a vote of confidence of four-fifths of the French chamber. "He had one interest, France," writes historian William E. Leuchtenburg, "and one concern, that Germany must never march again." He was seventy-eight and recalled the humiliating defeat of the Franco-Prussian War and the loss of Alsace-Lorraine as well as the cruelty of the recent conflict. . . .

Harsh Terms for the Vanquished

The Treaty of Versailles with Germany was not only harsh but added insult to injury. As he had intended, Clemenceau secured the reduction of the German army to a maximum of 100,000 men without heavy artillery and without an air force. Ironically, because it was to be a force of men on long service, it turned out to be capable of providing the nucleus for a rapidly trained conscript army. To compensate France for wartime devastation to its own industry, the mining reserves of the Saar valley were placed under international control. After fifteen years the people there would decide on their future affiliation—whether to France or Germany—by a plebiscite. As a safety precaution, the right bank of the Rhine was to be demilitarized. The left bank and its bridges and bridgeheads of Cologne, Coblenz, and Mainz on the right were to suffer an army of occupation for fifteen years that Germany had to maintain. Poland, which had disappeared as an independent state in the 1790s when it was partitioned by Russia, Austria, and Prussia, was revived as a nation state according to the Wilsonian principle of the self-determination of nations. But, contrary to the self-determination of nations, Germans were placed under Polish rule in Silesia and a corridor giving Poland access to the sea at Danzig (now Gdansk) separated East Prussia from Germany. On the insistence of Lloyd George, Danzig became a free city under the Polish Customs Union.

South Africa and Australia were not prepared to give up the German colonies they had acquired in the war, South West Africa and New Guinea. Thus they defied Wilson and, for the sake of appearances, the term "mandates" was used to cover the acquisitions. Britain took German East Africa and some other territory in West Africa. Japan was granted formal entitlement to Shandong in China.

Germany was forced to pay an immediate indemnity to the Allies of $5 billion and to agree to pay further reparations of an unspecified amount to be decided later. Moreover, the Treaty of Versailles in its "war guilt" clause pronounced Germany the sole cause of the war. Wilson could hardly repudiate the war guilt clause since his own wartime rhetoric had done so much to incriminate the kaiser and the whole German establishment. Rather than assent to the treaty, the German cabinet of Philipp Scheidemann resigned on June 23, 1919. "L'heure du lourd règlement de comptes est venue." "The hour has come for the serious settlement of debts," declared Clemenceau in the Hall of Mirrors at Versailles on June 28, 1919; and five years after the assassination of Franz Ferdinand at Sarajevo the event that had precipitated the war, peace with Germany was signed. . . .

A Confused Woodrow Wilson

Conferences are a matter of trade and barter and Wilson was not a wheeler-dealer—it was contrary to his open nature. Journalist William Allen White recalled how "Time and again, at Paris, he came out of the Council of Ten realizing belatedly and freely admitting in private that he had agreed to something too hastily.... His advisers sat silently aghast as he bartered away things which they knew were dear to him, in ignorance of the play on the board." In private Wilson admitted to George Creel that too much was expected of him, partly because of the great success of Creel's publicity, partly because "People will endure their tyrants for years, but they tear their deliverers to pieces if a millennium is not created immediately. Yet these ancient wrongs, these present unhappinesses, are not to be remedied in a day or with a wave of the hand. What I seem to see—I hope I am wrong—is a tragedy of disappointment." Moreover, during this period also Wilson's friendship with [his friend and adviser] Colonel House ended in a rift.

Wilson hoped that inequities of the settlements especially concerning the "successor" states would be reconsidered by the League of Nations, his mechanism to keep the peace.

Wilson mistakenly thought the Allies would oppose the League of Nations and was somewhat surprised that the British Foreign Office had anticipated him and had already drawn up a draft scheme. It provided the basis for the League Covenant and was duly written into the Treaty of Versailles before anything else. The Covenant of the League of Nations gave every member an equal vote in the Assembly while the United States, Britain, France, Italy, and Japan and four other countries elected for a limited period would constitute the Council, an executive body. League members were pledged to "respect and preserve as against external aggression the territorial integrity and existing political independence of all members"; to submit to arbitration all disputes and to refrain from hostilities until after a "cooling-off period" of three months after the arbiters investigating disputes had made their decision; and, if recommended by the League Council, to impose military, naval, and economic sanctions on nations disregarding the Covenant. . . .

When the terms of the peace treaties were published, the

editors of the *New Republic* forsook Wilson. The *New Republic's* attack of May 17 was headed "Is it Peace?" The editorial by Lippmann declared, "We do not see how this treaty is anything but the prelude to quarrels in a deeply divided and hideously embittered Europe." The following week, under the title "This is not peace," the editors recommended that America should withdraw from commitments to Europe. Thus Article Ten of the League Covenant about collective security was the hardest for them to accept. Undoubtedly, the most bitter draught of all for the liberals to swallow was the fact that Wilson's failure was theirs also, especially since it was America's inexpertise and ignorance that were under attack. They found it easier to blame Wilson than accept their own complicity. . . .

A Divided Senate

When Woodrow Wilson called Congress into special session in June 1919 to debate the treaty, he encountered ugly resistance. Because they had won the midterm elections the Republicans had been able to place one of Wilson's most bitter critics, Henry Cabot Lodge of Massachusetts, in the chair of the Senate Foreign Relations Committee. The prospect for the treaty was bleak. Lodge led a group of Republicans jealous of the president's prerogative in foreign affairs, determined on complete American independence from Europe, and anxious to resist the Democrats' intention of fighting the 1920 elections as the party that had led America through a victorious war to a conclusive peace.

Some historians believe that all available evidence suggests that in early 1919, despite widespread criticism, the majority of Americans were ready to approve the Treaty of Versailles and accept American membership of the League of Nations. The evidence is the accounts and opinions published in newspapers, especially of polls, and resolutions passed by thirty-two state legislatures, labor unions, women's groups, farm organizations, and professional societies. Even Wilson's most bitter critics, Lodge and Borah, conceded this. Such was Wilson's prestige and such was public support for the League that the Senate would probably have to accede to the treaty, despite the opposition of numerous isolationists within it.

Opinion in the Senate was divided into four schools of thought. Firstly, there were those who would accept the treaty without change. Later called the Non-Reservationists, this group comprised forty Democrats and one Republican, Porter J. McCumber of North Dakota. It was led by Gilbert B. Hitchcock of Nebraska, chairman of the Senate Foreign Relations Committee in 1918. Secondly there were those who would accept the treaty with minor alterations. These Mild Reservationists consisted of thirteen Republicans headed by Frank B. Kellogg of Minnesota, later secretary of state. Thirdly were those who would accept the treaty with major amendments. These Strong Reservationists consisted of twenty-one Republicans and four Democrats. Led by Henry Cabot Lodge, they included Warren Gamaliel Harding of Ohio, subsequently Wilson's successor as president. Fourthly were the Irreconcilables, consisting initially of fourteen Republicans and three Democrats, including the Republicans William E. Borah of Idaho, Philander C. Knox of Pennsylvania (Taft's secretary of state), Frank B. Brandegee of Connecticut, and Hiram W. Johnson of California, the Democrat James A. Reed of Missouri, and the Progressive Robert La Follette of Wisconsin.

The treaty went for examination to the Senate Foreign Relations Committee. Walter Lippmann cooperated with the Irreconcilables, feeding them information he had gained at the Inquiry and in Paris, that proved most embarrassing to Wilson. When Wilson appeared before the committee, he was asked why he had not insisted that the Allies repudiate the secret treaties before taking America into the war. Wilson answered that he did not know about the treaties until he was in Paris in December 1918. This was disingenuous bluff. As we have seen, in December 1917 Lippmann had been assigned the task of reconciling Wilson's principles with the aims of the treaties in order to provide the draft that became the Fourteen Points.

When William C. Bullitt appeared before the committee, he had his revenge on Wilson for rejecting the Russian overtures. With ill-concealed glee he revealed the bitter truth of the political maneuvers behind the scenes at Paris. He recalled Robert Lansing's private remarks to him that

At Last a Perfect Soldier!

Some publications opposed the war because of the regimentation demanded of soldiers. Individualism and thought, according to some, were subordinated to obedience. The following cartoon from the war years illustrates the point.

Editors of Time-Life Books. *This Fabulous Century: Volume II, 1910–1920.* New York: Time-Life Books, 1969.

the treaty was a disaster and the League useless. When Bullitt had finished his testimony, Wilson looked as unscrupulous as Lloyd George and not nearly so accomplished.

Wilson was unable to counter the personal and political resistance to his proposals, yet he was unwilling to accept more than mild amendments to his grand design. Thus he embarked on a speaking tour of the United States on September 4, 1919. This fateful tour was a forlorn attempt to appeal to the conscience of ordinary Americans across the country. But Wilson could make little headway against popular isolationism and intolerance. The Irreconcilables followed him wherever he spoke. They countered his conviction that, "I can predict with absolute certainty that within another generation there will be another world war if the nations of the world do not concert the method by which to prevent it," with ridicule.

Wilson Collapses

Wilson had little remaining strength to continue the struggle. On September 25, 1919, he collapsed at Pueblo, Colorado, and returned to Washington. On October 4 he was found half conscious on the bathroom floor, having suffered a second stroke. Thereafter, he was too ill even to be shaved. His second wife, Edith, and doctor kept all visitors from him, except for Joseph Tumulty who had to avoid exciting him. George Creel recalled later, "At sight of me he gestured pathetically, a tragic sweep of the hand that took in the whole of his helpless, wasted body, and great tears filled his eyes."

In the face of repeated assertions from Mrs. Wilson and Tumulty that Wilson was not disabled, the Senate despatched a "smelling committee," led by Senator Albert W. Fall of New Mexico, to ascertain the facts for themselves. On a second occasion Wilson exerted maximum effort to appear cogent and in control for half an hour before them. However, in a bitter rage he dismissed Secretary of State Robert Lansing on February 7, 1920, when he learned Lansing had been calling cabinet meetings without him.

Cut off from his allies and friends by his illness, Wilson nevertheless insisted on controlling a battle he could not even fight. As the historian of the League of Nations, F.P. Walters, puts it, "A difficult situation was thus converted into irretrievable defeat." To meet Wilson's arguments, Lodge and the Senate Foreign Relations Committee had reduced their numerous early criticisms to fourteen reservations by November 6, 1919. The most significant was about Article 10—by which the putative signatories agreed to respect and preserve the territorial integrity and political independence of all members of the League. The United States, they argued, could accept no such obligation without the specific assent of Congress for each and every instance. Two other reservations would have given the United States exclusive authority over the tariff and immigration. On November 19, 1919, the Treaty of Versailles was defeated in the Senate both *with* Lodge's reservations (which Wilson wanted his supporters to suppress) and *without* (which the Irreconcilables resisted). Thus ratification was denied in a paradoxical situation. Those voting against any Covenant at all were at one with those who voted for the Covenant as it stood. To both sides it was a case of all or nothing.

Whereas the Senate Democrats, led by Senator Gilbert Hitchcock, were willing to pay the Republican price for ratification and compromise, Wilson was not. He maintained that, if the reservations were accepted, one or other of the foreign powers would have refused ratification in turn. Britain, for instance, could have objected to a reservation in favor of Irish independence. And the United States would not want to be obligated by decisions in a council where the British Empire had six votes against its one. Latin American countries might object to United States' reluctance to relinquish its prerogatives in the Monroe Doctrine. It is probable the other signatories would have preferred even qualified American adherence to the League rather than its total abstention from it. This was certainly true of Britain and France. More important was Wilson's rejection of Lodge's reservation to Article 10. The United States could not send troops abroad without the approval of Congress, anyway, so the objection was not necessary. But underlying the semantic dispute was a chasm of different assumptions. Those Americans who favored supporting the League perhaps did so without fully understanding the implication of collective security. For membership of the League would involve a clear break with the prevailing myth of American isolation that had really outlasted the substance of policy. It meant that America would assume new responsibilities. Most Americans still thought they could maintain national security without making external commitments. For the ultimate weapon of the League against aggression would have to be an international force—an army. Most Americans could not accept this. The United States was not ready psychologically.

Yet a majority of Republicans and Democrats in the Senate still favored the ideal of membership of the League and blamed both Wilson and Lodge for their obduracy. When the next session opened in January 1920 attempts were made at the compromise. At a final vote on March 19, 1920, there was a substantial majority for ratification of the treaty with reservations but seven votes less than the necessary two-thirds. The thirty-five votes against the forty-nine in favor included twenty-three of Wilson's loyal followers agreeing with twelve Irreconcilables in accordance with the president's wishes. As Senator Frank Brandegee put it to Lodge, "We can always depend on Mr. Wilson. He never has failed us."

CHAPTER 5

A Nation Isolated

AMERICA'S DECADES

Changes Wrought by War:
World War I and Society

Page Smith

The Progressive Movement gave hope that society could be improved for everyone. Reformers strove to make changes that benefited not simply the upper classes, but the down-trodden as well. Spirits soared with each march, each speech, each law. That heady spirit of being able to create a better world crumbled in the face of World War I. Page Smith wrote a much-acclaimed multi-volume history of the United States. In his seventh volume, he mentions the destructive impact of the war on Progressive reformers.

T he war altered every aspect of American life. American capitalism emerged a hero for its remarkable accomplishments in providing the sinews of war, not only for the United States Army and Navy but for the Allies as well. Its prestige was enormously enhanced. Or perhaps, considering the bitter criticism to which it had been subjected since the Civil War, it might be more accurate to say that the reputation of capitalism was not so much enhanced as *created*. Moreover, capitalists, elated by their new popularity and their generally favorable press, took the offensive against those individuals and groups reckless enough to criticize them. Chambers of Commerce and the National Association of Manufacturers hired hundreds of highly paid publicists to proclaim the virtues of business, big and small, and to denounce their opponents as unpatriotic and, worst of all, as "Reds," unwitting dupes of Russia or wily agents of Bolsheviks. It was a novel notion—the idea that criticizing capitalism and capitalists constituted subversive activity. What had been, almost since the beginning of the Republic, a common exercise now fell under a ban. Criticizing capitalism could (and often did) result in the critics' being clapped in jail.

Capitalism, recently on the defensive in virtually every part of the globe, had seized the opportunity presented by the peace conference to create a new global financial order, in William Allen White's words "of cartels and trusts and interlocking international directorates." It was, of course, not a wholly new development. European capital had helped settle America, opened mines, built railroads, created many of the great ranches of the West, bought state bonds, and speculated in American commodities. It had preyed on the vast, defenseless body of China and built railroads for the Russians. Now, in the aftermath of the war, while diplomats and heads of state did their best to patch together the old order as they paid lip service to the new and while revolution bubbled away beneath the surface, the quietly efficient men of finance and industry, who knew exactly what they wanted and how to get it, conducted their own, largely sub rosa "Versailles"; it was in time to have more far-reaching consequences than the deliberations of politicians, which, in any event, were largely subservient to the interests of the men of power. It must be said to their credit that the cartel makers were ready to conceive of the world as, if not one great human family, one great trading entity bound together by pounds and dollars and francs, by cartels and commodities. In some ways it was a not unpromising beginning. Joel Barlow, the Federalist poet whose *The Vision of Columbus* was widely acclaimed as the first American epic, anticipated the day when the United States, through a "Source" of "creative Power," the nature of which was never clearly defined, would become a great nation, combining with other nations of the earth in "one great empire," connected by common ideals and commercial ties and ruled by "a general council" of "the fathers of all empires."

> See, thro' the whole, the same progressive plan,
> That draws, for mutual succour, man to man,
> From friends to tribes, from tribes to realms ascend,
> Their powers, their interests and their passions blend.

Although it may be doubted that international cartels were exactly what Joel Barlow had in mind (he believed that love would guide the "general council"), it was nonetheless striking that the captains of commerce, finance, and industry most boldly anticipated the practical interrelatedness of the world; that a Japanese or Chinese peasant might become, in fact, a customer rather than simply a wretched Oriental of unclean habits and inscrutable motivations.

"That organism," White wrote, "—somewhat financial, somewhat social, and of necessity more or less political— was growing conscious across national lines, even across ocean boundaries. Indeed it was passing the equator and spreading the sensitive pocket nerves of the well placed and overweening people of this globe . . . it sought unconsciously that world organization—that world sense of the power and the glory of the almighty dollar . . . which . . . makes a new kind of aim and purpose for the leaders of the world. . . ."

In a somewhat contradictory spirit the war demonstrated that the Federal government, faced by a severe crisis, could organize the human and material resources of the nation with remarkable speed and efficiency. The war thus helped shatter the states' rights myth and, with it, the notion that private initiative (or enterprise) was inherently superior to governmental action. The fact that the government could, in a time of national need, take over the productive facilities of the country and assume wide and even arbitrary powers was both a shock and a profoundly instructive lesson. Moreover, in exercising control over major segments of the economy, the government put into practice many of the labor practices that the unions and the reformers had been fighting for years, and it did it virtually overnight. To a euphoric William Allen White the war seemed for a time to have ushered in "the most dynamic epoch in the world; the time when the greatest social, political, industrial, and spiritual changes of men were made," an era to be compared with the birth of Christ and the discovery of America.

It seemed to White that "the world, and particularly the American part of the world, is adopting a new scale of living and a brand-new scale of prices all at the same time. It has given us the worst case of social bellyache that it has been my misfortune ever to see or hear about. By a prodigal wave of the hand, somewhere along during the war, we have raised the laboring man into middle-class standards of living and he is not going back. . . . It is a mess," he added. "We have jumped about a hundred years in less than ten months in our economic growth. . . ." To the editor of the *Survey* magazine, Paul Kellogg, who asked how the wartime economy could be adjusted to peacetime, White wrote: "It seems to me that our practical objective should be to keep every man who wants work in a job three hundred days in a year, and that he should be kept at work at a living wage, that is to say a wage upon which he may maintain a family of six in the enjoyment of all the comforts of our civilization, electric lights, central heat and power, modern plumbing, convenient fuel for cooking, decent housing, good clothing, clean and exhilarating amusements, time for reading, and money to make profitable reading possible, some leisure for seeing his city, his state, and his country, and at least a high school education for such of his children as desire it." White was confident that such goals could be achieved "under our present institutions," but a constitutional amendment would be required, in his view, to give "Congress unlimited powers over commerce and industry," along with "a minimum wage commission with full powers. . . . This would soon wipe out the revolutionary ideals of labor. I should not fight Bolshevism with guns, but with steady employment." Radical as such a program might seem to many standpat Republicans, White believed that "some forward movement must be taken, and taken quickly, or the situation will become vastly more dangerous than it is now."

Impact on Society

Aside from the radical curtailment of free speech (or the free curtailment of radical speech) and vastly increased pressures for social and political conformity, one of the more intangible consequences of the war was what we might call the democratization of American society. In the U.S. Army young men from different classes and different nationalities were drawn together in the "religion of combat," an experience, transcending all categories of civilian life, in which soldiers literally depended on each other, day after day, for their lives. The mystique of battle has been written of since the days of Homer. Distressing and terrible as war is, it engages the profoundest human emotions, and the trust, comradeship, and love that commonly characterize the relations of soldiers are, it seems safe to say, unique. Compared with all other armies, the American army was dramatically democratic. While most upper-class young Americans were given commissions, many on no better ground than the fact that they were college graduates, many middle-class voting men were also commissioned, and some young men with working-class backgrounds earned commissions on the basis of their performances as noncommissioned officers. In addition, many upper- and middle-class youths enlisted or were drafted as privates (a substantial portion of these earned commissions). Beyond that, the fact of simply being thrown together gave young Americans of widely divergent social and regional origins a new respect for each other. Much the same thing had been true, of course, in the Civil War and, to a far more modest degree, in the Spanish-American War, but the World War involved a very different America, one of far more cultural and even racial diversity. It thus worked as a powerful counterforce to the disintegrative tendencies of American life. Nowhere was this more evident than in the emphasis placed on the remarkable ethnic mix of the American army. It was a theme that, as we have seen, war correspondents delighted to dwell on. Many newspaper and magazine stories were built on that astonishing heterogeneity. Reporters would seek out soldiers of Polish, Irish, Czech, Russian, Hungarian, Chinese, or American Indian ancestry and feature their qualities as fighting men and loyal Americans. It was the major theme of the book by Theodore Roosevelt, Jr., *Rank and File*. Much of this was, of course, for home consumption to negate the resistance of a substantial number of ethnic Americans—Irish, Germans, and Austro-Hungarians especially—to the war. But whatever the motive, the fact was that propaganda corresponded to reality. It seems safe to say that America emerged from the war far more democratic than when it entered.

A Desire for Peace

One striking consequence of the war was the proliferation of organizations dedicated to the cause of peace. General Tasker Bliss, speaking at Edward Bok's Philadelphia forum— "What Really Happened at Paris"—reminded his audiences that the most imperative task facing the world was the limitation and, eventually, the abolition of all armaments. Modern wars, as distinguished from their predecessors, had become "total" wars, wars of extermination, "characterized by an intensity of national passions heretofore unknown . . . regarded by each side as wars for life or death, in which each, to save his life and destroy his adversary, will use every agent of destruction available to him; that, therefore, such agencies as the absolute blockade to starve people who heretofore were regarded as non-combatants, noxious gases, night and day bombing of cities from aeroplanes, the submarine, have come to stay until replaced by more destructive agencies."

William James had declared in 1906 in his lecture "The

Moral Equivalent of War" that wars had become so terrible that they could no longer be used as instruments of national policy. World War I had proved the point beyond dispute. In consequence, peace organizations multiplied exceedingly until there were dozens of them, many with overlapping memberships. Fannie Fern Andrews, a Bostonian, belonged to nineteen different peace organizations, among them the International Commission for Permanent Peace, the Women's Peace Party, the Neutral Conference for Continuous Mediation (a wartime organization), the Women's International League for Peace and Freedom, the American Union Against Militarism, the Association to Abolish War, the Women's Committee for World Disarmament, the Committee on Militarism in Education, the World Peace Foundation, and the Central Organization for a Durable Peace. Not surprisingly the American Legion, a reliable voice for Americanism and reaction, was soon attacking the peace groups as treasonous and un-American organizations, in league with the Communists to undermine the United States. Henry Ford's *Dearborn Independent,* an equally dependable spokesman for reaction, carried the headline in March, 1924, "Do Bolsheviks 'Use' Our Women's Clubs?" The resolutions of the Annual Conference of the Women's International League for Peace and Freedom, the paper charged, had been dictated by the Communist, or Third, International. A resolution against chemical warfare adopted by the conference was another example of Red influence, "since gas may be used to quell riots, and they [the Reds] plan the beginning of the Revolution in the United States with riots." The Red International was in the process of infiltrating Chautauquas, churches, and peace societies. One *Independent* headline proclaimed that the "Socialist-Pacificist Movement in America" was "an Absolutely Fundamental and Integral Part of International Socialism."

A poem reinforced the argument:

Miss Bolshevik has come to town
With a Russian cap and a German gown,

In women's clubs she's sure to be found,
For she's come to disarm America.
She uses the movie and lyceum too
And alters text-books to suit her view:
She prates propaganda from pulpit and pew,
For she's bound to disarm America.

Reform Momentum Crushed

Many Americans who had been caught up in the world of radical reform, reform in all its manifold aspects—in the arts, in politics, in social work—shared Hutchins Hapgood's mood of despair. "The years between 1914 and 1922," he wrote, "were for me years of deepest discouragement and unhappiness. It seemed as if my personal fate was a part of the world's woe. . . . I was rudderless, like the rest of the world." The effects were evident all around him, Friends in Greenwich Village and Provincetown, Massachusetts, fell out among themselves. They quarreled over the war and over more personal matters. They had grim and wounding affairs, joyless encounters in which beds became battlegrounds. "Drink and sex," Hapgood wrote, "become a despairing ideal, instead of the constructive forms we had dreamed about. It affected even the coolest and most balanced of us all." Oswald Garrison Villard abandoned the hope of reform of government concerted action of liberal spirits and placed what was left of hope in "Labor," the workingman as the final vessel of redemption. That the leadership of labor would "always be wise and just," he added, "would be preposterous to assume; I am only sure that it can never be worse than the political and economic leadership of the capitalist countries which I have observed at close range." He had lost "any hope that the capitalist system would redeem or reform itself, without, however, adopting any hard or fast creed, just clinging to my old-fashioned liberal doctrines modified by . . . the economic revolution." Villard wrote to Hapgood that he had suffered acutely during the preceding four years because of "the sense of spiritual outrage at the injustice and wickedness that we are seeing." It was evident to him that "all the nations of the world were drifting as steadily as a glacier, and as irresistibly, in the direction of greater control of business and private enterprise which cannot end before they have taken over the public services and basic industries."

When Frederic Howe asked Lincoln Steffens in 1920, "What has become of the pre-war radicals?" Steffens answered "smilingly: 'I am learning to be an intelligent father.'" Brand Whitlock turned back to literature, his first love. Newton D. Baker occupied himself with his law practice. When Howe and Whitlock met, they talked nostalgically of the old battles against corruption in Cleveland and Toledo, of Tom Johnson and Golden Rule Jones. Those days seemed dim and distant. "I have gone through every political philosophy," Whitlock told Howe. "I can see nothing in Socialism. The philosophy of Henry George of a free state in which the resources of the earth will be opened up to use is the only political philosophy that has ever commanded my adherence. But the world is not interested in such a simple reform. It wants too much government, too much regulation, too much policing. And it may never change.". . .

There was a strong disposition on the part of liberals to plead *mea culpa*. In Lincoln Steffens's view, "It was liberals who, in the liberal sense, made the war in all the allied countries, and who made the peace, too. That was why liberalism was fading out. . . 'it had been tried and found wanting.'" It had become a creed, and "that creed had been exposed as false." Steffens, for one, "was still of the opinion that only a revolution could do the job."

To Howe, as to many of his class of liberal intellectuals (for they formed a class of a kind), the war had disclosed the "hysterias, hatreds, passions of which democracy was capable"; the government had revealed a willingness to sanction the making of money from the ships and sufferings of the people. Wilson had failed dismally at Paris. Intelligence, idealism, "scientific" scholarship, the assiduous assembling of the pertinent "facts" by "experts"—all these, in which such hopes had been invested, had failed. "Men did not believe in the truth," a disillusioned Howe wrote. The liberal reformers had "believed in a discussion," he added, "in the writing of books and magazine articles, in making speeches. We liberals had the truth. If we talked enough and wrote it enough, it would undoubtedly prevail. . . . I believed in the mind and in facts. Facts were a Rock of Gibralter. . . . It was mind that would save the world, the mind of my class aroused from indifference, from money-making, from party loyalty and coming out into the clear light of reason. . . . I had built my life first around conventional morality, then about the mind. Conventional morals did not prevent men from making war, from corrupting the state, from destroying democracy. . . . And the mind had failed as completely as morals. Men did not think when social problems were involved. They did not use the mind. . . .

A Selfish World

Ray Stannard Baker believed the nation (and the world) were possessed by a fever of selfish ambition. "The world," he wrote in his journal in October, 1919, ". . . was never in such a state of disorganization and demoralization. All the passions of men seem to have been let loose; a far rebound from the discipline and sacrifice of war. At this moment in America we are facing a number of huge strikes; notably the steel strike. There have been fierce and brutal race-riots, only the other day one in Omaha in which the mob burned the courthouse and nearly killed the mayor." In Boston the police struck, an unheard-of event, and criminals rampaged through the city, unchecked. "Everyone is preaching rights rather than duties," Baker added; "each man is his own judge of what his rights are: if they are not instantly granted he tries to enforce them. No man thinks of sacrificing anything for any cause whatever. . . ."

From the perspective of the early 1940s Baker wrote: "Looking back along many years I can recall no period in which life in America looked bleaker than it did during the half dozen years following the close of the Peace Conference at Paris in 1918."

When Herbert Croly, who, Harold Laski wrote to Justice Holmes, "has the religious bug very badly," pressed William Allen White for an article for the *New Republic* on the election of 1920, White proposed as a topic "The Pharisees are running the temple and bossing the religion and handling the caucuses and the people are getting the worst of it." White's article was entitled "We Who Are About to Die.". . .

William Allen White wrote to his friend Victor Murdock, formerly editor of the *Wichita Eagle* and now a member of the Federal Trade Commission, that he was "very unhappy politically." It seemed to him that "any man is, who has any love of country or faith in its institutions, or hope for its future." He feared that if the "waters of progress" were damned, there would be in time "a tremendous breakover flood." He found comfort, nonetheless, in the "splurge" of progressive reform from 1903 to 1914. "We did get a lot of things done. Things that are well worth doing; things that are permanent. But I feel also that nobody much is paying attention to those things now." To Baker, White wrote: "What a God-damned world this is! I trust you will realize that I am not swearing; merely trying to express in the mildest terms what I think are the conditions that exist. What a God-damned world! Starvation on the one hand, and indifference on the other, pessimism rampant, faith quiescent, murder met with indifference . . . and the whole story so sad that nobody can tell it. If anyone had told me ten years ago that our country would be what it is today and the world would be what it is today, I should have questioned his reason. . . .

Everywhere there were strange incongruities. The phonograph was the rage, and an updated version of ragtime called jazz swept the country. William Allen White wrote of "the Gargantuan cricket-song of the phonograph." Dancing was more important than politics, and making money most important of all. Life seemed somehow geared to record lengths, three or four minutes of frantic sound and then a new record. The coonskin coat and hip flask were fixtures of college life and football games. Tin lizzies and flapper skirts, stockings rolled daringly below the knees, rumble seats and furtive sexual encounters. Unbuckled galoshes and tailcoats and white ties or tuxedoes for formal wear. . . .

We Came Out Self-Assured

Strangest of all, this new, crudely materialistic America—at least it seemed so to the generation that had reached maturity before the war—began to have a surprising influence on the rest of the world. American cars, American clothes, music (jazz), popular songs, above all American movies began to spread around the world to the astonishment and despair of the upper-class guardians of the cultures of those nations that fell under the spell of things American. What was most astonishing of all was that this influence was not limited to Europe; one of the nations that fell most completely and helplessly under the spell was Japan. "We found the whole world dancing to American jazz," Steffens wrote from abroad, "—the Germans, too. And economically they all were dancing to our pipers. We went into the war a conceited, but secretly rather humble, second-rate country; we came out self-assured. Our soldiers, our engineers, our organizers and managers, our industrialists and financiers—we had measured ourselves with our European competitors and discovered our competence: we were beaten only in diplomacy. In actual fighting, in work, in resources, in riches, management, we were first-rate people, 'the' first world power!" It was a curious phenomenon. Even the "hardest-boiled, least sentimental of observers," the American correspondents in Paris, perceived it.

America Overreacts:
The 1919 Red Scare

Burl Noggle

Following World War I, America had an intense feeling of nationalism that no longer could find an outlet in battling foreign enemies. Instead some Americans turned their patriotic zeal against real or perceived threats from political radicals and immigrants within the country. Historian Burl Noggle studied the years from war's end until the early 1920s. His description of the Red Scare illustrates how American society used its fear of communism to justify attacks on anyone suspected of Socialist leanings.

In this context of postwar economic readjustments, of wartime nationalism seeking new outlets of expression, and in a world where Bolshevik Revolution was—at least in Russia—a hard reality, the catalyst to panic came with a series of inexplicable bombings around the country. As Robert Murray has suggested, "the word 'radical' in 1919 automatically carried with it the implication of dynamite." The current stereotype portrayed the Red with "wild eyes, bushy, unkempt hair, and tattered clothes, holding a smoking bomb in his hands." In the spring of 1919, when some bombs began to go off, American radicals instantly became suspect. In March the *Chicago Tribune* announced discovery of a radical plot to plant bombs in Chicago. In Franklin, Massachusetts, where four men died from a bomb explosion, IWW

Excerpted from *Into the Twenties: The United States from Armistice to Normalcy*, by Burl Noggle. Copyright ©1974. Reprinted with permission from the author.

[Industrial Workers of the World, a socialist labor organization] literature was found in the room where they died. Already the IWW had been linked to bombings when, in Sacramento in January, forty-six Wobblies had been found guilty of sabotage, some of it with bombs, though the reconstructed ingredients of the bombs that the government offered as evidence were labeled "ol' rags an' bottles" by *Nation* magazine." On April 28 a homemade bomb arrived by mail at the office of Mayor Ole Hanson in Seattle. A leak in the package led to discovery of the bomb before it exploded. The next day, a similar package arrived at the home of former Georgia Senator Thomas W. Hardwick of Atlanta. The maid opened the package, the bomb exploded, and she lost both hands. Other people began to receive bomb packages. Sixteen of them turned up in a New York post office when a perceptive clerk discovered them in time. Post offices, now on the alert, finally intercepted eighteen more. The bombs, all alike and in uniform wrappers, had been mailed to men with reputations for anti-radicalism, such as Anthony J. Caminetti, commissioner of immigration; Senator Lee S. Overman, chairman of the Senate committee investigating Bolshevism; Postmaster General Albert S. Burleson, notorious for his wartime bans on radical literature; and Judge Kenesaw M. Landis, who had sentenced Victor Berger and Bill Haywood. Then on the evening of June 2, within the same hour, more bombs exploded in eight different cities. In at least six cases the evident target was a public official of some note, such as Attorney General Palmer. The Palmer family had just gone to bed that evening when the front of their Washington home was demolished by the explosive. The bomb-thrower had made a miscalculation. He evidently stumbled on the front step, set off the bomb prematurely, and blew himself to bits. Enough of his body and clothing remained intact to indicate that he was an Italian alien from Philadelphia. An anarchist pamphlet found near the door read in part: "We will destroy. . . . We are ready to do anything and everything to suppress the capitalist class. [signed] THE ANARCHIST FIGHTERS."

Newspapers publicized the bombings with glaring banners—and often with equally blaring emotion. Attorney General Palmer in June asked Congress for immediate funds to help protect the country from bombings. Senator Overman called a special session of his subcommittee on Bolshevik propaganda. Several bills designed to curb Bolshevism were introduced in a special session of Congress in May and June. And Ole Hanson gave voice to what soon became a widespread chorus: deport all radicals. At Fort Collins, Colorado, General Leonard Wood, a leading contender for the Democratic presidential nomination in 1920, asserted his motto, tactic, and rationale for dealing with Reds: "S.O.S.—ship or shoot. I believe we should place them all on ships of stone, with sails of lead and that their first stopping place should be hell. We must advocate radical laws to deal with radical people."

A Dangerous Over-Reaction

Even while the drive for deportation of alien radicals was gaining speed, sporadic raids on homegrown radicals began. In June, New York state officials raided the Rand School of Social Science in New York, as well as the headquarters of the IWW and the left-wing Socialists. The raids were the work of the Lusk Committee, created by the New York legislature in March "to investigate the scope, tendencies, and ramifications of . . . seditious activities and report the results of its investigations to the legislature." State Senator Clayton R. Lusk, committee chairman, declared that the purpose of the raids was "Names!—Names of all parlor bolsheviki, IWW, and socialists. They will be a real help to us later on."

Later the tactics of the Lusk Committee grew in popularity elsewhere in the nation, as did still other means of defending the republic. In July, Attorney General Palmer complained of any law enabling him to deport aliens. Under existing legislation only those guilty of advocating anarchist ideas could be expelled. Even so, the law (the Immigration Act of 1918) was so murky that it had already been used as the basis for deporting thirty-six Seattle Wobblies, who were put on board a "Red Special" and, amidst high publicity, rushed toward Ellis Island for deportation. There the Wobblies became caught up in a conflict between the Immigration Bureau and the Department of Labor that presaged further conflict to come between the two agencies when, following the massive raids in 1919 and early in 1920, the bureau would seek to deport virtually at will, while the Labor Department would act with much more restraint. But meanwhile, the Justice Department precipitated much of the federal government's anti-radical action of 1919. The key figure in that department was Attorney General Palmer.

Initially after the war Palmer was every inch the liberal. He even argued for [Eugene V.] Debs's release from prison [Debs was a socialist activist convicted under the Espionage Act]. But then, either out of growing presidential ambition or out of his own genuine mounting hysteria or both, he began to respond to the increasing public hostility toward radicals. That he himself had been the target of an anarchistic bombthrower could hardly have been irrelevant. In the summer of 1919 he began to move against radicalism. In August, he established a general intelligence, or anti-radical, division in the Justice Department. At its head he placed young J. Edgar Hoover, who promptly began to assemble an elaborate card index file of radical organizations, publications, and leaders. On November 7, Justice Department agents raided the headquarters and branches of a New York labor society, the Union of Russian Workers. State and local officials carried out smaller raids on suspected radicals throughout the country, and state legislatures passed a mass of "criminal syndicalism" laws, "red flag" laws, and other measures designed to stifle the IWW and other revolutionary movements.

A Flurry of Congressional Bills

Congress, in response to a barrage of petitions and appeals to "drive from these shores all disloyal aliens," began to formulate deportation bills. Senator Kenneth McKellar of Tennessee even proposed that radical native-born Americans be expelled to a special penal colony on Guam. As one contemporary critic observed, some of the proposed bills were "evidently struck off in the characteristically American reaction to unpleasant events—to pass a law to stop them, without much thought as to [the law's consequences and implementation]." For example, Congressman James B. Aswell of Louisiana prepared a bill to punish by death any aliens found guilty of throwing a bomb or committing "any act with the object to destroy life or property." Senator Harry S. New of Indiana introduced an anti-red flag bill, endorsed by the National Security League, to penalize by fine (up to $5,000) or imprisonment (five years) or both anyone displaying a red or black flag or emblem at a meeting or parade. The Kansas legislature carried this notion a step further and forbade use of any emblem of any hue if it was "distinctive of bolshevism, anarchism or radical socialism." A number of bills appeared in Congress to check immigration, forecasts of the 1921 and 1924 exclusion acts. Other bills, drawn to implement Americanization of aliens, were in fashion with the drive already begun to achieve "100% Americanism." During the 66th Congress fourteen bills dealing with naturalization or immigration were introduced. In December, Congressman Albert Johnson of Washington offered all of them as a single package. Another Johnson bill defined "anarchistic and similar classes" to include those who distributed handbills or displayed cartoons—and made such actions a deportable offense.

Not all of these bills met with unanimous approval. Senator Borah, who in February, 1919, had allowed his name to appear on the letterhead of an anti-Bolshevik newspaper association, was by 1920 alarmed over the course of events. He praised *New York World* editor Frank Cobb for his "splendid editorial upon the strange lunacy which is now prevalent . . . —this idea that you must destroy all guarantees of the Constitution in order to preserve the rights of the American people." To a correspondent who had evidently provoked him, Borah declared, "We cannot deal with the situation which now confronts us by deporting a few people. Besides, why should we deport people into Russia and then go to the great expense of sending troops over there to shoot them?" Opinion from a number of liberal journals was equally caustic. "What," asked a *Survey* editorialist, "is going to be the outcome of all this legislation? Will it stop unrest? Yes! Just as shaving the dog will keep his hair from growing. In fact, shaving is said to promote growth."

An Illegal Campaign

But Palmer had begun shaving. On December 21 some 250 deportees set sail for Russia from New York aboard the U.S.S. *Buford,* promptly labeled the "Soviet Ark." Then late in the afternoon on Friday, January 2, 1920, Justice Department agents, in a concerted raid on Communist (and reputedly Communist) headquarters, began arresting thousands of persons in major American cities. They poured into private homes and clubs, pool halls and cafes, and seized citizens and aliens, Communists and non-Communists, and tore apart meeting halls and damaged and destroyed property. In two days close to 5,000 persons were arrested, and possibly another 1,000 were jailed in the mopping up that followed during the next few weeks. The arrests were carried out with total disregard for due process, and the treatment of the masses under arrest was sometimes barbarous. Agents jailed their prizes, held them incommunicado and without counsel, and interrogated them. Those who could demonstrate American citizenship gained release, though often into the custody of state officials who hoped to try them under state syndicalist laws. Aliens were released a few days later unless they were members of the Communist party or the Communist Labor party. These the Justice Department hoped to deport.

Under existing immigration law, only the Department of Labor and its subordinate agencies, such as the Bureau of Immigration, had authority to arrest and deport aliens. For some time during and since the war the Immigration Bureau had cooperated with the Justice Department by launching deportation proceedings against aliens, once the Justice agents had arrested them. This was cooperation, but it was illegal, and J. Edgar Hoover admitted as much. There was, he said, "no authority under the law permitting this Department to take any action in deportation proceedings relative to radical activities." But Anthony Caminetti, commissioner general of the Immigration Bureau, was seemingly as committed to an anti-radical drive as were Palmer and Hoover, and by January, 1920, the Justice Department and the Immigration Bureau had evolved a technique: raid swiftly, seize evidence, and, while holding them in isolation, cross-examine aliens before they could gain legal counsel, and then deport. As William Preston suggests, "Like a pig in a Chicago packing plant, the immigrant would be caught in a moving assembly line,

Fear of a Communist takeover contributed to the public's racist attitude toward all immigrants.

stripped of all his rights, and packaged for shipment over-seas—all in one efficient and uninterrupted operation." Yet, as Preston then shows, Hoover's and Caminetti's efficiency was their undoing. They were administrators, not policy-makers or judges, and the very excesses of the raids, their blatant disregard for fundamental rights, aroused opposition from individuals and organizations that, until now, had not been vocal in opposition to the Red hysteria. Suddenly a renewed appreciation for toleration and freedom of expression arose. The Interchurch World Movement denounced the lawlessness of the raids. A committee of twelve prestigious lawyers and law professors issued a *Report* which censured the department for its infractions of the Bill of Rights.

The Scare Dies Down

Perhaps most crucial was the response within the Department of Labor. Secretary William B. Wilson had never condoned the anti-radicals in his department, but he was unaware of their machinations until the raids occurred. He promptly repudiated them, restored due process in deportations, and improved control over hearings for aliens. Assistant Secretary of Labor Louis F. Post, who carefully and personally reviewed case after case, refused to adopt the sweeping definition of the law that Palmer, Hoover, and Caminetti had wanted to apply. Secretary Wilson ruled that mere membership in the Communist party was not sufficient justification for deportation. Post, who had final authority to sign deportation orders, refused to deport the hundreds of aliens who, though arrested, were obviously unfamiliar with illegal doctrines. Post estimated that the Department of Labor, on behalf of the Justice Department's detectives, had issued about 6,000 warrants of arrest for alien "Reds." Palmer's agents had carried out some 4,000 arrests, but after hearings Post cancelled the warrants for about 3,000 of these. Less than 1,000 deportations resulted from the Palmer raids. The earlier cooperation between the Justice and Labor departments turned to bitter enmity, and

Palmer finally forced an investigation of Post and Secretary Wilson. The inquiry aborted, and Post, if anything, emerged with an enhanced reputation. Palmer continued to aspire for higher office.

Meanwhile, the Red Scare abated. The great labor conflicts of 1919 had eased off, leaving American workers discouraged and defeated. If the strikes of 1919 had fed the fear of social revolution, labor's retreat into quiescence now created a reassuring calm, as American labor entered the "lean years" of the Twenties. The final withdrawal of American troops from Russia in 1920 and the failure of Communist revolutions in Germany and Central Europe brought at best a certain reassurance, though one student of American attitudes toward Soviet Russia sees the violence of the Red Scare settling into "an apolitical complacency" soon after the raids. The stereotyped Russian, "though still bearded," became "simply a plaintive old man, vulnerable to intoxicating theories." Palmer himself kept on raising the spectre of Bolshevism, and in the weeks before May Day, 1920, he issued elaborate warnings against violence, terror, and plots that might erupt on that historic day. When nothing of the sort occurred, Palmer promptly claimed credit—his timely warnings had staved off revolution. By now even Congress (at least some of it) was irritated with the attorney general. Just as it wound up its investigations of Louis Post, it invited Palmer to appear before the House Rules Committee and defend his actions. Palmer read a long speech, one that required two sessions of the committee. The committee decided to drop its inquiry, and the attorney general went on working for the presidential nomination.

A Revival of Hate: The Ku Klux Klan Reawakens

David M. Chalmers

As part of the reaction against supposed un-American elements within the nation, the Ku Klux Klan enjoyed renewed popularity. The Klan appealed to common fears and bigotries and, under the leadership of William J. Simmons, enrolled thousands of members. An expert on the Ku Klux Klan, historian David M. Chalmers wrote of the revival in his 1987 book, *Hooded Americanism.*

T he stories of the Klan's rebirth differ. There were those on the inside who claimed that it was suggested by [D.W.] Griffith's picture. Colonel Simmons, its founder, maintained that he had thought for twenty years of creating a fraternal order that would stand for "comprehensive Americanism." He spoke variously about childhood stories and fancies, about an illness and a vision: "On horseback in their white robes they rode across the wall in front of me. As the picture faded out I got down on my knees and swore that I would found a fraternal organization that would be a memorial to the Ku Klux Klan."

The Story of Colonel Simmons

William J. Simmons was born in the little central Alabama town of Harpersville, in 1880, and grew up on his father's farm. His father had given up doctoring for a spell as a mill owner, but when the floods of 1886 washed away his wealth, he returned to the practice of medicine. He died not too many years afterwards, and young William had to abandon the dream of becoming a doctor, but his father and life on an Alabama farm had initiated him into the love of place and heritage which has long been a major factor in Southern life. A part of this, in a society less than two decades removed from the tumultuous days of Reconstruction, was the Ku Klux Klan. "My father was an officer of the old Klan in Alabama back in the 60s," he later told an interviewer. "I was always fascinated by Klan stories. . . . My old Negro mammy, Aunt Viney, and her husband, used to tell us children about how the old Reconstruction Klansmen used to frighten the darkies.

"'Why, dat Klansman was shore twelve foot high,' I heard Aunt Viney say to Uncle Simon."

"'Go 'long with you, Viney,' said Uncle Simon. 'Dat Klansman was twenty foot tall, on his hawse!'"

When he was eighteen, Simmons enlisted as a private in the 1st Alabama Volunteers to fight against the Spaniards. The title of colonel, which he later liked to attribute to his wartime service, was still a thing of the future. Released from the army, inspired by patriotism and Americanism, too poor to study medicine, he turned to the career traditionally open to talent, the church. It was not a happy choice but it was a useful one in developing his talents. The ministry did not pay. He rode circuit and was given only backwoods districts in Alabama and Florida, never the big churches, such as Mobile or Montgomery for which he yearned. He developed his oratory and his eloquence, and gave popular lectures at revival meetings on "Women, Weddings, and Wives," "Red Heads, Dead Heads, and No Heads," and the "Kinship of Kourtship and Kissing." And he went deeper and deeper into debt on his $200 to $300 yearly stipend, each year attending the church conference with hopes that this would be his year to get the "big" church. The bishops of the Methodist Church South, however, recognized their man. The call was missing, and they failed to move him upward.

After twelve years, the 1912 Alabama Conference voted to deny him a pulpit because of inefficiency and moral impairment, and he was pushed out to tread the secular path to fame and fortune. First he tried his hand as an ordinary salesman. His detractors later said that he had been a garter salesman and a poor one at that, but he soon found his calling in the attractive commercial field of fraternal organizing. Here was proper employment for his talents, and he rose to the youngest colonelcy of the Woodmen of the World, in command of five regiments. Within two years, he later boasted, he was out of debt and was earning $15,000 a year as a district manager. In addition, he belonged to several varieties of Masons and to the Knights Templar. He was a post commander and a national aide-de-camp of the Spanish-American War Veterans, and was a member of perhaps half a score other organizations, including both the Congregational and Missionary Baptist churches. "I am a fraternalist," he was to explain whenever anyone asked his profession.

During all of this time he dreamed of founding his own fraternal order based upon the Ku Klux Klan. When an automobile accident laid him up in bed for three months he worked out all the details, which he duly copyrighted. It remained only to pick the time. In the fall of 1915 the right moment seemed at hand. With *The Birth of a Nation* scheduled to open in Atlanta, Simmons sprang into action. He gathered together nearly two-score men from various fraternal orders, including two members of the original Klan and the speaker of the Georgia legislature. They agreed to found the order, and Simmons picked Thanksgiving Eve for the formal ceremonies.

When the members gathered at Atlanta's Piedmont Hotel, Simmons had a surprise prepared. The ceremonies were to be held on Stone Mountain, an immense, striking, granite slab, rising from the earth sixteen miles outside of Atlanta. The late-November nights are cold in northern Georgia and some of those present refused to go, but fifteen piled into the hired sight-seeing bus which Simmons had waiting at the door. Using flashlights they picked their way to the top of Stone Mountain, and, under Simmons' direction, his shivering company gathered stones to make a crude altar and a base for the cross of pine boards which Simmons had brought there that afternoon. He touched a match to the cross which he had padded with excelsior and drenched with kerosene. Then, "Under a blazing, fiery torch the Invisible Empire was called from its slumber of half a century to take up a new task and fulfill a new mission for humanity's good and to call back to mortal habitation the good angel of practical fraternity among men."

When *The Birth of a Nation* opened a week later, an Atlanta paper carried Simmons' announcement of "The World's Greatest Secret, Social, Patriotic, Fraternal, Beneficiary Order" next to the advertisement for the movie. And so, with an assist from D.W. Griffith, Colonel Simmons' "HIGH CLASS ORDER FOR MEN OF INTELLIGENCE AND CHARACTER" was launched.

Simmons Builds a Following

Within a short time, Simmons had ninety followers to whom he sold membership, raiment, and life insurance. The Ku Klux Klan was incorporated as a "purely benevolent and eleemosynary" institution, intended to be not unlike the Elks, the Masons, and the Odd Fellows. Despite the crudeness of its early advertising—A CLASSY ORDER OF THE HIGHEST CLASS—it drew good, solid middle-class members. Among the first were Robert Ramspect, future congressman from Georgia, and Paul Etheridge, lawyer and long-time member of Atlanta's Fulton County Board of Commissioners of Roads and Revenues. In its initial stages, the Klan was not a night-riding organization but merely a fraternal one which stressed 100 per cent Americanism and the supremacy of the Caucasian race. It was Protestant rather than anti-Catholic, and to favor "keeping the Negro in his place" was little more than the meaning of the term, Caucasian. In these characteristics the Klan was not unlike the multitude of other fraternal organizations to which Colonel Simmons and his new Klansmen were accustomed. The word "fraternity," in its most common usage, had long since come to mean the exclusiveness of the in-group, rather than the commonality and brotherhood of mankind.

When America entered the war in 1917, Simmons and the Klan found a purpose and a role. The nation had to be defended against alien enemies, slackers, idlers, strike leaders, and immoral women, lest victory be endangered. The Klan accepted the challenge. Simmons was not asked to join the elite government-sponsored American Protective League, but as a member of the lesser Citizens' Bureau of Investigation he entered the fray. Klansmen in Georgia and Alabama secretly kept tabs on local goings on and reported back. It was all very exciting. Warnings against evil-doing were posted. Robed Klansmen intervened in a shipyard strike in Mobile, hunted draft dodgers, and occasionally marched in patriotic parades. Public sentiment seemed favorable. By 1919 the Klan had several thousand members, whose dues were naturally Simmons' wages of entrepreneurship. Secrecy had become its pattern.

To have garnered only several thousand members after five years of work, was not, somehow, tapping the full potential of as big an idea as the Klan. There was much more money in it than Colonel Simmons had touched thus far. His talent lay in the realm of fraternal ideas and rituals. As his whole life was to show, he lacked the ability of generalship to execute his logistical ideas, the capacity to master a situation and achieve victory in the end. In reality, his was not a fighting spirit, and under pressure he tended to retreat. Gutzon Borglum, sculptor of mountains, student of men, and once high in the inner circles of the Klan, assessed Simmons as a dreamer who tended to surround himself with weak men.

Perhaps realizing his limitations and yearning for success, Simmons, the mystic, looked for apostles to spread his gospel. They came in the persons of Edward Young Clarke and Mrs. Elizabeth Tyler. Together, they were the Southern Publicity Association. Clarke had drifted from newspaper work into fraternal salesmanship, and then went on to become a not very successful publicist. He was slim, graceful, with a mass of curly dark hair. The eyes behind his horn-rimmed glasses looked cultured, and his nervous intensity passed for drive and intellectuality. Bessie Tyler was a large woman, with blue eyes and auburn hair. She favored black, from her patent-leather pumps to her broadcloth cape, and her definiteness and decisive manner of speech gave her an air of forcefulness. Clarke was running a Harvest Home Festival in Atlanta and Mrs. Tyler had handled the "Better Babies Parade." They were attracted to each other, and they saw a future in it. Their business venture was the Southern Publicity Association. They handled fund drives for the Anti-Saloon League, the Theodore Roosevelt Memorial Fund, and Near East relief. The accounts differed on who found whom first, but Simmons was in need, and he had what Clarke and Mrs. Tyler considered to be a potentially good thing going. "He was a minister and a clean living man," Mrs. Tyler later told the newspapers. "After we had investigated it from every angle, we decided to go into it with Colonel Simmons."

The expenses of mass recruitment and high-class publicity would not be small, but Klan affairs were stagnant and if they could get things going it would be worth the 80 per cent they asked. As the colonel later remembered it, Clarke seemed insightful as to the nature of the movement that he was about to join. "I have lots of friends among the Jews and Catholics," Clarke told him. They had helped him in drives such as the Red Cross, and he could not afford a break with them unless the price was right.

In June of 1920 the contract was struck. Clarke was to be in full charge of recruitment. His department was to receive eight dollars of the ten dollars paid by each recruit it brought in, plus two dollars from the membership fee of those who were signed up by the already organized Klans. Mrs. Tyler explained that their hopes had been modest and primarily directed toward the South. "But the minute we said 'Ku Klux,' editors from all over the United States began literally pressing us for publicity." The news value of the Klan initially caught them all by surprise. When Simmons and Clarke refused to pose for a press photographer, he rigged up his own costumes after those he had seen in *The Birth of a Nation* and hired Negroes to pose in them for two bits a man. The picture sold like wildfire.

The Klan was doing better than anyone had dreamed. Fraternity, secrecy, and white supremacy were not enough. A broader program of action was necessary and Simmons, Clarke, and Bessie Tyler responded to the need. From the lip-service to the traditional racial values of the white South, the Klan shifted into a pyrotechnically aggressive defense of one-hundred-per-cent Americanism.

Upon being introduced to an audience of Georgia Klansmen, Colonel Simmons silently took a Colt automatic from his pocket and placed it on the table in front of him. Then he took a revolver from another pocket and put it on the table too. Then he unbuckled his cartridge belt and draped it in a crescent shape between the two weapons. Next, still without having uttered a word, he drew out a bowie knife and plunged it in the center of the things on the table. "Now let the Niggers, Catholics, Jews, and all others who disdain my imperial wizardry, come on," he said. The Jews, Mrs. Tyler told newspapermen during a shopping trip in New York, were upset because they know that the Klan "teaches the wisdom of spending American money with American men." To be for the white race, she continued, means to be against all others. Clarke suggested sterilizing the Negro. Simmons explained that the Japanese were but a superior colored race. Never in the history of the world, the Klan believed, had a "mongrel civilization" survived. The major theme, however, was the rich vein of anti-Catholicism, which the Klan was to mine avidly during the 1920s, and it was this more than anything else which made the Klan. . . .

The Klan Is Organized

By the summer of 1921, almost a hundred thousand Klansmen had paid their money and stepped across the mystic threshold to take their chances in the Invisible Empire. Clarke, in his newly created role of Imperial Kleagle, or chief of staff, sent a small army of recruiters fanning out across the country. The nation was divided up into regional sales districts or domains, each headed by a district sales manager, the Grand Goblin. Each region was divided into state realms, headed by King Kleagles, under whom the ordinary Kleagles, or recruiters, worked. To aid them the national and state organizations sent out lecturers, usually ministers, to spread the more exalted parts of the Klan gospel. Of every ten-dollar initiation fee (Klectoken), four dollars went to the Kleagle responsible. The King Kleagle of the state realm got one dollar. The Grand Goblin got fifty cents and the rest went back to Atlanta: two dollars and fifty cents for Clarke and Mrs. Tyler, and two dollars for Simmons.

The newly recruited Klansman, with or without sheeted regalia (two dollars for costs and three to four dollars for Klan headquarters), belonged to a provisional Klan, headed by the appointed Kleagle. Only when the region had been thoroughly combed for members did the Klan chapter receive a charter. With it came the right to elect its own officers and, subject to veto by a new hierarchy appointed from Atlanta, conduct its own affairs. As subsequent history was to prove, that chartered independence was often too long in coming and even then too greatly subject to interference.

Wherever possible, Clarke selected his salesmen from among members of other lodges, since they would be likely to be skilled in the world of ritualism and fraternal dynamics. He particularly favored Masons because of the size of their own order and because the chances were they would not be overly friendly toward Roman Catholicism. Many Masonic leaders bitterly denounced and fought the Klan both for its divisive effects within their lodges and because they disapproved of its violent intolerance. However, the rank and file turned to the Klan by the thousands, and the Scottish Rite Masons and Orange Lodges were particularly rich hunting grounds.

The usual Klan pattern was to approach the local Protestant minister. He would be offered a free membership and urged to take office in the to-be-formed local, either as its chaplain (Kludd) or higher up in the leadership structure. Hundreds upon hundreds did join, and in some areas constituted a major portion of the local officialdom. Others left their flocks for the wider Klan calling as either organizers or speakers. Almost all of the national Klan lecturers were ministers. Usually the presence of a Klan in a town was announced by a Saturday night parade of hooded horsemen down Main Street, a cross blazing on a nearby hillside, or a sudden appearance in the midst of the Sunday service. Robed in white, masked, they would divide into three columns and march silently down the aisles congregating in front of the pulpit to present a purse of thirty-five or forty dollars to the minister. If their appearance was not completely unexpected or unwelcome, they might file into the front rows that had been left vacant, while the minister or one among them propounded the principles of the Klan and read from the Twelfth Chapter of Romans, calling upon them to present their bodies, through the Klan, as "a living sacrifice, holy, acceptable unto God." Or, having made the donation, they might march out again while the church choir sang "The Old Rugged Cross" or "Onward, Christian Soldiers."

By the late summer of 1921 the Klan was a flourishing concern. In the first fifteen months of the Clarke-Tyler regime, approximately eighty-five thousand members had been added, worth, at ten dollars a head, over three quarters of a million dollars. Naturally expenses were high, but since the Klan was a benevolent and charitable enterprise, taxes were not a worry. Colonel Simmons' share was $170,000. In token of his past devotion during the lean years prior to 1920, the Klan rewarded him with $25,000 back pay and a $33,000 suburban home, which he named Klan Krest.

The Coming of Prohibition

Herbert Asbury

While the Progressive Movement and World War I battled for the headlines through much of the decade, another force steadily gained momentum. Advocates of prohibition gained sufficient support to have a Constitutional amendment passed to outlaw alcohol. Before it took effect, thousands of people embarked upon a final "legal" drinking spree. Social historian Herbert Asbury wrote of those last days in his book, *The Great Illusion*.

At exactly 12:01 A.M. on January 17, 1920, constitutional prohibition went into effect everywhere in the United States, and the American people, 105,000,000 strong, began the joyous march into the never-never land of the Eighteenth Amendment and the Volstead Act. Everything was ready for the great transformation. More than fifteen hundred enforcement agents, badges shined, guns oiled, and fingers trembling upon the triggers, were on their toes, ready to pounce upon the rum demon wherever he showed his ugly mug. The Coast Guard, the Customs Service, and the various agencies of the Bureau of Internal Revenue were standing by. The police of a thousand cities and the sheriffs of a thousand counties were on the alert. Judges were pondering the probability of history-making decisions, and prosecuting attorneys were thumbing their lawbooks and briefing their publicity staffs. Political bosses

Excerpted from *The Great Illusion: An Informal History of Prohibition*, by Herbert Asbury (New York: Doubleday, 1950). Copyright ©1950 by Herbert Asbury. Reprinted with permission from Edith Asbury.

were happily grabbing jobs for the faithful in the many departments of the new Prohibition Bureau. Statements, predictions, and pronunciamentos were flying thick and fast. And behind this imposing array, their nostrils quivering eagerly to catch the first faint whiffs of illegal hooch, crouched the Allied Citizens of America and the embattled members of the Women's Christian Temperance Union, the latter more dangerous to the politicians than ever, now that Congress had passed the woman-suffrage amendment to the constitution and submitted it to the states for ratification. The Allied Citizens, formed by the Anti-Saloon League to help the government enforce the law, had long since served notice upon prospective evildoers that it was a militant organization that would tolerate no nonsense.

Board Uncle Sam's Water Wagon

Entranced by the shining vision of an America forever free from the thralldom of the rum pot, the Anti-Saloon League of New York enthusiastically announced that "a new nation will be born," and wished every man, woman, and child "a Happy Dry Year." William H. Anderson, superintendent of the New York league and an important figure in the councils of the drys, sternly admonished the wets to be good sports and take their medicine. "Shake hands with Uncle Sam," he said, "and board his water wagon." Had Anderson been able to look four years into the future, he would have seen himself taking a little medicine—a prison sentence for forgery. In New York, Colonel Daniel Porter, supervising revenue agent temporarily in charge of enforcement, expressed the opinion that the penalties provided by the Volstead Act were so severe that the people would not attempt to violate the law; no one, he declared, would risk a fine up to one thousand dollars and imprisonment up to six months (for first offenders) for the sake of a few drinks. "There will not be any violations to speak of," he said.

From Washington came the ominous warning that prohibition officials would keep the liquor traffic, or what was left of it, under close scrutiny at all times. The United States Government, through Daniel C. Roper, Commissioner of Internal Revenue, urged every clergyman in the country to observe January 18 as Law and Order Sunday, and "participate in the moral suasion movement for the upholding of law and order with reference to making America dry under the Eighteenth Amendment." John F. Kramer, the new Prohibition Commissioner, said that he had virtually completed the organization of his anti-liquor forces, and was prepared to handle any problem which might arise. He supplemented the prosaic official statements with a ringing personal pronouncement which reached new heights of rhetoric and optimism. "This law," he proclaimed, "will be obeyed in cities, large and small, and where it is not obeyed it will be enforced. . . . The law says that liquor to be used as a beverage must not be manufactured. We shall see that it is not manufactured. Nor sold, nor given away, nor hauled in anything on the surface of the earth, or in the air."

The brewers and the distillers, cowering among their barrels and bottles, said nothing, or at least nothing that was recorded for posterity.

The Victorious "Drys" Celebrate

In thousands of Protestant churches throughout the country, and in every town which had a chapter of the W.C.T.U., the drys greeted the coming of the great day with thanksgiving and watch-night services, at which the Lord was publicly praised for His share in the victory. In Tennessee there were parades and mass meetings as well. In Denver and San Francisco the ceremonies were elaborate and the meetings remained in session for several days; in the latter city a national official of the W.C.T.U. described prohibition as "God's present to the nation," and the head of the California State Anti-Saloon League declared that San Francisco was "complacently joyful that John Barleycorn had been laid to rest." In Chicago the W.C.T.U. announced that, having brought prohibition to America, it would now proceed to dry up the rest of the world. In Washington,

D.C., temperance reformers from all parts of the United States, in the capital to attend meetings of the National Temperance Council and the National Legislative Conference, attended a watch-night service and cheered a rousing oration by William Jennings Bryan. The great Commoner spoke from Matthew 2:20: ". . . for they are dead which sought the young child's life." His audience included such notables as Wayne B. Wheeler, Bishop James Cannon, Jr.; Josephus Daniels, Secretary of the Navy; Clarence True Wilson, of the Methodist Board of Temperance, Prohibition, and Public Morals; Representative Andrew J. Volstead of Minnesota, author of the Volstead Act; and Senator Morris Sheppard of Texas, author of the Eighteenth Amendment. Incidentally, only a few months after the dry era began, a moonshine still was found neatly hidden in a thicket on Senator Sheppard's farm near Austin. It was producing one hundred and thirty gallons of alcohol a day.

There were a few meetings in New York churches, but no extensive ceremonies had been planned, a circumstance which, among other things, impelled one thousand rural clergymen to sign a statement denouncing the metropolis as "the center of nullification and seditious activity designed to prevent the enforcement of the Eighteenth Amendment." The upstate pastors also reminded would-be nullifiers that "the same power that brought about enactment of prohibition is pledged to its enforcement," a bit of information which didn't make the wets any easier in their minds. The statement further implied that the ministers of New York were cringing before the wealthy, guzzling members of their congregations, and shielding them "from realizing and discharging their responsibility as citizens and as Christians."

The governor of New Jersey had rashly promised, when running for re-election, that he would ignore the Eighteenth Amendment and make the state as wet as the Atlantic Ocean; the drys laughed at him and celebrated with a great victory banquet in Newark and the ringing of church bells in Atlantic City. In Norfolk, Virginia, Billy Sunday, noted evangelist and always a master showman, entertained a congregation of ten thousand with a funeral service for John Barleycorn. From the Norfolk railroad station, where it had arrived "on a special train from Milwaukee" in a casket twenty feet long, the body of old John was hauled in a truck to Sunday's tabernacle, escorted by twenty pallbearers and followed by a man dressed as a devil and simulating extreme sorrow. Sunday conducted the service while the devil and a group of liquor addicts, sottish and bedraggled, gabbled and squirmed on the mourner's bench and bemoaned the untimely death of their old pal. "Good-by, John," said the evangelist. "You were God's worst enemy; you were hell's best friend. I hate you with a perfect hatred. I love to hate you." Sunday then preached a sermon on the glories of prohibition. "The reign of tears is over," he cried. "The slums will soon be only a memory. We will turn our prisons into factories and our jails into storehouses and corncribs. Men will walk upright now, women will smile, and the children will laugh. Hell will be forever for rent."

A Mad Rush for Alcohol

The wets, or at any rate the drinking segment of the population, appeared to have no doubt whatever that prohibition would really prohibit; they envisioned the future, once hoarded stocks of liquor had been consumed, as dry and bleak and well-nigh unbearable. And governmental action on January 15 didn't make them feel any better. Supported by a decision handed down by Judge John C. Knox of the United States District Court in New York, enforcement officials in Washington announced that all privately owned booze in warehouses and safety-deposit vaults would be liable to seizure when prohibition became effective. There was never any way of knowing how much liquor had been squirreled away in anticipation of the great drought, but everybody who could afford it had been buying feverishly since the ratification of the Eighteenth Amendment by the thirty-sixth state in January 1919. For months the hoarding of whiskey and other drinkables had been one of the principal subjects of conversations; a common greeting was, "Got any good stuff put away?" Few admitted possessing more than "a little."

Editions of the newspapers containing the government's ukase and an account of Judge Knox's decision were scarcely off the presses when a great rush began to get the supplies of liquor into their owners' homes, the only sanctuaries. Vehicles of every description were pressed into service; the New York *Tribune* noted an eagerness "to hire trucks or baby carriages or anything else on wheels." The New York *Evening Post* said that "probably never before had so much liquor been in transit in this city." A dispatch from Chicago said that "trucks and automobiles and vans scurried over the city all day transporting liquor." The San Francisco *Chronicle* described the movement of liquor as "gigantic"; the streets were jammed with trucks and wagons, and the sidewalks were crowded with men lugging heavy suitcases and boxes. "Fair ladies sat in limousines behind alluring barricades of cases," said the *Chronicle*. "Business men in runabouts had cases on their knees. . . . On every face was stamped that extraordinary and inexplicable expression of triumph mingled with apprehension which the possession of irreplaceable treasure in a predicament of extraordinary peril is wont to imbue." This passage would seem to mean that in San Francisco, at least, liquor hoarders were proud but scared. In a list of dry law "don'ts" published in the New York *Tribune* of January 16 was the warning that only in the home could intoxicating beverages be given away, and that the recipient of the gift must drink it immediately. This was probably the only provision of the Volstead Act that was universally obeyed.

As the fateful hour approached, many of the activities of the liquor people took on a quality of desperation. A brewery in Providence, Rhode Island, announced that in lieu of a final dividend, two barrels of beer would be shipped to every stockholder. "Many members of the General Assembly," said the New York *Tribune*, "also shared in the distribution, being among the first to be cared for." In New

Jersey a brewer threatened to dump his entire stock into the Passaic River, whereupon hundreds of men hurried to the stream with buckets and pans, hoping to salvage at least a little foam. However, the brewer changed his mind and said that instead he would "de-authorize" his beer. In Denver bootleggers said that they "were through with the game forever," and would sell their liquors at reduced prices; they changed their minds also. In California the owner of a vineyard, convinced that prohibition would bankrupt him and every other grape grower in the country, committed suicide; he had failed to foresee the golden years that lay ahead. In New York two prohibition agents were threatened by a crowd when they seized a truck loaded with twenty thousand dollars' worth of whiskey; but it was never clear whether the crowd wanted to manhandle the officers or grab the liquor. Another hopeful crowd gathered on a Hudson River pier when a big cake of ice sank a barge loaded with whiskey worth one hundred and fifty thousand dollars. The owners of the liquor, the Green River Distilling Company, tried desperately to raise the barge and get it out of the harbor before prohibition became effective. They failed, and the liquor was confiscated by the government.

When the prohibition authorities notified the vintners of western New York State that they could legally sell their stocks of wine, thousands of motorists set out for the wine districts with the enthusiasm of prospectors rushing to a new Klondike. Many headed for the village of Hammondsport, in Steuben County, where seventy thousand cases of champagne had been placed on sale, but found the highways blocked by the heaviest snowfall of the year. Their yelps of despair were heard by the State Highway Department, and crews and emergency equipment were hurriedly sent to clear the roads. In the forlorn hope that something might happen, members of retail liquor dealers' associations in New Jersey decided to keep their saloons open and sell near beer, an insipid but legal beverage containing a maximum of one half of one per cent of alcohol. More general, however, was the feeling expressed by John S. Bennett, counsel for saloonkeepers' organizations in Brooklyn, which before prohibition had supported some two thousand saloons. Bennett declared that at least 75 per cent of the Brooklyn saloonkeepers would close their doors. "As sensible men," he said, "most of our members know that the public will not buy this one half of one per cent stuff. As law-abiding citizens they cannot sell anything else. So there is nothing to do but close up."

One Last Party

Everybody expected that on the night of January 16, 1920, saloons, cafés, cabarets, restaurants, and hotels all over the country would be crowded with liquor slaves having a last fling before prohibition settled "like a blight upon the entire joyous side of human existence," as Senator W. Cabell Bruce of Maryland put it in testifying before a congressional committee in 1926. But the nation-wide binge failed to occur. Newspaper reports described the last fling as "very tame," even in such notoriously wet cities as New York, Chicago, Detroit, Louisville, Baltimore, New Orleans, Philadelphia, and San Francisco. In Boston it was excessively tame; policemen were stationed in all of the well-known drinking places to prevent guzzling after midnight, and to seize all liquor on tables or otherwise in sight after that hour. In Atlantic City, home of the famous boardwalk and as wet a town as could be found anywhere, virtually every place that sold liquor closed at midnight after a quiet evening; some of the resorts gave their customers milk bottles as souvenirs. Things were a little better in San Francisco; the *Chronicle* reported that many "saw it through with glorious festivals wherein corks popped and siphons fizzled and glasses clinked long after the legal hour." Nothing out of the ordinary occurred in New Orleans; that city simply ignored prohibition, both on the night of January 16 and thereafter. In Washington, D.C., the saloons were crowded all day and all evening, especially those of the Wet Mile, a stretch of Pennsylvania Avenue between the Capitol and the White House, which boasted forty-seven bar-rooms. When midnight struck on January 16, a final toast was drunk, and glasses and partially emptied bottles were given to favorite customers with the compliments of the saloonkeepers. The bars of the Willard, the Raleigh, and other big Washington hotels had closed several days before the Eighteenth Amendment became effective.

A dispatch to the New York *Times* said that in Chicago drinkers "cheered the final moments of a moist United States in a more or less tame celebration in the cafés and restaurants." But a gang of six masked men gave Chicago a foretaste of what was to come within another few years; they invaded a railroad yard, bound and gagged a yardmaster and a watchman, locked six trainmen in a shanty, and stole whiskey valued at one hundred thousand dollars from two boxcars. In a smaller enterprise of the same sort, several men held up a watchman and rolled four barrels of alcohol from a warehouse into a truck. More than a hundred thefts of large quantities of liquor had been reported during the two or three months prior to the advent of constitutional prohibition; the authorities at Washington admitted that they were investigating seventy-five cases in which whiskey worth several hundred thousand dollars had been stolen, or at least removed, from warehouses heavily guarded by watchmen and enforcement agents. In one of these thefts sixty-one barrels of fine bourbon, valued at one hundred and fifty thousand dollars, disappeared from a government warehouse at Bardstown, Kentucky. The news that so much good liquor had fallen into the hands of men who, presumably, would sell it was greeted by drinkers with quiet chuckles of contentment, but screams of anguish came from the distillers who owned the whiskey. Under the bond placing the liquor in the warehouses, they were required to pay a tax of $6.40 a gallon if it was withdrawn for sale. The Prohibition Bureau ruled that thefts would count as withdrawals. . . .

New York Says Good-Bye

When New York, the nation's nightlife and amusement center and by far the wettest city in the country, was preparing to welcome the Eighteenth Amendment, the newspapers and the police predicted that Broadway would usher the rum demon into limbo with the biggest drunk of all time. The police had announced, unofficially, that since New York had no state prohibition law, they would not attempt to enforce the federal statutes. They prepared to handle crowds larger than those which surge through Times Square on election nights and on New Year's Eve. But none of the prophets had considered the weather. At six o'clock on the morning of January 16, 1920, the official Weather Bureau temperature was six degrees above zero. At noon it was fourteen, with a cold, raw wind blowing from the north. By 11 P.M. the mercury had risen to twenty degrees, but the wind was still howling through the streets and a fine, stinging snow was falling. It was not a fit night for man or drunkard. . . .

Whatever lamentations there were occurred in New York's famous restaurants and cabarets, many of which had promised special programs of "great daring, originality, and imagination." At most of the resorts these ceremonies consisted of mock funerals, and skits involving coffins, death, gloom and despair and hopelessness, all of which caused Billy Sunday's admirers to complain indignantly that the booze hounds had stolen the master's ideas. Considerable originality was displayed, however, at a farewell party given in one of the large dining rooms of the Park Avenue Hotel by a Philadelphia publisher. The walls were covered with black cloth, as were the tables and other fixtures, the waiters, musicians, and all the guests wore solid black, the napkins were black, the tableware had black handles, the main dish was black caviar, and the liquor was served in black glasses specially manufactured for the occasion. In the center of the floor was a huge black coffin filled with black bottles. During the evening the orchestra alternated dance tunes and funeral dirges. At midnight the publisher and his guests marched solemnly around the coffin, and after they had resumed their seats the lights were extinguished and the orchestra played a few bars of a dirge. Then a spotlight picked up the final spectacle—two young men and two girls, all clad in black, sitting at a black table and pouring the last drops from four black bottles, while they held their pocket handkerchiefs before their streaming eyes. A newspaperman who wandered into this party for a few minutes reported that it was "the damnedest thing I ever saw."

The only free liquor in New York on prohibition night, as far as the reporters could discover—and it is reasonable to suppose that they would have found it—was available in the Della Robbia Room of the Hotel Vanderbilt. According to the *Herald,* "one hundred cases of the finest champagne ever held in any cellar" were served to the celebrants at midnight, while the orchestra played "Good-by, Forever." This was the only unusual feature offered by the Vanderbilt. At Thomas Healey's Golden Glades Restaurant, famous for its iceskating entertainment, a coffin was wheeled around as the clock struck twelve, and the customers filled it with broken bottles and glassware. Mock funerals were held at Maxim's and Murray's Roman Gardens, and songs and skits were presented at the Café des Beaux Arts operated by André Bustanoby, a celebrated restaurateur of the period. At the Pré Catelan, run by André Bustanoby's brother, Jacques, the program was climaxed at midnight by a burlesque funeral oration. A similar celebration was staged at the Garden Cabaret. Both the Garden and the "Pré Cat" were notoriously "fast" resorts and favorite rendezvous for college boys and chorus girls; their farewells to booze were noisy and a bit rowdy. Alderman Louis Zeltner acted as master of ceremonies at Little Hungary, a noted winehouse on the lower East Side, and led the mourners in drinking toasts to every notable who had ever entered the place, from Theodore Roosevelt to Alderman Louis Zeltner. At Delmonico's, Sherry's, Churchill's, Jack's, and Luchow's, among the city's finest restaurants, there were no special ceremonies; the diners just sat and ate and drank and sorrowed.

Life in 1919

Frederick Lewis Allen

The ten years from 1910–1920 produced enormous changes which affected the lives of every American. The famous social historian, Frederick Lewis Allen, brilliantly recreates an imaginary couple and takes them through an "ordinary" day in 1919. At each step, the reader sees how American society had changed by decade's end.

I f time were suddenly to turn back to the earliest days of the Post-war Decade, and you were to look about you, what would seem strange to you? Since 1919 the circumstances of American life have been transformed—yes, but exactly how?

Let us refresh our memories by following a moderately well-to-do young couple of Cleveland or Boston or Seattle or Baltimore—it hardly matters which—through the routine of an ordinary day in May, 1919. (I select that particular date, six months after the Armistice of 1918, because by then the United States had largely succeeded in turning from the ways of war to those of peace, yet the profound alterations wrought by the Post-war Decade had hardly begun to take place.) There is no better way of suggesting what the passage of a few years has done to change you and me and the environment in which we live.

Around the Table

From the appearance of Mr. Smith as he comes to the breakfast table on this May morning in 1919, you would

Excerpted from *Only Yesterday: An Informal History of the Nineteen-Twenties*, by Frederick L. Allen. Copyright ©1931 by Frederick Lewis Allen, renewed 1959 by Agnes Rogers Allen. Reprinted by permission of HarperCollins Publishers, Inc.

hardly know that you are not in the nineteen-thirties (though you might, perhaps, be struck by the narrowness of his trousers). The movement of men's fashions is glacial. It is different, however, with Mrs. Smith.

She comes to breakfast in a suit, the skirt of which—rather tight at the ankles—hangs just six inches from the ground. She has read in *Vogue* the alarming news that skirts may become even shorter, and that "not since the days of the Bourbons has the woman of fashion been visible so far above the ankle"; but six inches is still the orthodox clearance. She wears low shoes now, for spring has come; but all last winter she protected her ankles either with spats or with high laced "walking-boots," or with high patent-leather-shoes with contrasting buckskin tops. Her stockings are black (or tan, perhaps, if she wears tan shoes); the idea of flesh-colored stockings would appall her. A few minutes ago Mrs. Smith was surrounding herself with an "envelope chemise" and a petticoat; and from the thick ruffles on her undergarments it was apparent that she was not disposed to make herself more boyish in form than ample nature intended.

Mrs. Smith may use powder, but she probably draws the line at paint. Although the use of cosmetics is no longer, in 1919, considered *prima facie* evidence of a scarlet career, and sophisticated young girls have already begun to apply them with some bravado, most well-brought-up women still frown upon rouge. The beauty-parlor industry is in its infancy; there are a dozen hair-dressing parlors for every beauty parlor, and Mrs. Smith has never heard of such dark arts as that of face-lifting. When she puts on her hat to go shopping she will add a veil pinned neatly together behind her head. In the shops she will perhaps buy a bathing-suit for use in the summer; it will consist of an outer tunic of silk or cretonne over a tight knitted undergarment—worn, of course, with long stockings.

Her hair is long, and the idea of a woman ever frequenting a barber shop would never occur to her. If you have forgotten what the general public thought of short hair in those days, listen to the remark of the manager of the Palm Garden in New York when reporters asked him, one night in November, 1918, how he happened to rent his hall for a pro-Bolshevist meeting which had led to a riot. Explaining that a well-dressed woman had come in a fine automobile to make arrangements for the use of the auditorium, he added, "Had we noticed then, as we do now, that she had short hair, we would have refused to rent the hall." In Mrs. Smith's mind, as in that of the manager of the Palm Garden, short-haired women, like long-haired men, are associated with radicalism, if not with free love.

The breakfast to which Mr. and Mrs. Smith sit down may have been arranged with a view to the provision of a sufficient number of calories—they need only to go to Childs' to learn about calories—but in all probability neither of them has ever heard of a vitamin.

As Mr. Smith eats, he opens the morning paper. It is almost certainly not a tabloid, no matter how rudimentary Mr. Smith's journalistic tastes may be: for although Mr. Hearst has already experimented with small-sized picture papers, the first conspicuously successful tabloid is yet to be born. Not until June 26, 1919, will the New York *Daily News* reach the newsstands, beginning a career that will bring its daily circulation in one year to nearly a quarter of a million, in five years to over four-fifths of a million, and in ten years to the amazing total of over one million three hundred thousand.

Strung across the front page of Mr. Smith's paper are headlines telling of the progress of the American Navy seaplane, the NC-4, on its flight across the Atlantic *via* the Azores. That flight is the most sensational news story of May, 1919. (Alcock and Brown have not yet crossed the ocean in a single hop; they will do it a few weeks hence, eight long years ahead of Lindbergh.) But there is other news, too: of the Peace Conference at Paris, where the Treaty is now in its later stages of preparation; of the successful oversubscription of the Victory Loan ("Sure, we'll finish the job!" the campaign posters have been shouting);

of the arrival of another transport with soldiers from overseas; of the threat of a new strike; of a speech by Mayor Ole Hanson of Seattle denouncing that scourge of the times, the I.W.W. [Industrial Workers of the World, a socialist labor organization]; of the prospects for the passage of the Suffrage Amendment, which it is predicted will enable women to take "a finer place in the national life"; and of Henry Ford's libel suit against the Chicago *Tribune*—in the course of which he will call Benedict Arnold a writer, and in reply to the question, "Have there been any revolutions in this country?" will answer, "Yes, in 1812."

If Mr. Smith attends closely to the sporting news, he may find obscure mention of a young pitcher and outfielder for the Boston Red Sox named Ruth. But he will hardly find the Babe's name in the headlines. (In April, 1919, Ruth made one home run; In May, two; but the season was much further advanced before sporting writers began to notice that he was running up a new record for swatting—twenty-nine home runs for the year; the season had closed before the New York Yankees, seeing gold in the hills, bought him for $125,000; and the summer of 1920 had arrived before a man died of excitement when he saw Ruth smash a ball into the bleachers, and it became clear that the mob had found a new idol. In 1919, the veteran Ty Cobb, not Ruth, led the American League in batting.)

The sporting pages inform Mr. Smith that [Tex] Rickard has selected Toledo as the scene of a forthcoming encounter between the heavyweight champion, Jess Willard, and another future idol of the mob, Jack Dempsey. (They met, you may recall, on the Fourth of July, 1919, and sober citizens were horrified to read that 19,650 people were so depraved as to sit in a broiling sun to watch Dempsey knock out the six-foot-six-inch champion in the third round. How would the sober citizens have felt if they had known that eight years later a Dempsey-Tunney fight would bring in more than five times as much money in gate receipts as this battle of Toledo?) In the sporting pages there may be news of Bobby Jones, the seventeen-year-old Southern golf champion, or of William T. Tilden, Jr., who is winning tennis tournaments here and there, but neither of them is yet a national champion. And even if Jones were to win this year he would hardly become a great popular hero; for although golf is gaining every day in popularity, it has not yet become an inevitable part of the weekly ritual of the American business man. Mr. Smith very likely still scoffs at "grown men who spend their time knocking a little white ball along the ground"; it is quite certain that he has never heard of plus fours; and if he should happen to play golf he had better not show his knickerbockers in the city streets, or small boys will shout to him, "Hey, get some men's pants!"

Did I say that by May, 1919, the war was a thing of the past? There are still reminders of it in Mr. Smith's paper. Not only the news from the Peace Conference, not only the item about Sergeant Alvin York being on his way home; there is still that ugliest reminder of all, the daily casualty list.

Mr. and Mrs. Smith discuss a burning subject, the High Cost of Living. Mr. Smith is hoping for an increase in salary, but meanwhile the family income seems to be dwindling as prices rise. Everything is going up—food, rent, clothing, and taxes. These are the days when people remark that even the man without a dollar is fifty cents better off than he once was, and that if we coined seven-cent pieces for street-car fares, in another year we should have to discontinue them and begin to coin fourteen-cent pieces. Mrs. Smith, confronted with an appeal from Mr. Smith for economy, reminds him that milk has jumped since 1914 from nine to fifteen cents a quart, sirloin steak from twenty-seven to forty-two cents a pound, butter from thirty-two to sixty-one cents a pound, and fresh eggs from thirty-four to sixty-two cents a dozen. No wonder people on fixed salaries are suffering, and colleges are beginning to talk of applying the money-raising methods learned during the Liberty Loan campaigns to the increasing of college endowments. Rents are almost worse than food prices, for that matter; since the Armistice there has been an increasing shortage of houses and apartments, and the profiteering landlord has become an object of popular hate along with the profiteering middleman. Mr. Smith tells his wife that "these profiteers are about as bad as the I.W.W.'s." He could make no stronger statement.

To the Office

Breakfast over, Mr. Smith gets into his automobile to drive to the office. The car is as likely to be a Lexington, a Maxwell, a Briscoe, or a Templar as to be a Dodge, Buick, Chevrolet, Cadillac, or Hudson, and it surely will not be a Chrysler; Mr. Chrysler has just been elected first vice-president of the General Motors Corporation. Whatever the make of the car, it stands higher than the cars of the nineteen-thirties; the passengers look down upon their surroundings from an imposing altitude. The chances are nine to one that Mr. Smith's automobile is open (only 10.3 per cent of the cars manufactured in 1919 were closed). The vogue of the sedan is just beginning. Closed cars are still associated in the public mind with wealth; the hated profiteer of the newspaper cartoon rides in a limousine.

If Mr. Smith's car is one of the high, hideous, but efficient model T Fords of the day, let us watch him for a minute. He climbs in by the right-hand door (for there is no left-hand door by the front seat), reaches over to the wheel, and sets the spark and throttle levers in a position like that of the hands of a clock at ten minutes to three. Then, unless he has paid extra for a self-starter, he gets out to crank. Seizing the crank in his right hand carefully, (for a friend of his once broke his arm cranking), he slips his left forefinger through a loop of wire that controls the choke. He pulls the loop of wire, he revolves the crank mightily, and as the engine at last roars, he leaps to the trembling running-board, leans in, and moves the spark and throttle to twenty-five minutes of two. Perhaps he reaches the throttle before the engine falters into silence, but if it is a cold morning perhaps he does not. In that case, back to the crank again and the loop of wire. Mr. Smith wishes Mrs. Smith would come out and sit in the driver's seat and pull that spark lever down before the engine has time to die.

Finally he is at the wheel with the engine roaring as it should. He releases the emergency hand-brake, shoves his left foot against the low-speed pedal, and as the car sweeps loudly out into the street, he releases his left foot, lets the car into high gear, and is off. Now his only care is for that long hill down the street; yesterday he burned his brake on it, and this morning he must remember to brake with the reverse pedal, or the low-speed pedal, or both, or all three in alternation. (Jam your foot down on any of the three pedals and you slow the car.)

Mr. Smith is on the open road—a good deal more open than it will be a decade hence. On his way to work he passes hardly a third as many cars as he will pass in 1929; there are less than seven million passenger cars registered in the United States in 1919, as against over twenty-three million cars only ten years later. He is unlikely to find many concrete roads in his vicinity, and the lack of them is reflected in the speed regulations. A few states like California and New York permit a rate of thirty miles an hour in 1919, but the average limit is twenty (as against thirty-five or forty in 1931). The Illinois rate of 1919 is characteristic of the day; it limits the driver to fifteen miles in residential parts of cities, ten miles in built-up sections, and six miles on curves. The idea of making a hundred-mile trip in two and a half hours—as will constantly be done in the nineteen-thirties by drivers who consider themselves conservative—would seem to Mr. Smith perilous, and with the roads of 1919 to drive on he would be right.

In the course of his day at the office, Mr. Smith discusses business conditions. It appears that things are looking up. There was a period of uncertainty and falling stock prices after the Armistice, as huge government contracts were canceled and plants which had been running overtime on war work began to throw off men by the thousand, but since then conditions have been better. Everybody is talking about the bright prospects for international trade and American shipping. The shipyards are running full tilt.

There are too many strikes going on, to be sure; it seems as if the demands of labor for higher and higher wages would never be satisfied, although Mr. Smith admits that in a way you can't blame the men, with prices still mounting week by week. But there is so much business activity that the men being turned out of army camps to look for jobs are being absorbed better than Mr. Smith ever thought they would be. It was back in the winter and early spring that there was so much talk about the ex-service men walking the streets without work; it was then that *Life* ran a cartoon which represented Uncle Sam saying to a soldier, "Nothing is too good for you, my boy! What would you like?" and the soldier answering, "A job." Now the boys seem to be sifting slowly but surely into the ranks of the employed, and the only clouds on the business horizon are strikes and Bolshevism and the dangerous wave of speculation in the stock market.

The State of Business

"Bull Market Taxes Nerves of Brokers," cry the headlines in the financial pages, and they speak of "Long Hours for Clerks." Is there a familiar ring to those phrases? Does it seem natural to you, remembering as you do the Big Bull Market of 1928 and 1929, that the decision to keep the Stock Exchange closed over the 31st of May, 1919, should elicit such newspaper comments as this: "The highly specialized machine which handles the purchase and sales of stocks and bonds in the New York market is fairly well exhausted and needs a rest"? Then listen; in May, 1919, it was a long series of *million-and-a-half-share* days which was causing financiers to worry and the Federal Reserve Board to consider issuing a warning against speculation. During that year a new record of six two-million-share days was set up, and on only 145 days did the trading amount to over a million shares. What would Mr. Smith and his associates think if they were to be told that within eleven years there would occur a sixteen-million-share day; and that they would see the time when three-million-share days would be referred to as "virtual stagnation" or as "listless trading by professionals only, with the general public refusing to become interested"? The price of a seat on the New York Stock Exchange in 1919 ranged between $60,000 and a new high record of $110,000; it would be hard for Mr. Smith to believe that before the end of the decade seats on the Exchange would fetch a half million.

In those days of May, 1919, the record of daily Stock Exchange transactions occupied hardly a newspaper column. The Curb Market record referred to trading on a real curb—to that extraordinary outdoor market in Broad Street, New York, where boys with telephone receivers clamped to their heads hung out of windows high above the street and grimaced and wigwagged through the din to traders clustered on the pavement below. And if there was anything Mrs. Smith was certain not to have on her mind as she went shopping, it was the price of stocks. Yet the "unprecedented bull market" of 1919 brought fat profits to those who participated in it. Between February 15th and May 14th, Baldwin Locomotive rose from 72 to 93, General Motors from 130 to 191, United States Steel from 90 to 104½, and International Mercantile Marine common (to which traders were attracted on account of the apparently boundless possibilities of shipping) from 23 to 47⅝.

When Mr. Smith goes out to luncheon, he has to proceed to his club in a roundabout way, for a regiment of soldiers just returned form Europe is on parade and the central thoroughfares of the city are blocked with crowds. It is a great season for parades, this spring of 1919. As the transports from Brest swing up New York Harbor, the men packed solid on the decks are greeted by Major Hylan's Committee of Welcome, represented sometimes by the Mayor's spruce young secretary, Grover Whalen, who in later years is to reduce welcoming to a science and raise it to an art. New York City has built in honor of the homecoming troops a huge plaster arch in Fifth Avenue at Madison Square, toward the design of which forty artists are said to have contributed. ("But the result," comments the

New York *Tribune*, sadly, "suggests four hundred rather than forty. It holds everything that was ever on an arch anywhere, the lay mind suspects, not forgetting the horses on top of a certain justly celebrated Brandenburg Gate.") Farther up the Avenue, before the Public Library, there is a shrine of pylons and palms called the Court of the Heroic Dead, of whose decorative effect the *Tribune* says, curtly, "Add perils of death." A few blocks to the north an arch of jewels is suspended above the Avenue "like a net of precious stones, between two white pillars surmounted by stars"; on this arch colored searchlights play at night with superb effect. The Avenue is hung with flags from end to end; and as the Twenty-seventh Division parades under the arches the air is white with confetti and ticker tape, and the sidewalks are jammed with cheering crowds. Nor is New York alone in its enthusiasm for the returning soldiers; every other city has its victory parade, with the city elders on the reviewing stand and flags waving and the bayonets of the troops glistening in the spring sunlight and the bands playing "The Long, Long Trail." Not yet disillusioned, the nation welcomes its heroes—and the heroes only wish the fuss were all over and they could get into civilian clothes and sleep late in the mornings and do what they please, and try to forget.

Social Hour

Mr. and Mrs. Smith have been invited to a tea dance at one of the local hotels, and Mr. Smith hurries from his office to the scene of revelry. If the hotel is up to the latest wrinkles, it has a jazz-band instead of the traditional orchestra for dancing, but not yet does a saxophone player stand out in the foreground and contort from his instrument that piercing music, "endlessly sorrowful yet endlessly unsentimental, with no past, no memory, no future, no hope," which William Bolitho called the *Zeitgeist* of the Post-war Age. The jazz-band plays "I'm Always Chasing Rainbows," the tune which Harry Carroll wrote in wartime after Harrison Fisher persuaded him that Chopin's "Fantasie Impromptu"

271

had the makings of a good ragtime tune. It plays, too, "Smiles" and "Dardanella" and "Hindustan" and "Japanese Sandman" and "I Love You Sunday," and that other song which is to give the Post-war Decade one of its most persistent and wearisome slang phrases, "I'll Say She Does." There are a good many military uniforms among the fox-trotting dancers. There is one French officer in blue; the days are not past when a foreign uniform adds the zest of war-time romance to any party. In the more dimly lighted palm-room there may be a juvenile petting party or two going on, but of this Mr. and Mrs. Smith are doubtless oblivious. F. Scott Fitzgerald has yet to confront a horrified republic with the Problem of the Younger Generation.

After a few dances, Mr. Smith wanders out to the bar (if this is not a dry state). He finds there a group of men downing Bronxes and Scotch highballs, and discussing with dismay the approach of prohibition. On the 1st of July the so-called Wartime Prohibition Law is to take effect (designed as a war measure, but not signed by the President until after the Armistice), and already the ratification of the Eighteenth Amendment has made it certain that prohibition is to be permanent. Even now, distilling and brewing are forbidden. Liquor is therefore expensive, as the frequenters of midnight cabarets are learning to their cost. Yet here is the bar, still quite legally doing business. Of course there is not a woman within eyeshot of it; drinking by women is unusual in 1919, and drinking at a bar is an exclusively masculine prerogative. Although Mr. and Mrs. Smith's hosts may perhaps serve cocktails before dinner this evening, Mr. and Mrs. Smith have never heard of cocktail parties as a substitute for tea parties.

As Mr. Smith stands with his foot on the brass rail, he listens to the comments on the coming of prohibition. There is some indignant talk about it, but even here the indignation is by no means unanimous. One man, as he tosses off his Bronx, says that he'll miss his liquor for a time, he supposes, but he thinks "his boys will be better off for living in a world where there is no alcohol"; and two or three others agree with him. Prohibition has an over-whelming majority behind it throughout the United States; the Spartan fervor of war-time has not yet cooled. Nor is there anything ironical in the expressed assumption of these men that when the Eighteenth Amendment goes into effect, alcohol will be banished from the land. They look forward vaguely to an endless era of actual drought.

At the dinner party to which Mr. and Mrs. Smith go that evening, some of the younger women may be bold enough to smoke, but they probably puff their cigarettes self-consciously, even defiantly. (The national consumption of cigarettes in 1919, excluding the very large sizes, is less than half of what it will be by 1930.)

After dinner the company may possibly go to the movies to see Charlie Chaplin in "Shoulder Arms" or Douglas Fair-banks in "The Knickerbocker Buckaroo" or Mary Pickford in "Daddy Long Legs," or Theda Bara, or Pearl White, or Griffith's much touted and much wept-at "Broken Blossoms." Or they may play auction bridge (not contract, of course). Mah Jong, which a few years hence will be almost obligatory, is still over the horizon. They may discuss such best sellers of the day as *The Four Horsemen of the Apocalypse*, [Booth] Tarkington's *The Magnificent Ambersons*, [Joseph] Conrad's *Arrow of Gold*, Brand Whitlock's *Belgium*, and [H.G.] Wells's *The Undying Fire*. (The *Outline of History* is still unwritten.) They may go to the theater: the New York successes of May, 1919, include "Friendly Enemies," "Three Faces East," and "The Better 'Ole," which have been running ever since war-time and are still going strong, and also "Listen, Lester," [William] Gillette in "Dear Brutus," Frances Starr in "Tiger! Tiger!" and—to satisfy a growing taste for bedroom farce—such tidbits as "Up in Mabel's Room." The Theater Guild is about to launch its first drama, [John] Ervine's "John Ferguson." The members of the senior class at Princeton have just voted "Lightnin'" their favorite play (after "Macbeth" and "Hamlet," for which they cast the votes expected of educated men), and their favorite actresses, in order of preference, are Norma Talmadge, Elsie Ferguson, Marguerite Clark, Constance Talmadge, and Madge Kennedy.

One thing the Smiths certainly will not do this evening. They will not listen to the radio.

For there is no such thing as radio broadcasting. Here and there a mechanically inclined boy has a wireless set, with which, if he knows the Morse code, he may listen to messages from ships at sea and from land stations equipped with sending apparatus. The radiophone has been so far developed that men flying in an airplane over Manhattan have talked with other men in an office-building below. But the broadcasting of speeches and music—well, it was tried years ago by DeForest, and "nothing came of it." Not until the spring of 1920 will Frank Conrad of the Westinghouse Company of East Pittsburgh, who has been sending out phonograph music and baseball scores from the barn which he has rigged up as a spare-time research station, find that so many amateur wireless operators are listening to them that a Pittsburgh newspaper has had the bright idea of advertising radio equipment "which may be used by those who listen to Dr. Conrad's programs." And not until this advertisement appears will the Westinghouse officials decide to open the first broadcasting station in history in order to stimulate the sale of their supplies.

One more word about Mr. and Mrs. Smith and we may dismiss them for the night. Not only have they never heard of radio broadcasting; they have never heard of Coué, the Dayton Trial, cross-word puzzles, bathing-beauty contests, John J. Raskob, racketeers, Teapot Dome, Coral Gables, the *American Mercury*, Sacco and Vanzetti, companionate marriage, brokers' loan statistics, Michael Arlen, the Wall Street explosion, confession magazines, the Hall-Mills case, radio stock, speakeasies, Al Capone, automatic traffic lights, or Charles A. Lindbergh.

The Post-war Decade lies before them.

Chronology

1910

June 18—The Mann-Elkins Railroad Act hands increased power to the Interstate Commerce Commission to regulate certain industries.

November 1—The first issue of black activist W.E.B. Du Bois's *The Crisis* appears.

November 14—Eugene Ely flies the first aircraft from the deck of a ship, bringing air power and sea power together for the first time.

December 14—Norwegian explorer Roald Amundsen reaches the South Pole.

1911

January 26—Pilot Glenn H. Curtiss takes off and lands an airplane from the waters near San Diego, California.

March 25—Fire breaks out in the Triangle Shirtwaist Company of New York, killing 146 workers. The incident leads to a government investigation of shoddy factory conditions.

May 15—The Supreme Court breaks up the Standard Oil Company of New Jersey because of monopolistic practices.

September–November—Pioneer aviator Cal Rodgers flies coast to coast.

1912

January 6—New Mexico becomes the forty-seventh state.

January–February—Bitter labor strike occurs at Lawrence, Massachusetts.

February 14—Arizona becomes the forty-eighth state.

February 25—Former president Theodore Roosevelt announces he will again seek the Republican Party's nomination for president.

April 15—More than fifteen hundred passengers drown in the Atlantic after the ocean liner *Titanic* hits an iceberg and sinks.

April–November—Workers' rights activist Mother Jones leads a strike in West Virginia. Though unsuccessful, she brings national attention to the labor movement.

June 19—The federal government extends the eight-hour workday to all federal employees.

July—Jim Thorpe wins two Olympic gold medals but is subsequently stripped of them when it is revealed that he once played sports as a professional.

August 5–7—Theodore Roosevelt runs for president as the Progressive Party candidate after his former party, the Republican Party, nominates William Howard Taft.

October 14—John Schrank, a disturbed individual seeking notoriety, unsuccessfully attempts to assassinate former president Theodore Roosevelt in Milwaukee.

November 5—Woodrow Wilson, the Democratic Party nominee, is elected president.

1913
March 13—Suffragettes march in Washington, D.C., to demand the right to vote for females.

March 26—Disastrous floods devastate large portions of Ohio and Indiana.

May 10—Suffragettes march in New York City.

May 31—The Seventeenth Amendment to the Constitution takes effect, providing for the direct election of U.S. senators.

1914
January 5—Henry Ford stuns the automotive world by announcing that he will pay his laborers the then–unheard-of sum of five dollars per day.

April 21—U.S. Marines land in Mexico and seize Veracruz in retaliation for the arrest of American marines by Mexican authorities.

May 7—Congress passes a resolution designating the second Sunday of May as Mother's Day.

June 28—World War I erupts in Europe when Austrian archduke Franz Ferdinand is assassinated.

August 15—The Panama Canal opens and thereby shortens the travel time and distance from the Atlantic to the Pacific Ocean.

1915

January 25—In New York, Alexander Graham Bell, inventor of the telephone, conducts the first transcontinental telephone conversation when he talks to his assistant, Thomas A. Watson, in San Francisco.

February 8—D.W. Griffith's motion picture *The Birth of a Nation* opens.

April 5—Jack Johnson loses his heavyweight fight against Jess Willard.

May 7—Over one hundred Americans drown when a German submarine sinks the passenger ship *Lusitania* in the Atlantic Ocean; this incident brought the neutral United States to the brink of war with Germany.

July 29—U.S. Marines land in Haiti to stabilize the shaky political situation there and protect American interests in the Caribbean.

1916

March 9—Francisco "Pancho" Villa, rebel Mexican leader, leads a raid into New Mexico that results in the death of seventeen Americans; in response to the Villa raid, President Woodrow Wilson sends an American military force into Mexico led by General John J. Pershing; the troops pursue Villa in Mexico until the following January.

November 7—Woodrow Wilson is reelected president when he defeats the Republican candidate, Charles Evans Hughes.

1917

March 16—Three American ships are sunk in the Atlantic Ocean by German submarines.

April 6—The United States declares war on Germany when the European nation refuses to stop its unrestricted submarine warfare in the Atlantic Ocean.

June 15—Congress passes the Espionage Act, which makes it a crime for an American citizen to assist an enemy nation in any way.

November 7—The communist Bolshevik Party seizes control in Russia and removes the nation from the war.

1918

January 18—Woodrow Wilson delivers his "Fourteen Points" speech to Congress, in which he proposes his plan for world peace.

June 3–6—U.S. troops defeat the Germans at Chateau-Thierry.

June 6–July 1—U.S. troops defeat the Germans in the bitter fighting at Belleau Wood.

September—An influenza epidemic breaks out in Europe and spreads to the United States; over half a million Americans die from the disease worldwide.

November 11—World War I ends when Germany agrees to cease hostilities.

1919

January 18—Peace talks open in Paris.

January 29—The Eighteenth Amendment to the Constitution, banning the manufacture and sale of alcohol, is ratified; Prohibition goes into effect the next year.

June 28—Treaty of Versailles is signed in France, officially ending World War I.

September 22—Massive strike occurs against U.S. Steel and other companies that use the twelve-hour workday; military force is finally required to break the strike.

September 25—Woodrow Wilson suffers a stroke, which incapacitates him for the rest of his term.

October 28—The Volstead Act, which hands power to the police to enforce Prohibition, is passed; when it takes effect on January 16, 1920, Prohibition becomes the law of the land.

October—The Black Sox scandal tarnishes baseball's image when members of the Chicago White Sox accept money to lose ball games.

December 22—Attorney General A. Mitchell Palmer plans a series of raids against suspected subversive Americans.

For Further Reading

Primary Sources

H.H. Arnold, *Global Mission*. New York: Harper & Brothers, 1949.

Ray Stannard Baker, *American Chronicle: The Autobiography of Ray Stannard Baker*. New York: Charles Scribner's Sons, 1945.

William Benton, *The Annals of America: Volume 13, 1905–1915*. Chicago: Encyclopædia Britannica, Inc., 1968.

Henry Steele Commager, ed., *Documents of American History, Volume II*. Englewood Cliffs, NJ: Prentice-Hall, 1973.

Clarence Darrow, *The Story of My Life*. New York: Charles Scribner's Sons, 1932.

W.E.B. Du Bois, *The Autobiography of W.E.B. DuBois*. New York: International Publishers, 1968.

Elizabeth Gurley Flynn, *The Rebel Girl: An Autobiography*. New York: International Publishers, 1955.

Elizabeth Frost and Kathryn Cullen-DuPont, *Women's Suffrage in America: An Eyewitness History*. New York: Facts On File, 1992.

Richard Hofstadter, ed., *The Progressive Movement, 1900–1915*. Englewood Cliffs, NJ: Prentice-Hall, 1963.

Jack Johnson, *Jack Johnson—In the Ring and Out*. Chicago: National Sports, 1927.

Douglas MacArthur, *Reminiscences*. New York: McGraw-Hill, 1964.

Edward V. Rickenbacker, *Rickenbacker*. Englewood Cliffs, NJ: Prentice-Hall, 1967.

Lincoln Steffens, *The Autobiography of Lincoln Steffens*. New York: The Literary Guild, 1931.

Robert I. Vexler, ed., *Woodrow Wilson, 1856–1924: Chronology, Documents, Bibliographical Aids*. Dobbs Ferry, NY: Oceana Publications, 1969.

Secondary Sources

Frederick Lewis Allen, *Only Yesterday*. New York: Harper & Row, 1931.

Herbert Asbury, *The Great Illusion: An Informal History of Prohibition*. Garden City, NY: Doubleday & Company, 1950.

Ruth Brandon, *The Life and Many Deaths of Harry Houdini*. New York: Random House, 1993.

H.W. Brands, *T.R.: The Last Romantic*. New York: Basic Books, 1997.

David M. Chalmers, *Hooded Americanism: The History of the Ku Klux Klan*. Durham, NC: Duke University Press, 1987.

Dale Fetherling, *Mother Jones: The Miners' Angel*. Carbondale: Southern Illinois University Press, 1974.

Philip S. Foner, *History of the Labor Movement in the United States, Volume IV*. New York: International Publishers Co., 1965.

David Levering Lewis, *W.E.B. DuBois: Biography of A Race*. New York: Henry Holt and Company, 1993.

Walter Lord, *The Good Years*. New York: Bantam Pathfinder Editions, 1960.

Ernest R. May, *The Progressive Era*. New York: Time-Life Books, 1974.

David McCullough, *The Path Between the Seas: The Creation of the Panama Canal, 1870–1914*. New York: Simon and Schuster, 1977.

Allan R. Millett, *Semper Fidelis: The History of the United States Marine Corps*. New York: Macmillan, 1980.

Burl Noggle, *Into the Twenties: The United States from Armistice to Normalcy*. Urbana: University of Illinois Press, 1974.

William Preston, Jr., *Aliens and Dissenters: Federal Suppression of Radicals, 1903–1933*. Cambridge: Harvard University Press, 1963.

Henry F. Pringle, *Theodore Roosevelt: A Biography*. New York: Harcourt, Brace & World, 1956.

Clark G. Reynolds, *Admiral John H. Towers*. Annapolis, MD: Naval Institute Press, 1991.

Randy Roberts, *Papa Jack: Jack Johnson and the Era of White Hopes*. New York: The Free Press, 1983.

Kenneth Silverman, *Houdini!!!: The Career of Ehrich Weiss*. New York: HarperCollins, 1996.

Gene Smith, *Until the Last Trumpet Sounds: The Life of General of the Armies John J. Pershing*. New York: John Wiley & Sons, 1998.

Page Smith, *America Enters the World*. New York: McGraw-Hill, 1985.

Robin Langley Sommer, *Hollywood: The Glamour Years, 1919–1941*. New York: Gallery Books, 1987.

Irving Stone, *Clarence Darrow for the Defense*. Garden City, NY: Garden City Publishing Co., 1941.

Mark Sullivan, *Our Times, Volume IV: The War Begins, 1909–1914*. New York: Charles Scribner's Sons, 1932.

———, *Our Times, Volume V: Over Here, 1914–1918*. New York: Charles Scribner's Sons, 1933.

This Fabulous Century: Volume II, 1910–1920. New York: Time-Life Books, 1969.

John Toland, *No Man's Land: 1918, The Last Year of the Great War*. Garden City, NY: Doubleday & Company, 1980.

Michael V. Uschan, *A Cultural History of the United States Through the Decades: The 1910s*. San Diego, CA: Lucent Books, Inc., 1999.

Geoffrey C. Ward, *Baseball: An Illustrated History*. New York: Alfred A. Knopf, 1994.

Index

Index